FAMILIES IN EASTERN EUROPE

CONTEMPORARY PERSPECTIVES IN FAMILY RESEARCH

Series Editor: Felix M. Berardo

Recent Volumes:

CONTEMPORARY PERSPECTIVES IN FAMILY RESEARCH
VOLUME 5

FAMILIES IN EASTERN EUROPE

EDITED BY

MIHAELA ROBILA

Family Science, Queens College, City University of New York
Flushing, NY, USA

2004

ELSEVIER
JAI

Amsterdam – Boston – Heidelberg – London – New York – Oxford
Paris – San Diego – San Francisco – Singapore – Sydney – Tokyo

ELSEVIER B.V.   ELSEVIER Inc.   **ELSEVIER Ltd**   ELSEVIER Ltd
Radarweg 29   525 B Street, Suite 1900 **The Boulevard, Langford** 84 Theobalds Road
P.O. Box 211   San Diego   **Lane, Kidlington**   London
1000 AE Amsterdam   CA 92101-4495   **Oxford OX5 1GB**   WC1X 8RR
The Netherlands   USA   **UK**   UK

First edition 2004

Library of Congress Cataloging in Publication Data
A catalog record is available from the Library of Congress.

British Library Cataloguing in Publication Data
A catalogue record is available from the British Library.

ISBN: 0-7623-1116-9
ISSN: 1530-3535 (Series)

⊗ The paper used in this publication meets the requirements of ANSI/NISO Z39.48-1992 (Permanence of Paper). Printed in The Netherlands.

CONTENTS

LIST OF CONTRIBUTORS

Marina A. Adler	Department of Sociology & Anthropology, University of Maryland, Baltimore, USA
Valentina Bodrug-Lungu	Department of History and Psychology, State University of Moldova, Chisinau, Moldova
Suzana Bornarova	Institute for Social Work and Social Policy, Faculty of Philosophy, St. Cyril and Methodius University, Skopje, Republic of Macedonia
Dmitry Y. Borodin	Department of Sociology and Political Science, Tver State University, Tver, Russia
Danuta Duch	Research Unit on Women and Family, Institute of Philosophy and Sociology, Polish Academy of Sciences, Warszava, Poland
Parsla Eglite	Institute of Economics, Latvian Academy of Sciences, Riga, Latvia
Jarmila Filadelfiová	Bratislava Centre for Work and Family Studies, Bratislava Slovak Republic
Irena Juozeliūnienė	Department of Sociology, Faculty of Philosophy, Vilnius University, Vilnius, Lithuania
Loreta Kuzmickaitė	Department of Sociology, Vilnius University, Vilnius, Lithuania
Divna Lakinska-Popovska	Institute of Social Work and Social Policy, Faculty of Philosophy, St. Cyril and Methodius University, Skopje, Republic of Macedonia
Hana Maříková	Institute of Sociology, Gender & Sociology Department, Academy of Sciences of the Prague, Czech Republic

Mihaela Robila	Family Science, Department of Family, Nutrition and Exercise Sciences, Queens College, City University of New York, NY, USA
Raya Staykova	Center for Science Studies and History of Science, Bulgarian Academy of Sciences, Sofia, Bulgaria
Anna Titkow	Research Unit on Women and Family, Institute of Philosophy and Sociology, Polish Academy of Sciences, Warszava, Poland
Olga Tóth	Institute of Sociology, Hungarian Academy of Sciences, Budapest, Hungary
Mirjana Ule	Faculty of Social Sciences, University of Ljubljana, Slovenia
Valentina I. Uspenskaya	Department of Sociology and Political Science, Tver State University, Tver, Russia
Tatiana Zhurzhenko	Department of Philosophy, V. Karazin Kharkiv National University, Ukraine

PREFACE

In order to develop our understanding of the diversity of family processes, social scientists require research on a wide range of national settings and ethnic groups. However, systematic scholarship regarding families in Eastern European countries has been lacking, due primarily to dramatic changes in their socio-political systems. This has impeded the elaboration of cross-cultural comparisons essential to a more complete family social sciences.

The present volume, the fifth in our series on *Contemporary Perspectives in Family Research*, is an initial attempt to rectify this gap by focusing on timely and critical issues confronting families in Easter Europe. Throughout an emphasis is placed on describing the major socio-historic and economic factors that have oriented family functioning in the past and the role they play in fashioning marriage and family life today. Contributors present detailed data on culture-specific influences on human development in countries about which relatively little prior knowledge exists. As such, they make available a range of information that is often difficult to locate and analyze.

The scientific study of the family in this part of the world was long discouraged. Some social science departments – such as sociology and psychology – were closed and research initiatives suppressed. Such actions affected the level of scholarship conducted in the region. Even today governmental support for social science research – especially on family processes – is low. Nevertheless, a broad family research agenda, mostly descriptive, is emerging.

This volume makes an important contribution by providing Western scholars with greater knowledge of the past and current traditions in the literature on families and youth in Eastern Europe. It also creates an opportunity for these investigators to integrate this knowledge among themselves, and with other social scientists. Moreover, this work fills an important niche by reflecting the transformation within the Eastern European academic community toward a Western style of research and analysis.

Readers will come to appreciate the timeliness of this work, given the rapid economic and socio-political changes occurring in this part of the world, and the profound they impact they have on family structure and relationships. Accordingly, the compilation presented here establishes a necessary baseline against which future scholarly work will be assessed. With this publication, the role of the larger environmental contexts within which their development is embedded will become more visible to families and youth and to the social scientists studying these changes.

Felix M. Berardo
Series Editor

FAMILIES IN EASTERN EUROPE: CONTEXT, TRENDS AND VARIATIONS

Mihaela Robila

ABSTRACT

Eastern Europe has been recognized as a region that has experienced major socio-political and economic changes in the last decades. The impact of these transitions on families and their functioning has also been significant. Although understanding of families in different cultures in the last years has considerably increased, little has been written on Eastern European families. This book fills the void in literature and provides a timely and comprehensive analysis of family issues in Eastern Europe. It brings together scholars from fourteen Eastern European countries. The authors explain family processes in that particular country focusing on the historic, social and economic contexts and the impact they have on families. The scholars also provide demographic information about families and discuss cultural traditions, marital and gender roles, parenting processes, family policy and programs within the society, and the state of research on family issues. The first chapter provides both an overview of family changes in Eastern Europe and an introduction to the subsequent chapters.

SOCIO-HISTORIC AND ECONOMIC CONTEXT

In the last century, Eastern Europe has been marked by very dynamic geo-political changes brought about by World Wars I and II and by the fall of communism.

Families in Eastern Europe
Contemporary Perspectives in Family Research, Volume 5, 1–14
Copyright © 2004 by Elsevier Ltd.
All rights of reproduction in any form reserved
ISSN: 1530-3535/doi:10.1016/S1530-3535(04)05001-0

Throughout this period, countries were formed and boundaries were reconfigured (see Tóth et al., this volume). Significantly, following World War II, several countries and regions were annexed to the Soviet Union and Soviet regimes were installed in the others, imposing a communist political framework throughout Eastern Europe (see Eglite, this volume).

For over 40 years, communism had a powerful impact not only at the level of society as a whole, but at the family level as well. Industrialization, which was one of the most prevalent features, determined an institutional transformation of the family through the migration of populations from rural to urban areas, thereby encouraging the formation of the nuclear family and the decline of the traditional extended family (see Filadelfiová, this volume). Accompanying these processes were changes in family roles such as an increase in the educational level of women and the large scale entry of women into the labor market. Thus, the only acceptable family model was the one in which both spouses worked. During communism, the State had a powerful controlling function over the family. The level of intrusiveness was so deep that it controlled basic needs and family functions such as housing, reproductive behaviors (by forbidding contraceptive measures and abortions) and parenting.

In late 1980s and early 1990s, several social and political protest movements developed across Europe that had a crucial role in undermining communism (Gal & Kligman, 2000; Roberts et al., 2000). While some of them were peaceful (such as the one in the Czech Republic), others were more violent (over 1,000 people died in the confrontations in Romania). At the same time, the region has gone through a significant geo-political reorganization through the dissolution of the Soviet Union, Yugoslavia and Czechoslovakia into their constituent states and the reunification of East and West Germany. The transition from communism to democracy was accompanied by a general state of confusion, since there have been no similar changes previously, and therefore there were no "experts or strategies to be followed" (Roberts et al., 2000, p. 1). The transition brought a wide array of socio-political changes, but the economic transformations had the most profound impact at the family level.

When the transformation phase began, all the ex-communist countries started the new era from similar positions, after spending decades with basically the same systems of political authority and central economic planning (Roberts et al., 2000). As soon as communism collapsed, inter-national and intra-country differences/inequalities began to widen rapidly, due partly to the different speeds at which the market economies were developing, and due partly to a resuscitation of national characteristics in policies (Mestrovic, 1994; Roberts et al., 2000). Thus, for example, the former East Germany and Slovenia rank among the most successful transition economies, while Moldova and Bulgaria are still struggling economically (CIA, 2003).

The major problem of the post-communist transition towards democracy is the high level of poverty that persists in the region. Profound economic reforms were necessary to create market economies. Among them, privatization is usually regarded as the primary means by which command economies were transformed into market-regulated economies (Szalai, 2000; Zhurzhenko, this volume). An immediate consequence of the development of the labor market while the centrally planned economic sectors were in rapid decline was the spread of unemployment. Coupled with high inflation, wages have decreased significantly. Fifty-one percent of people in Moldova and 25% in Russia live below the poverty level (see Bodrug-Lungu, this volume; CIA, 2003; World Bank, 2003). Similarly, in Bulgaria the transition from communism has led to mass impoverishment: four-fifths of the population subsist below the minimum standard of living (Daskalova, 2000). After the optimism and enthusiasm of the first transition period, pessimism and dissatisfaction with living conditions followed. Many people indicated that they currently lived in worse conditions than before (see Staykova, this volume). Studies examining the impact of regime change have regularly found that a great part of the population associates change with disappointment (see Tóth, this volume).

Research shows that throughout Eastern Europe, poverty is most closely associated with family type (e.g. single-parent families are the most affected) and number of children (families with many children have a higher probability of experiencing poverty) (Nauck & Joos, 1999; Tesliuc et al., 2001). For example, at the time of the political unification of both German states, a study conducted amongst the adult population of East Germany showed that unmarried women (who had a poverty risk nearly four times as high as for married adults) and divorced men (who had a poverty risk nearly five times as high as for married adults) were increasingly affected by poverty (Nauck & Joos, 1999). The number of children is an even stronger factor influencing poverty. In 1990, the poverty risk for adults with four or more children was already five times as high as for childless adults, and by 1993 the poverty risk was more than ten times as high (Nauck & Joos, 1999). Similarly, research conducted in Ukraine indicates that the risk of poverty increases with the number of children (Zhurzhenko, this volume).

Economic changes had the most widely and directly devastating effects on young people. Youth were affected by the disappearance or degradation of many careers which, under communism, they would have entered, and for which their education had prepared them (Morris, 1998; Roberts et al., 2000). Young families are also constrained in their efforts to become independent of their family of origin. The shortage of housing and high prices force young families to live, at least for several years, with their parents. This creates difficulties for young people wishing to own or rent an apartment independently, and places families under intolerable pressure (Lakinska & Bornarova; Robila, this volume).

In general, the deterioration of living conditions affects women more than men, both in private (e.g. increased amount of time women spend on housework and childcare) and public spheres. Discrimination against women in the labor market appears in several forms and is frequently a continuation of patterns established in the communist period (Daskalova, 2000). This is reflected in low average wage levels as well as in high unemployment rates. For example, in Hungary in the last decade, women's employment has dropped by 20% (Kovacs & Varadi, 2000) and in East Germany women's full-time employment fell from 91% to about 62% (Adler, this volume).

Overall, the historic, political and economic changes have affected all aspects of people's lives, including work-related and household economic strategies, the value of social relationships, patterns of family life, and childrearing practices (Szalai, 2000). Each of the following chapters presents an in-depth analysis of the impact of these changes on family life.

FAMILY DEMOGRAPHICS IN EASTERN EUROPE

The transition period was characterized by several transformations at the population and family level. One of the major issues is the demographic crisis, with the population declining significantly due to several factors. One of them is the short life expectancy, mainly a consequence of harsh living conditions. For example, in 2003, life expectancy at birth was 64.88 years in Moldova, 69.31 in Latvia, 70.60 in Romania, and 75.51 in Slovenia (CIA, 2003). While these values are above the world average (63.95), they are below the average in more developed countries (U.S., 77.14; Japan, 80.93; Australia, 80.13) (CIA, 2003). Since 1990, a new phenomenon has emerged which contributes to population decline: the migration of Eastern Europeans towards Western, more developed countries, looking for work (see Bodrug-Lungu, this volume).

Another phenomenon is the declining birth rates throughout the region to 1.13 in Bulgaria, 1.25 in Hungary, 1.33 in Russia, or 1.43 in Lithuania (CIA, 2003) (also see Eglite; Staykova, this volume). The decrease in the fertility rate is due mainly to economic uncertainty and cutbacks on welfare support for child-rearing families (e.g. maternity leave), making young people unwilling to have children (see Juozeliûnienë & Kuzmickaitë, this volume).

New family trends include the increased age at marriage and at the birth of the first child, and increased cohabitation. For example, the mean age for marriage in Hungary is 27.8 years for men and 25.2 years for women and in Slovenia it is 31.8 for men and 28.8 years for women (see Tóth; Ule, this volume). Closely related to the increased age at marriage is the increased age at first birth, which, in East Germany, for example, is 28.4 years (Adler, this volume). Bulgaria is among the countries where women continue to give birth to their first child at an early age (23.8 years) (Staykova, this volume). While cohabitation was a relatively rare phenomenon, during the last decade there has been an increase in the acceptance and practice of cohabitation (see Juozeliûnienë & Kuzmickaitë, this volume). In 2001, 11% of all partner relationships in Bulgaria and 11% in Hungary were cohabitations (see Staykova; Tóth, this volume). Increased cohabitation has produced an increase in the number of out of wedlock births. For example, in 2001, 22.5% of Moldavian babies and more than 50% of East German children were born out of wedlock (Adler; Bodrug-Lungu, this volume).

FAMILY RELATIONS

Although there is very limited research on the family during the communist era, the family maintained a central role in people's lives, acting as a buffer and protector from the intrusiveness of external forces. Several studies conducted throughout Eastern Europe during the transition period indicate that the family remains an institution of very high value for people, providing stability and resources, and minimizing the effects of societal changes on the individual (see Robila; Tóth; Zhurzhenko, this volume). For example, successful marriage was mentioned by Poles as a very important value, strongly related to having children (Titkow & Duch, this volume). For younger generations, although the family remains very important, having a professional career appears to hold equally important value (Uspenskaya & Borodin, this volume).

Research conducted on marital relations indicated that the factor identified as provoking the most marital distress is economic hardship (see Lakinska & Bornarova; Robila, this volume). Increased economic pressure is associated with higher psychological distress (depression, anxiety), which in turn is associated with a higher level of marital conflict and a lower quality of parenting behaviors (Robila, this volume).

As mentioned earlier, young families are more seriously impacted by economic struggles, due mainly to their inability to own or rent a place to live. This has significant consequences for intergenerational relationships between parents and adult children who are not able to become independent, creating, at times, intergenerational tensions (for Macedonia, see Lakinska & Bornarova; for Romania, see Robila; for Hungary, see Tóth, this volume).

Gender Roles

Under communism, gender and ideology interacted, with socialist ideology proclaiming (at times only for propaganda) gender equality, ensured by equal opportunities for men and women in education, professional training and employment (Kerig et al., 1993). However, patriarchal views of women were maintained since they were primarily responsible for childcare and household duties.

While both spouses were expected to work, the woman was also expected to assume housework and childrearing responsibilities. Immediately after the fall of communism, there was a revival of patriarchal attitudes toward families, underlying women's return to the home (e.g. in Lithuania see Juozeliûnienë and Kuzmickaitë; in Russia see Uspenskaya & Borodin, this volume). However, during the last decade, changes toward more symmetric gender role models are evident (see Eglite; Juozeliûnienë & Kuzmickaitë, this volume). Thus, the younger (and urban) generation presents clear trends towards more egalitarian gender roles, while older people and those residing in rural areas maintain more traditional perspectives that attribute the burden of domestic work and childrearing to women (see Bodrug-Lungu; Lakinska & Bornarova; Maøíková; Uspenskaya & Borodin, this volume).

Traditions

Many of the traditions and practices (especially in the customs related to life cycles: birth, marriage, and death) in the area are linked to religious affiliations. Economic struggles might sometimes challenge the continuation of certain traditions, pushing people to adapt them (or reduce, or even cancel) (see Moldova, Bodrug-Lungu, this volume). The role of religion in people's lives is important, especially since during communism the States encouraged atheism, forbade religious education and practices, destroyed churches and punished religious leaders and worshipers. Democracy brought back the religious freedom that encouraged people to revisit their cultural roots and beliefs (see Bodrug-Lungu; Eglite; Lakinska & Bornarova, this volume).

CHILDREARING PRACTICES

In Eastern Europe, children play a central role in family life (Robila & Krishnakumar, 2004a). For example, in Romania, the majority of the participants in a national survey indicated that a family needed to have a child in order to consider itself fulfilled (see Robila, this volume). Similarly for Poles, children are so important that not having children is perceived negatively (Titkow & Duch, this volume). While research indicates that the preferred number of children in a family is two, the fertility rate is actually lower throughout Eastern Europe (e.g. in Slovenia; see Ule, this volume). When asked about the reasons for not having more children, parents indicated being concerned about their ability to provide enough economic resources for their children (Zhurzhenko, this volume).

Parents are very involved in the lives of their children. Children perceive their families as highly supportive and talk about their parents making financial sacrifices for their happiness, thereby protecting them from the negative effects of the changes in society (Van Hoorn et al., 2000; Wallace & Kovatcheva, 1998). Children express a high level of closeness and trust towards their families (Robila, 2003; Robila & Krishnakumar, 2004b; Tóth, this volume). The relationship with the mother is especially warm, with the child talking and sharing more with the mother than with the father (Maříková; Tóth, this volume). Ule (this volume) also discusses the self-sacrificing role of mothers, women being expected to be more involved than men in childrearing activities (Lakinska & Bornarova; Titkow & Duch, this volume).

Childrearing practices in Eastern Europe have been changing gradually over the years, reflecting the overall societal transformations, with parents moving from focusing on child obedience and submission to using strategies designed to promote independence and self-reliance. However, teaching obedience remains an important practice, the child being expected to listen to his/her parents. For example, research conducted in Moldova (see Bodrug-Lungu, this volume) indicates that teenagers have little room to negotiate with their parents, and although parents' attitudes are based on their desire to help their children and to meet society's standards, this might impede their children's development of independence and initiative. Similarly in Ukraine, it is expected that parental authority will be respected and not questioned (Zhurzhenko, this volume); however, more liberal parental attitudes are evolving, and children are enjoying more freedom and decision-making powers (see Lakinska & Bornarova, this volume). In eastern Germany, for example, this pattern existed even right after the unification, when parents considered that promoting independence (52%) and diligence (44%) were more important child-rearing goals than promoting obedience (4%) (Adler, this volume).

Another important issue is the child's responsibility towards his/her parents. Thus, when compared to youth in Western Europe, adolescents from Eastern Europe rated social responsibility (including taking care of one's parents) significantly higher than did their Western peers (Alsaker & Flammer, 1999).

As in the West, parenting is influenced by the child's gender, parents being stricter with girls than with boys. Similarly, boys are socialized to be more active and assertive while girls are encouraged to be more sensitive and caring (e.g. in Moldova; see Bodrug-Lungu, this volume).

Parents frequently act like filters, insulating and protecting their children from the effects of the transitions (e.g. giving priority to children's needs when allocating financial resources) (see Staykova; Robila, this volume). A study of Eastern European adolescents indicated that their psychosocial identity was grounded in the private/family sphere and rarely extended to the public world (Van Hoorn et al., 2000). The central and positive nature of family relationships in adolescents' descriptions of themselves explains why their families are so influential in the way adolescents respond to societal changes.

Providing the child with the best education possible is a major preoccupation. While education is not necessarily perceived as ensuring considerable economic advancement any more, it still assures social respectability and prestige. The high competition for educational advancement, evidenced through the considerably difficult college admission examinations, suggests that having a good education is still valued very highly. Parents give much-needed support, sometimes enduring economic adversities to provide their children with all they need to succeed (Robila, this volume).

FAMILY POLICIES

Before the 1990s, throughout Eastern Europe the State provided a limited, although uniform, family support system, represented by child-care facilities, maternity leave, and child allowance. The transition period is characterized by significant revisions of policies. For example, Latvia (see Eglite, this volume) started its own family policies after regaining its independence from the Soviet Union. Those most closely related to family functioning are maternity leave, birth grants, childcare allowance, childcare leave, and family allowance. German family policy entitles women to a 14-week paid maternity leave (Adler, this volume), while in Latvia childcare allowance is paid to a mother or a father for up to 2 years (Eglite, this volume). Sometimes the childcare allowance is insufficient to meet a family's needs and parents decide to go back to work earlier (e.g. in Romania; see Robila, this volume). Among the most discussed changes is the introduction of paternity leave, although, unfortunately, there is not much data suggesting fathers actually take up this opportunity. In Germany, while fathers can apply for paternity leave, 95% of applicants are women (see Adler, this volume).

A trend regarding family policy is in using family issues as a political factor. Throughout the region, political programs, regardless of their orientation, use family in their platforms in order to gain public support (Uspenskaya & Borodin; Zhurzhenko, this volume). Family policies across the area need considerable restructuring and orientation towards meeting the needs of the contemporary family.

RESEARCH ON FAMILY

Under communism, research on family was practically nonexistent. During the transition period, several research endeavors commenced, the main themes in Eastern Europe being those related to major societal concerns. One of these is the demographic problem (e.g. fertility rate, changing family forms) that has been widely explored (e.g. in Latvia see Eglite); in Slovakia (see Filadelfiová); in Hungary (see Tóth, this volume). Research has also been conducted on the support system dedicated to families, especially those with economic problems (e.g. in Slovakia; see Filadelfiová, this volume). Another major topic is the changes in gender roles and family relationships (see Uspenskaya & Borodin), with several programs on gender issues being developed (e.g. in Ukraine; see Zhurzhenko, this volume).

An important research development is the international collaboration on a diverse range of family issues (e.g. family policies, demographic development, gender roles) (e.g. in Slovakia, see Filadelfiová; Czech Republic, see Maříková). These projects are supported by several centers focused on families, such as the Centre for Work and Family Studies in Bratislava, or the Tver University Center for Women's History and Gender Studies in Russia. After decades of physical, social and intellectual isolation, international collaborations are now of significant importance (Roberts et al., 2000). Multinational exchanges have demonstrated the benefits of research on individual development and social transitions that includes investigators that provide "the native (emic) perspective as well as others who provide the outsider (etic) perspective" (Van Hoorn et al., 2000, p. 10).

However, throughout Eastern Europe, research on family issues is rather limited. Family Science (e.g. family psychology, family sociology) as a specific field needs to be recognized in order to create a scientific support system for the family. Family Science and Family Counseling academic departments need to be created in order to prepare educators, researchers, and practitioners who would be able to develop systematic, scholarly work on families and to assist them to be successful in their endeavors. Moreover, Institutes and/or Centers for Family Studies need to be developed in order to conduct research projects on family relationships, to attract funding and collaborations, and to meaningfully influence family-related policies.

ORGANIZATION OF THE VOLUME

Each of the following chapters examines families in specific Eastern European countries. Each chapter addresses the impact of the historic and socio-economic context on families. The effects of the post-communist transition on family functioning are also underlined, since the transformation of the political climate has dictated significant changes in all of these countries. Further, family demographics and their changing trends are presented. Family processes such as marital relationships, gender roles, or child-rearing practices are also examined. Additionally, details are provided on family policies and programs in each country, as well as on the state of research on family issues.

Marina Adler, in "Continuity and Change in Familial Relationships in East Germany since 1990," discusses the transformations in family patterns in East Germany compared to those in West Germany. German unification brought a restructuring of the socio-economic context based on West German standards. This transformation had multiple implications on family life. Adler's analysis indicates that, after more than 10 years of unification, families in eastern Germany continue to present distinctive characteristics. Thus, rather than adopting the more traditional West German family roles, East German families maintained non-traditional patterns such as women's high work orientation (combined with family care) and an appreciation of a wide diversity of family forms.

Hana Maříková ("The Czech Family at Present and in the Recent Past") and Jarmila Filadelfiová ("Families in Slovakia") discuss the impact of the splitting of Czechoslovakia in January 1993 on families' lives. Maříková explores the family situation during the communist period as well as in the present, indicating that, after the Velvet Revolution, the predictability and uniformity of family life was disrupted, having a significant effect upon lifestyles. These differences are even stronger when considering urban and rural families. Czech families living in the countryside are more traditional, stable, religious and cohesive, using more "passive/defensive" strategies (such as savings – a considerable amount of housework replaces market goods and services) to achieve success. Families in urban areas use active strategies (focus on entrepreneurship, assertiveness) to accomplish their goals. Filadelfiová explains the changes in the structure and functions of the Slovak family. The family based on marriage is still considered to have a fundamental social value. One of the major factors impacting contemporary young families is the impossibility of living independent lives (due to high prices of houses), pushing them to live with their family of origin for several years after their marriage.

Anna Titkow and Danuta Duch (in "The Polish Family: Always an Institution?") focus on the changes in the demographic characteristics of Polish families. These authors indicate that, despite the transformations undergone, the Polish family continues to filter the impact upon the individual of societal challenges. While women adopt more progressive gender roles and attitudes, Polish men still favor traditional gender patterns. In terms of parenting, the authors indicate that during the 1990s Polish parents started to adopt more liberalized childrearing styles, characterized by using more partnered/collaborative approaches and fewer punishing strategies.

Two chapters focus on countries from the former Yugoslavia, Slovenia and Macedonia. In "Changes in Family Life Courses in Slovenia," Mirjana Ule reviews the developmental trends of contemporary Slovenian families which, due to the country's proximity to Western Europe and the high pre-transition standards of living, rank among the most economically successful countries in the area. However, they are no longer able to rely on the past security of everyday life; Slovenians need to adjust their lifestyles to change and dynamism. Ule elaborates on the uncertainty of youths' transition to adulthood, which impacts partnership relations and decisions about creating families and having children.

Divna Lakinska and Suzana Bornarova in "Families in the Republic of Macedonia" address issues of family functioning, suggesting that, besides the challenges inherited from the country's dependence on the central government of Yugoslavia (e.g. centralism, lack of experience in policy development), the difficulties of the transition process (e.g. urban overpopulation, economic migration) created considerable hardships for Macedonian families. The authors also elaborate on the ethnic and religious diversity of the environment and on the important role that traditions play in family life.

Olga Tóth (in "The Hungarian Family") indicates that contemporary Hungarian families change, not only demographically, but also ideologically. For example, as part of child socialization, the practice of value propagation presents new challenges to parents due to the differences at times between their values and those of the outside world. Tóth also addresses the role of parents in childrearing, indicating that while mothers have a determining role in a child's upbringing, the father's role in the family has decreased, and he is no longer such a figure of authority.

Mihaela Robila's chapter on "Child Development and Family Functioning within the Romanian Context" provides an overview of the impact of recent political and socio-economic changes on families. The transition from communism to democracy brought, along with its appealing social liberties and decentralized and competitive economy, inherent challenges and insecurities. In their efforts to adapt to these changes, Romanians endeavor to develop coping strategies, relying heavily on their families as filters and support mechanisms.

Raya Staykova, in "The Bulgarian Family: Specifics and Development from Liking at the Village Square to Love in the 'Chat,'" examines families from a historical perspective. Staykova presents an analysis of the traditional family form, "zadruga" (a household of several generations of monogamous families), as well as the modern transformation of the contemporary family.

Several chapters present family evolution in countries under former Soviet rule. The chapter on Moldova by Valentina Bodrug-Lungu, for example, discusses the country's past and present considerable economic struggles and their impact on families. Significant reforms of social and family policies are necessary in order to support family statutes and improve individual and family quality of life in Moldova.

In "Families in Ukraine: Between Postponed Modernization, Neofamilism, and Economic Survival," Tatiana Zhurzhenko focuses on the changes and new family patterns in that region. Most Ukrainian families are confronted with economic hardships and insecurities. Zhurzhenko addresses the current "neofamilism" as state ideology, which underlines the importance of "traditional family values" for the nation building process. "Postponed" modernization (due to liberalization and uncensored information flows) in the private sphere brought new family patterns as well as new challenges.

Parsla Eglites's chapter on "Marriage and Families in Latvia" outlines the recent transformation of the family there. Eglite addresses the impact of the Soviet regime and of the transition towards democracy on family issues. Patriarchal norms of family life in Latvia are being replaced by egalitarian relations between spouses and democratic attitudes toward children as equal members. In "Families in Lithuania," Irena Juozeliûnienë and Loreta Kuzmickaitë delineate the evolution of families in Lithuania. One of the demographic changes, the decline in the fertility rate, is associated with a considerable increase in "children's value," with more attention and resources being provided to them.

Valentina Uspenskaya and Dmitry Y. Borodin (in "Family Relations in 20th Century Russia as a Projection of Popular Beliefs, Scholarly Discourse and State Policies") examine the impact of socio-political changes on families in Russia using a social constructivist perspective. The authors provide a comprehensive historical analysis of families during the 1920s and 1930s, during the Soviet period, and during the contemporary era.

In the context of globalization and the intermingling of world cultures, this book expands the knowledge about families in Eastern Europe. Written mainly by Eastern European scholars, this book promotes a better understanding of family issues in this region, at the same time setting the stage for more systematic research. Throughout Eastern Europe, the family is perceived both as a buffer for the impact of society's problems on individuals and as a resource provider. As in other parts of the world (e.g. USA, Australia), Eastern European families need to be supported in their endeavors to be successful. Through education, influence on public policy, dissemination of information, and development of applied programs, family science can improve the quality of family life. This volume hopes to stimulate the development of family science in Eastern Europe.

REFERENCES

Alsaker, F. D., & Flammer, A. (Eds) (1999). *The adolescent experience: European and American adolescents in the 1990s*. Mahwah, NJ: Lawrence Erlbaum.

Central Intelligence Agency (CIA) (2003). Countries reports.

Daskalova, K. (2000). Women's problems, women's discourses in Bulgaria. In: S. Gal & G. Kligman (Eds), *Reproducing Gender: Politics, Publics and Everyday Life After Socialism* (pp. 337–370). Princeton, NJ: Princeton University Press.

Gal, S., & Kligman, G. (2000). *Reproducing gender: Politics, publics and everyday life after socialism*. Princeton, NJ: Princeton University Press.

Kerig, P. K., Aloyshina, Y. Y., & Volovich, A. S. (1993). Gender-role socialization in contemporary Russia: Implication for cross-cultural research. *Psychology of Women Quarterly, 17*, 389–408.

Kovacs, K., & Varadi, M. (2000). Women's life trajectories and class formation in Hungary. In: S. Gal & G. Kligman (Eds), *Reproducing Gender: Politics, Publics and Everyday Life After Socialism* (pp. 176–200). Princeton, NJ: Princeton University Press.

Mestrovic, S. G. (1994). *The Balkanization of the West: The confluence of postcommunism and postmodernism*. London: Routledge.

Morris, E. W. (1998). Household responses to major economic change in Poland: A theoretical framework. *Journal of Family and Economic Issues, 19*(3), 199–220.

Nauck, B., & Joos, M. (1999). Child poverty in East Germany – The interaction of institution transfer and family type in the transformation process. In: R. K. Silbereisen & A. von Eye (Eds), *Growing Up in Times of Social Change* (pp. 73–90). Berlin: Gruyter.

Roberts, K., Clark, S. C., Fagan, C., & Tholen, J. (2000). *Surviving post-communism: Young people in the former Soviet Union*. Cheltenham, UK: Edward Elgar.

Robila, M. (2003). Romania. In: J. J. Ponzetti, Jr. (Ed.), *International Encyclopedia of Marriage and Family* (pp. 1370–1373). New York, NY: Macmillan.

Robila, M., & Krishnakumar, A. (2004a). The role of children in Eastern European families. *Children & Society, 18*(1).

Robila, M., & Krishnakumar, A. (2004b). The impact of financial strain on marital conflict in Romania. *Journal of Family Psychology.*

Szalai, J. (2000). From informal labor to paid occupations: Marketization from below in Hungarian women's work. In: S. Gal & G. Kligman (Eds), *Reproducing Gender: Politics, Publics and Everyday Life After Socialism* (pp. 200–225). Princeton, NJ: Princeton University Press.

Tesliuc, E. D., Pop, L., & Tesliuc, C. M. (2001). *Poverty and the social security system*. Iasi: Polirom.

Van Hoorn, J. V., Komlosi, A., Suchar, E., & Samelson, D. A. (2000). *Adolescent development and rapid social change: Perspectives from Eastern Europe.* Albany, NY: State University of New York Press.

Wallace, C., & Kovatcheva, S. (1998). *Youth in society: The construction and deconstruction in East and West Europe.* London: Macmillan.

World Bank (2003). Country Reports.

CONTINUITY AND CHANGE IN FAMILIAL RELATIONSHIPS IN EAST GERMANY SINCE 1990

Marina A. Adler

The unprecedented economic and political transformation processes in Eastern Europe, which began in 1989, have had profound effects on regional economic, social, and political structures. In the case of East Germany, the major shift from a socialist to a capitalist political economy meant the superimposition of West German structures, policies, and values on the former German Democratic Republic (GDR). This process has brought about industrial restructuring based on West German social market economy standards and changes in social policy in line with West German social and family values, which have dramatically changed the everyday work and family lives of the East German population.

The sudden move from a "centrally planned life" to a "high risk society" has completely overturned the predictable life course of most East Germans (Adler, 2002; Dölling, 1998). To a population, who for 40 years took for granted the right to work, extensive social provisions for the integration of work and family, and a generous social safety net, the newly found uncertainties have threatened a formerly safe and predictable future. Consequently, unification has led to drastic changes in family formation behaviors in the East German population. And yet research also shows a continuation of various GDR-based family values and attitudes (Adler, 2002, 2004; Dölling, 1998; Kolinsky, 1998). Of particular interest are changes in the variety of family forms and the gendered nature of social change since unification. This chapter explores to what extent the observed economic, policy and demographic shifts have affected the various forms of living together

Families in Eastern Europe
Contemporary Perspectives in Family Research, Volume 5, 15–28
© 2004 Published by Elsevier Ltd.
ISSN: 1530-3535/doi:10.1016/S1530-3535(04)05002-2

and family-related attitudes since the *Wende* (turning point, unification). Are we witnessing a general assimilation to West German patterns or do East Germans remain distinctive in maintaining their appreciation for a plurality of family forms and family values?

SOCIO-HISTORIC AND ECONOMIC CONTEXT

Among the Eastern European nations East Germany occupies both a typical and a unique position. It is typical in the sense that it was part of the Soviet-dominated Eastern Bloc, and as such its political, social and economic structure resembled that of other state socialist countries. Nevertheless, due to its geographical, cultural and socio-historical proximity to West Germany, the GDR evolved into the most advanced Eastern European socialist state, and served as model for the rest of the region. This special status also entailed numerous problems, such as the high social and economic cost associated with maintaining the East-West German border, preventing the intrusion of capitalist cultural (media) influences from the West, and counteracting differences in living standards to the West and other Eastern bloc nations.

In 1990, the GDR and FRG (Federal Republic of Germany) were officially reunited after being separate countries with different political economies and constitutions for 40 years. After World War II, Germany was divided into the capitalist Western Germany (FRG) and the state socialist Eastern Germany (GDR). While the West German "social market economy" and its social democratic culture was strongly influenced by the economic and military presence of the United States, the centralized state apparatus of the GDR was shaped and controlled by the Soviet Union's vision of the ideal socialist worker state.

Ideologically, the GDR regime endorsed the Marxist idea that women's emancipation presupposes their full integration into the labor market as workers. Practically, the state needed to increase its population and a stable labor supply to counteract acute shortages produced by postwar emigration. Consequently, in order to draw women into the labor market while at the same time encouraging fertility, the ideal of the "employed mother" was created (see Adler, 2002). In order to realize this ideal, the GDR state put in place a number of work-family related institutional support systems. They included inexpensive state-run childcare centers, generous child allowances, marriage and child grants, housing preferences for marriage and child bearing, and generous maternity leave policies (Kreyenfeld, 2001). GDR ideology promoted gender equality and social policies supported the equal importance of women's' family and work roles. Because the state proclaimed every citizen's constitutional right and duty to work, both men and women, disregarding family status, were expected to be lifelong full-time workers. In return the state provided a lifelong safety net, free health care, housing and family subsidies, and an extensive infrastructure in support of maternal employment.

These policies had a significant impact on the biographies of East Germans in general and on women's life course in particular (Adler, 2002). They have led to a "double life orientation" (Geissler & Oechsle, 1996) among women (work and family are considered to be equally important features of the life course), a demographic pattern entailing early marriage and childbirth, and a phenomenon called the "double burden" (full-time employed women also have to do most housework). The latter was the result of the double "Vergesellschaftung" (integration into society) of women – via a double socialization to become workers and mothers, but not necessarily wives. This process did not have a parallel for men – while women participated in the labor market in almost equal numbers as men, men did not equally (or even significantly) participate in family responsibilities (Kolinsky, 1998). Generous state policies and supportive infrastructure granted married and unmarried employed mothers the ability to reconcile work and family. Consequently, women did not – as is the case in the West – leave the labor market for extended periods to become "stay-at-home mothers."

The shift from socialism to capitalism has caused changes in the gender contract and in everyday work and family experiences. The term "gender contract" entails a classification of societies in terms of the societal social and institutional arrangements that define and reinforce their dominant gender division of labor as male breadwinner or dual earner regimes (e.g. Pfau-Effinger, 1993). Whereas in West Germany the male-breadwinner/female homemaker model predominates, the GDR subscribed to the dual earner/employed mother model. Since unification the two public/private sphere arrangements have clashed rather than merged. Even 10 years after unification, the role model of employed mother persists in the East and research on young women shows that they are not recasting their identity in the image of the West German homemaker (Adler, 2002, 2004). According to Kolinsky, "In accepting women's employment alongside motherhood and endorsing women's material independence, post-communist Germany eschews the breadwinner and housewife model of the west and sets a new agenda of family development" (Kolinsky, 1998, p. 207).

DEMOGRAPHIC CHANGES SINCE 1990

One of the most problematic post-unification changes occurred in the East German labor market: due to massive plant closings, workplace restructuring, deindustrialization, downsizing and economic streamlining of "inefficient"

Table 1.   Employment Patterns of East Germans Since 1991.

	Percent of...	
	1991	2000
Women aged 15–64 who are employed		
Total[b,c]	77.2	72.4
Total full time (>36 hrs)[b]	91.0 [1989][d]	62.2 [1999]
Who are married women[a]	73.0	63.7 [2001]
Who are lone mothers[c]	89.0 [1989][d]	64.0
Who are mothers[c]	80.6	71.3
Who have kids under 3	75.9	52.2
Who have kids 3–5	82.8	63.7
Who work full time (>36 h)[c]	64.6	47.8
	1991	2001
Women aged 15–64 who are unemployed[a]	12.3	19.4
Men who are unemployed, total[a]	8.5	18.4
Women who are employed[a]		
Aged 15–20	46.3	30.6
Aged 21–25	87.2	71.7
Aged 26–30	96.2	83.8

Note: In official statistics, "current employment" can take the form of (1) employed (part or full time), (2) employed but temporarily on leave (sick leave, maternity leave, parental leave), or (3) in the labor force but currently unemployed and looking for work. "Erwerbstätigenquote" includes only the first two options and "Erwerbsquote" adds the unemployed.
[a] Statistisches Bundesamt, 2002 Tab.2, 3, 9 ("Erwerbstätigenquote").
[b] Winkler, 2000, p.22 ("Erwerbsquote," includes the currently unemployed), p. 27.
[c] Engstler und Menning, 2003 Tab A4–1, A4–2 ("Erwerbsquote" for all employed in 2000), Tab 32.
[d] Bundesanstalt für Arbeit, quoted in Adler, 1997.

socialist work processes, an unprecedented number of people became unemployed or marginally employed. Despite various government efforts to alleviate the unemployment crisis by offering early retirement incentives, retraining, and further training opportunities, the number of workers affected by layoffs, reduced work hours, and unemployment grew to over 3 million people after unification (Kolinsky, 1998). As Table 1 illustrates, employed women were particularly affected. In the 10 years following unification, the proportion of full time employed women fell from 91% to about 62%. The percentage of married women and mothers in the labor force also fell in this time period. The reduction in employment of young women under age 30 is particularly interesting because they are of traditional childbearing age. Many in this age group are extending their educational and occupational training in an effort to more successfully compete in the tight labor market. As the

Table 2. Demographic Trends in Eastern Germany Since 1989.

	1989	1995	2000
TFR[a]	1.56	0.84	1.22
Births per 1,000 population[c]	12.0	5.4	7.3
Marriages per 1,000 population[b]	7.9	3.5	3.5 [1997]
Average age at first marriage, Women/Men	23.7/25.8	26.4/28.5	28.0/30.7
Average age at first birth,[a] Women	22.9	27.2[b]	28.4 (married)
			26.5 (unmarried)
Percent of all births non-marital[c]	33.6	41.8	51.5
Percent remaining single,			
Women age 20–24 and 25–29[a]	67.6/24.9 [1991]	84.8/42.6	91.3/59.8 [1999]
Men age 20–24 and 25–29[a]	87.0/46.2 [1991]	94.9/67.9	97.2/79.3 [1999]

Note: Not available – 1997 from Mau and Zapf, 1998.
[a]Engstler & Menning, 2003, Table 10, 11, 13, 15.
[b]Statistisches Bundesamt, in Mau & Zapf, 1998.
[c]Winkler, 2000, Abb 1.2 and 1.4.

high unemployment rate for women demonstrates (19.4 in 2000), this departure from the labor market was not voluntary. Overall, the labor force participation of women in East Germany remains much higher than that in West Germany.

These economic realities, combined with dramatic shifts in social and family policy have affected family formation decisions in the population. Table 2 shows the drastic reduction in total fertility from 1.56 to a 1995 low of 0.84 to 1.22 in 2000. In addition, the birth rate dropped from 12 per 1,000 to 7.3. Marriage rates were also cut in half in the last decade. The standardized life plan for women and men produced by state pressures during GDR times has become more diverse since unification (Adler, 1997, 2002). While GDR women followed a biography typically including having a child before age 20, before or after marriage, and often during education and occupational training, contemporary East German women postpone marriage and childbearing to their 30s (Adler, 2004). Table 2 shows that in 1989 the average age at first marriage was 23.2 (women) and 25.8 (men) years and the age at first birth was 22.9. The higher average age at first marriage relative to that of first birth indicates that these life events were not sequenced in the normative Western way. These ages have moved up considerably and resembled West German averages in 2000. Currently the average age for first marriages and births appears to be around 28 for women on both sides of the former border.

Elder (1995) makes the connection between social change and individual development by combining a life course model with an ecological perspective to explain how dramatic changes in society can affect individual biographical trajectories. Unification – or the *Wende* – quite literally was a *turning point* for millions of East Germans. While a "transition" in the life course implies a gradual change, a "turning point" occurs rapidly and includes a shift in direction. In the past GDR citizens "transitioned" more or less automatically into various temporally sequenced life stages, monitored by the state. After unification a plurality of life plans opened to East Germans, "privatizing" not only the economy but also individual decision-making about their lives. Consequently, the timing of transitions across the life course was influenced. "Thus, young couples may schedule work and family events to minimize financial, time, and energy pressures, as when children are postponed until the mid-to late −30 s" (Elder, 1995, p. 114).

Because the human life course is situated in a specific historical time and place, each age cohort experiences shifts at the societal level differently. Analysis of age-specific fertility rates indicates that the most drastic "baby bust" after unification occurred among 18–28 year olds (Münz & Ulrich, 1995). The most pronounced fertility decrease was for second births, and among women under age 30 (Grünheid & Roloff, 2000). Thus, it appears that women under age 30 are postponing their first birth and women over 30 are forgoing additional births. While during GDR times about 10% of women never had children, about 25% of the 1965 birth cohort is expected to remain childless (Bundesinstitut für Bevölkerungsforschung, 2000). The percentage of women under age 30 choosing not to marry also reveals a dramatic upward trend (see Table 2). Whereas around the time of unification only 67.6% of East German 20–24 and 24.9% of 25–29 year old women were unmarried, by 1999 these numbers had risen to 91.3 and 59.8%, respectively. These trends indicate that young women are prioritizing family differently than before unification.

Table 2 also shows that the proportion of all births occurring outside of marriage has increased, and currently more than half of all births are non-marital births. Since unification, the definition of what constitutes a family in Germany has been modified to reflect the fact that there is an increasing diversity in family forms, including cohabiting couples, single parents, and same-sex couples. Consequently, the German Constitutional Court ruled that cohabiting partners are in a "marriage-like relationship" if they are in a committed long-term relationship (see Henneck, 2003). Before unification marriage did not have the provider function for East German women as it did in West Germany. Due to easily accessible and affordable divorce, East German marriage was an even less stable institution than in the West and thus women, with the help of the state, chose not to be dependent on it as the sole source of economic stability. Even in the new "risk society" based on individualization principles women continue to insist on their self-reliance (Adler, 2003).

Adler (2002) confirmed Lenz' (1997) claim that in contemporary Germany household and family formation are not necessarily synchronized life events anymore. Biographies are less standardized than in the past, with major life events

Table 3.   East German Women in Marital and Non-marital Unions with and without Children (2000).

	% Of Women ...
Who are in a non-marital union	
Of women under age 25	15.5
With/without kids	3.6/11.9
Of women 25–29	28.1
With/without kids	14.5/13.6
Who are mothers without a partner	
Of women under age 25	3.7
Of women 25–29	10.8
Who are married	
Of women under age 25	4.9
With/without kids	3.1/1.8
Of women 25–29	32.1
With/without kids	24.5/7.6

Source: Engstler & Menning, 2003, Tables A 1–6.

less temporally dependent, variable in sequence, and sometimes even optional. Thus, marriage and household formation do not necessarily occur concurrently or subsequently, and are not necessarily the precondition of the birth of a child. The GDR pattern of a pluralization of family forms continues today – East Germans insist on a multitude of family forms even though the male breadwinner family is preferred by the state (Adler, 2002, 2004).

Cohabitation among East German couples has increased by 37% since 1991 (Engstler & Menning, 2003, Table A1–22) and is particularly popular among those under age 30; in fact 76.1% of all couples under age 25 cohabit (Engstler & Menning, 2003, Table A1–25). By the year 2000, 15.5% of East German women under 25 and 28.1% of those aged 25–29 lived in non-marital unions (see Table 3). In addition, 3.6% of East German women under 25 and 14.5% of women aged 25–29 lived in non-marital unions with children, clearly regarding cohabitation as an alternative to marriage. Approximately 50% of non-marital unions included children (Engstler & Menning, 2003, Table A1–22). This unexpected increase in cohabitation and non-marital births has lead some to speculate that changes in family policies and tax laws, unfavorable labor market developments, higher educational levels, women's work orientation, and rejection of the institution of marriage may be the causes (Grünheid, 2003; Konietzka & Kreyenfeld, 2002).

Adler (2002, 2004) examined the biographies of East German women in order to assess the effects of unification on the life course by age cohort and specifically for young women. It was found that although the life plans of women under 30 differed significantly from the standard GDR biography, they have kept the work orientation of their mothers, are postponing family formation, and reject the West German notion of full-time homemaker. Economic necessity and the desire for independence make employment a priority, and prompt many women to delay or forgo marriage and child bearing until they secure a stable employment situation (Adler, 2004; Kreyenfeld, 2001).

FAMILY PATTERNS

In the GDR family was considered very important – partly because it provided a private retreat from public life and state surveillance (Keiser, 1995; Kolinsky, 1998; Uhlendorff, 2003). The question is whether this strong "family orientation" intensified after unification as a mechanism of social support in times of insecurity or whether it was reduced when state pressures in the public sphere disappeared. After unification, East German families, which were accustomed to predictability under the old system, were being challenged in numerous ways by changed material conditions, conflicts in reconciling work and family, changed values, and by having to assume functions that formerly were held by the state.

From an ecological perspective, familial resources, such as economic (income), human capital (education and employment), and personal psychosocial resources (emotional and social support) have been strained since unification. In addition, policy shifts and life style changes have reduced community resources and external supports, such as childcare, employment opportunities, leisure time, and social networks. Combined, these changes have led to a shift in culture towards a "risk society," which necessitated a resocialization process (Dölling, 1998). Not only are people objectively feeling the strain on resources (unemployment, higher cost of living), their perceptions about resource limitations (feelings of insecurity, fears for the future, lack of predictability) may affect their family decision-making and change their priorities. Historically, East Germans have developed an array of survival strategies designed for the old system and some of these skills, such as resilience and stubbornness (Eigensinn), have served them well in meeting the challenges presented by the changed conditions (Adler, 2002; Dölling, 1998). Moen and Erickson (1995) argue that in order to counteract risk factors and vulnerability in times of social change, coping skills are an important personal resource. In addition to personal coping skills, adult family members represent an important emotional and economic network in times of crisis.

Family formation, however, may be regarded as a risky venture in times of economic insecurity. Recent attitude data from the Allbus Database 2002 reveal that among childless East Germans, 79% report eventually wanting children

(Statistisches Bundesamt, 2002, Table 11.4). Nevertheless, among those who already have children very few (9%) want further children. In addition, 30% of the respondents want only one child and the average number of children wanted is 1.8. These numbers indicate a desire to have children and a preference for fewer children in the East than the West. The survey also shows that 79% of East Germans (70% of West Germans) indicate that "one needs family to be truly happy." Furthermore, 61.9% agree strongly that "watching ones children grow up is the greatest joy in life" (42.3% in the West), and 21.9% of East Germans strongly agree that "people who have no children have empty lives" (only 13.4 in the West). These attitudinal data not only reflect the continued high importance given to children in the life of East Germans, it shows a lack of convergence with West Germany.

Numerous studies (reviewed in Uhlendorff, 2003) also show that in the years immediately following unification, the family ties between partners, and between parents and adult children have become closer. While the majority of survey respondents said their family relationships had not changed, 20% indicated their partnerships had become closer and 15% said their relationship with their grown children had intensified (see Uhlendorff, 2003). Nevertheless, when considering more distant relationships, 22% indicated that other relatives had become less close, 35% considered their friendships less close, and 45% said their relationships with colleagues were less close. Overall, it appears that the turmoil experienced after unification actually intensified the family orientation of East Germans and that whereas ties to immediate family have gained in importance, contacts to colleagues were diminished in importance (Uhlendorff, 2003). Various scholars (see Dennis, 1998; Uhlendorff, 2003) do not anticipate the importance of close family ties to erode in the near future.

CHILDREARING GOALS AND PARENTING PRACTICES

Historically speaking, Germany has ranked higher than other European nations in regards to "authoritarian" child rearing values directed at achieving conformity (Reuband, 1997). Empirical data, collected approximately every 5 years since 1950, show the relative changes in childrearing goals in Germany (Reuband, 1997). The key survey question in these studies asks respondents to select the most important among the following goals: "independence and free will; love for order and diligence; obedience and submission." In West Germany the percentage of survey respondents choosing obedience shrank dramatically from about 25% in 1951 to 7% in 1995. During the same period, independence and free will rose from 28% to 60% (Reuband, 1997).

Considering that the GDR and FRG had a very different ideological framework and value system one might expect that their values regarding child-rearing goals would also differ significantly. The 1966 Family Code in the GDR outlined the model of the "socialist family," which was defined as the smallest cell of socialist society (Dennis, 1998). As such it featured key elements, such as a life-long marital union, gender equality, family-employment compatibility, and the socialization of children as socialist citizens (Dennis, 1998). This demand for conformity by the centralized government may have led to equally authoritarian parenting practices. Nevertheless, survey results for 1991 show that these values were very similar in the East and West at unification: in the East 52% (compared to 57% in the West) consider independence and free will as the most important child-rearing goal, 44% emphasized order and diligence (West: 35%), and only 4% (compared to 8% in the West) focus on obedience and submission (Reuband, 1997). This surprising similarity has been explained by various sources as the result of the Western media influences, which showed child-rearing practices guided by fostering independence, and by a fundamentally similar culture. In 1995, 46% of East Germans preferred independence, 48% preferred diligence, and 6% obedience. The comparable West German numbers were 60, 33, and 7%, respectively. The observed reduction of independence in favor of diligence may be attributable to the perception that, in order to reconstruct East Germany, much effort is needed (Reuband, 1997).

Nevertheless, these survey data reflect attitudes rather than behaviors. In order to examine what types of sanctioning are used in parenting, retrospective survey data on how respondents were raised are helpful. Among East German respondents, who were aged 16 in the years 1978–1991, 22% said they were raised very strictly, 49% said good manners were emphasized at home, 57% said punctuality was important, 28% said they had received beatings, 27% said they received a lot of praise from their parents, and 33% said their parents gave them everything they wanted (see Reuband, 1997). These data are very similar to those in the West. Hence, the expected large difference between the two regions in terms of parenting again did not materialize.

SOCIAL POLICIES SUPPORTING FAMILIES

Overall, while East Germans, especially women who want to reconcile work and family, had reason to complain about a reduction in benefits supporting families after unification, family policy in contemporary Germany is in line with other European nations. The main benefits lost to East Germans were: (1) interest-free marriage loans and birth grants; (2) housing preferences for marriage and children;

(3) the "baby year" with full pay; and (4) convenient and free childcare for all ages. These generous entitlements were replaced by shorter leaves with less pay, tax exemptions, and a more expensive child care system with less coverage and inconvenient opening hours (see Kreyenfeld, 2001). The following summarizes the current provisions in Germany:

Maternity leave. German family policy currently entitles women to a 14-week, paid maternity leave (Mutterschaftsurlaub) with job protection. Of this time, six weeks are taken before the birth of the child. During maternity leave employed women are paid 100% of their net earnings through their statutory health insurance overage (Henneck, 2003).

Parental leave. Either parent can apply for paid parental leave to care for a child up to age 3 (since 2000 called Elternzeit, formerly Erziehungsurlaub). The amount of the federal child rearing support (Erziehungsgeld) during the leave is income-based, with the full amount being €307/month, and after 6 months lower income limits are used to assess benefits (Bundesregierung, 2003). This benefit is available at the end of the maternity leave and has to be applied for each year until the child's third birthday. During the leave, parents can work up to 30 hours per week (Engstler & Menning, 2003). While fathers are eligible for this leave, more than 95% of applicants are women (Henneck, 2003). In East Germany, 100% of new parents apply for benefits and 76.6% receive the full amount (Engstler & Menning, 2003). That means that in these cases at least one parent does not work or is only employed part-time. In 2000, of these applicants 46.8% were married, 31% were cohabiting, and 22.2% were single mothers (Engstler & Menning, 2003). In general, research shows that East German women are more likely to take parental leave than West German women, but they are more likely to return to work, and to do so more rapidly than West German women (Engstler & Menning, 2003). In addition, for each child under age 12, employed parents get ten days paid child sick leave per year (Henneck, 2003).

Child allowances. Every parent, disregarding income level, is entitled to a child allowance for each child under age 18, which can be extended for unemployed dependents up to age 21 or for dependents in training or schooling up to age 27 (Henneck, 2003). In 2003, the amount was €154/month for the first to third child and €179/month for subsequent children (Bundesamt für Finanzen, 2003). In addition, there are tax exemptions for families (Kinderleistungsausgleich), which in 2001 amounted to a maximum of €5,808/year per child (Küppers, 2002). Due to the fact that, on average, incomes in the East remain under Western levels, more East Germans qualify for child-related tax exemptions than West Germans.

Public childcare. Since 1996, every child aged three through six has a constitutional right to a place in *Kindergarten* (child care for 3–6 year olds), which has led to a high coverage of part-time care for 3–6 year olds with limited opening hours and relatively high prices (Kreyenfeld, 2001). The *Krippe* (child care for under 3 year olds) and the *Hort* (after school care for 6–10 year olds) have very limited coverage. In 2000, 35.1% of East German children under age 3 were in a Krippe, 86.8% of 3–6 year olds were in Kindergarten, and 55.1% of over 6 year olds attended a Hort (Engstler & Menning, 2003). These numbers were 5.5%, 74% and 8.6% in the West, respectively. In general there is a higher coverage of childcare needs for pre-schoolers in the East, mainly because of the higher demand from women who want to combine employment with motherhood.

CONCLUSION

This chapter intended to review currently available evidence in order to examine whether East Germany has assimilated to West German standards in terms of family patterns since 1990. Overall the evidence presented here indicates that more than a decade after unification East Germany remains distinctive in a number of ways. The review of demographic and survey data and research results shows that the dramatic changes in aggregate demographic statistics (reduced birth and marriage rates) cannot be interpreted as a rejection of, or reduction in significance of, familial relationships. Indeed, rather than forgoing partnership and childbirth, the patterns reveal a continued importance assigned to familial relationships – albeit not of the traditional (nuclear family) variety. Rather than accepting the West German pressure to conform to nuclear family formation and the male breadwinner gender contract, East German women continue to have high employment, cohabitation and nonmarital birth rates. These non-traditional familial patterns are part of the legacy of the GDR gender contract, which entailed support for employed mothers and for diverse family forms.

Familial relationships continue to occupy a high priority in the lives of East Germans. Similarly, having children remains an important life goal but childbirth is postponed until women are in their 30s, and fewer children are anticipated. East German women continue to show a very high work orientation and a strong desire to combine work and family. While the supportive state policy and infrastructure has largely been removed, a large number of children are in public daycare so that women can remain economically independent. Furthermore, rather than lacking "modernity," East German childrearing goals and practices are quite similar to those in the West.

It appears that East German definitions of what constitutes a family are clearly more diverse than those in the West. In fact the increasing diversity in family forms has already informed policy by expanding some benefit coverage to nontraditional unions. This moves East German thinking to the forefront of a new tolerance of diversity in postindustrial societies. Clearly this is part of the trend in postindustrial societies: families are more varied in form, they are getting smaller, births and marriages are becoming fewer and later, and divorce rates are high. It may be time West Germany assimilates to East German standards and embraces the development of new family concepts in the new millennium.

REFERENCES

Adler, M. A. (1997). Social change and declines in marriage and fertility in Eastern Germany. *Journal of Marriage and the Family, 59,* 37–49.

Adler, M. A. (2002). German unification as a turning point in East German women's life course: Biographical changes in work and family roles. *Sex Roles: A Journal of Research, 47,* 83–98.

Adler, M. A. (2004). "Child-free" and unmarried: Changes in the life planning of young East German women. *Journal of Marriage and Family, 66,* 1167–1176.

Bundesamt für Finanzen (2003). *Merkblatt Kindergeld* (Pamphlet about child allowances) Bundesamt für Arbeit (Ed.) Steuern und zentrale Dienste http://www.bffonline.de/kige/KGMB2003.pdf.

Bundesinstitut für Bevölkerungsforschung (Bib) (2000). *Bevölkerung. Fakten Trends – Ursachen-Erwartungen.* [Population, Facts-trends-causes-expectations] Mai. Wiesbaden.

Bundesregierung, die. (2003). Einkommensgrenzen für Erziehungsgeld werden geändert. (13.08.2003) http://www.bundesregierung.de/Themen-A-Z/Familie,9973/Erziehungsgeld.htm.

Dennis, M. (1998). Family policy and family function in the German Democratic Republic. In: E. Kolinsky (Ed.), *Social Transformation and the Family in Post Communist Germany* (pp. 37–56). New York: St. Martin's Press.

Dölling, I. (1998). Structure and Eigensinn: Transformation processes and continuities of Eastern German women. In: P. J. Smith (Ed.), *After the Wall. Eastern Germany since 1989* (pp. 183–202). Boulder, CO: Westview Press.

Elder, G. (1995). The life course paradigm: Social change and individual development. In: P. Moen, G. H. Elder, K. Lüscher (Eds), *Examining Lives in Context* (pp. 101–140). Washington, DC: American Psychological Association.

Engstler, H., & Menning, S. (Eds) (2003). *Die Familie im Spiegel der amtlichen Statistik.* (The family in official statistics) Bundesministerium für Familie, Senioren, Frauen und Jugend und Statistisches Bundesamt: Berlin.

Geissler, B., & Oechsle, M. (1996). Lebensplanung junger Frauen (Life planning among young women). Weinheim: Deutscher Studien Verlag.

Grünheid, E. (2003). Junge Frauen in Deutschland – Hohe Ausbildung contra Kinder? (Young women in Germany – high qualifications versus children?). *Bundesinstitut für Bevölkerungsforschung (Bib) Mitteilungen, 24,* 9–15.

Grünheid, E., & Roloff, J. (2000). Die demographische Lage 1999 in Deutschland mit dem Teil B Die demographische Entwicklung in den Bundesländern – ein Vergleich. *Zeitschrift für Bevölkerungswissenschaft, 25,* 3–150.

Henneck, R. (2003, May). *Family policy in the US, Japan, Germany, Italy and France: Parental leave, child benefits/family allowances, child care, marriage/cohabitation and divorce.* Briefing Paper. Council on Contemporary Families.

Keiser, S. (1995). Die familien in den neuen Bundesländern zwischen individualisierung und 'Notgemeinschaft' (The families in the new federal states between individualization and relations based on need). In: R. Hettlage & K. Lenz (Eds), *Deutschland nach der Wende. Eine Bilanz* (Germany after Unification. A Summary) (pp. 171–193). München: Verlag C. H. Beck.

Kolinsky, E. (1998). The family transformed: Structures, experiences, prospects. In: E. Kolinsky (Ed.), *Social Transformation and the Family in Post-communist Germany.* (pp. 207–217). New York: St. Martin's Press.

Konietzka, D., & Kreyenfeld, M. (2002). Women's employment and non-marital childbearing: A comparison between East and West Germany in the 1990s. *Population, 57,* 331–372.

Kreyenfeld, M. (2001, November). *Employment and fertility – East Germany in the 1990s.* Doctoral Dissertation at the Economics and Social Science Faculty of the University of Rostock, Rostock.

Küppers, T. (2002). *Konzepte der familienbesteuerung. (Concepts of family taxation).* Unpublished manuscript. University of Köln, Institut für Steuerrecht. http://www.uni-koeln.de/jur-fak/inststeu/sem-ws-2001–17.pdf.

Lenz, K. (1997). Ehe? familie? – beides, eines oder keines? Lebensformen in Umbruch. (Marriage? Family? Both, one or neither? Changing life forms). In: L. Boehnisch & K. Lenz (Eds), *Familien. Eine interdisziplinäre Einführung* (Families. An interdisciplinary introduction) (pp. 181–197). Weinheim und München: Juventa Verlag.

Mau, S., & Zapf, W. (1998). Zwischen schock und anpassung (Between shock and assimilation). *Informationsdienst Soziale Indikatoren (ISI), 20,* 1–4.

Moen, P., & Erickson, M. A. (1995). Linked lives: A transgenerational approach to resilience. In: P. Moen, G. H. Elder, K. Lüscher (Eds), *Examining Lives in Context* (pp. 169–207). Washington, DC: American Psychological Association.

Münz, R., & Ulrich, R. E. (1995). Depopulation after unification? Population prospects for East Germany, 1990–2010. *German Politics and Society, 13,* 1–29.

Pfau-Effinger, B. (1993). Modernization, culture and part-time employment: The example of Finland and West Germany. *Work Employment and Society, 7,* 383–410.

Reuband, K. H. (1997). Aushandeln statt Gehorsam? Erziehungsziele und Erziehungspraktiken in den alten und neuen Bundesländern im Wandel. (Bargaining instead of obedience? Changes in the goals and practices of childrearing in the old and new federal states) In: L. Boehnisch & K. Lenz (Eds), *Familien. Eine interdisziplinäre Einführung* (pp. 129–154). Weinheim: Juventa Verlag.

Statistisches Bundesamt (Ed.) (2002). *Datenreport 2002.* Destatis. de. Wiesbaden.

Uhlendorff, H. (2003). Family and family orientation in East Germany. In: E. Kolinsky & H. M. Nickel (Eds), *Reinventing Gender: Women in Eastern Germany since Unification* (pp. 209–228). London: Frank Class Publishers.

Winkler, G. (Ed.) (2000). *Frauen in Deutschland. 10 Jahre nach der Einheit.* Sozialwissenschaftliches Forschungszentrum Berlin-Brandenburg e. V.: Berlin.

THE CZECH FAMILY AT PRESENT AND IN THE RECENT PAST

Hana Maříková

SOCIO-HISTORIC AND ECONOMIC CONTEXT

Both the Czech family and the institution of marriage have gone through certain changes during the period of transformation for Czech society in the nineties. This has been influenced by the changed political, economic and social situation in our country. This chapter focuses on revealing these changes affecting the family and showing their relationship to the transformation of Czech society.

The Czech Republic was established as an independent state on the 1st of January 1993. From 1918 to 1993, it formed part of Czechoslovakia, which was established after World War I when the Austro-Hungarian Empire broke up. In 1948, the democratic regime in this country was replaced with a communist, totalitarian system. This was characterized by the absence of civic society, government supervision of the activities of citizens, the so-called national planning of the economy, the absence of a labour market with free movement of the work force,[1] significant state intervention in the private sphere (the family), "information embargo,"[2] blurring of social differences among classes and social groups (e.g. social equalization), very limited possibility of travel abroad and a low level of migration within the country. Socialist Czechoslovakia was a relatively closed society.

The leading political power in the country was the Communist Party. Participation in elections was monitored and if somebody did not participate, they were prosecuted. Even though the majority of the population was not politically active, it was politically loyal. Everybody was a member of a social organization

Families in Eastern Europe
Contemporary Perspectives in Family Research, Volume 5, 29–47
© 2004 Published by Elsevier Ltd.
ISSN: 1530-3535/doi:10.1016/S1530-3535(04)05003-4

governed by the Party and the government. Membership in these organizations was "voluntarily obligatory," so to speak. Membership was compulsory rather than voluntary because it guaranteed the absence of political prosecution and offered certain types of benefits (although they were relatively small compared with the advantages and privileges accorded to Party members). Children in elementary and middle school were organized into the Pioneer movement (otherwise, they could face difficulties when applying to high school or to an attractive vocational training course). Young people were required to be members of the Socialist Youth Movement in order even to be considered for acceptance into university or to be able to get a "good" job. Similarly, adults had to be members of at least one trade union organization (the so called ROH – Revolutionary Trade Union Movement) if they wanted to avoid political discrimination. Major advantages and privileges were given to Party members such as the possibility of career growth, management positions at work, better financial remuneration, preference in assignment of flats, the possibility to travel abroad, etc.

In the economy, state companies and organizations prevailed, along with cooperative organizations. The private sector did not exist. Redistribution of economic resources leading to the blurring of social differences[3] was a distinct feature of the socialist system. This was efficiently achieved by the gradual expropriation of private property and by an egalitarian distribution of payroll funds. The income differentiation in the former Czechoslovakia was one of the lowest within the socialist bloc (Večerník, 1991). Wage differences were minimized both on the horizontal level (by economic sectors) and on the vertical level (by education, achieved qualifications, profession prestige, and actual performance), and distinctions were made by age and gender. Manual work was remunerated identically or even better than intellectual work. Equalization of wages resulted in extensive development of the economy, as it enabled the employment of the maximum number of people.

In the 1950s, many more women became involved in the economy. Their employment level was and still is one of the highest in the world.[4] Although women's income level represented 66–68% of men's wages, their salary became necessary to the family due to the man's low income. With a single income, the family would not be able to maintain the required living standard. Employment of women was supported by state measures that tried to help women fit work and family together. Maternity leave was introduced and its duration was progressively extended (from 3 months in the 1950s up to 2 years by the end of the 1980s), together with financial assistance. Nursery schools were established for the youngest children (initially from 3 months of age, later from 6 months, and in the 1980s from 12 months to approximately 3 years of age) and kindergartens for pre-school children (from 3 years of age). School children were provided with lunch at school and after school could go to various centres for leisure activities as well as to the "youth club" at the school (where children were taken care of while their parents were at work and also before lessons started in the morning). All these measures remained in force after 1989.[5]

As the socialist economy (the so-called "supply economy") was unable to produce or provide certain types of goods and services, people secured these by "self-help," most frequently through the network of the extended family. In socialist Czechoslovakia, "self-supply" (farming for one's own consumption or for the consumption of the closest family members) was rather common, but there were also other forms of assistance replacing missing services and craft works (frequently in the form of subsistence exchange; not just reciprocal exchange of services or goods, but also information). According to Večerník (1991), the scope of economic activity of the family in our country, or the volume and composition of needs supplied from outside the market, was substantially higher and broader compared with the advanced market economies and was necessary for the achievement of an elementary living standard (e.g. acquiring an apartment).

The state "expropriated" the family because it was trying to substitute it to a large extent (particularly in terms of the care and education of children); on the other hand, the families in socialism colonized the state (Možný, 1991), which is expressed in the slogan, "who does not prey on the state, he preys on his own family." The family provided the individual with economic support as well as the possibility of self-realization (as other types of self-realization were rather problematic under socialism). People learned to strictly separate the spheres of the public and the private. Different rules applied in these spheres (e.g. what can be said at home and is not to be said in public) as well as different morals (e.g. lying in public was justifiable, whereas it was not justifiable at home).

FAMILY DEMOGRAPHICS IN THE CZECH REPUBLIC

The Czech Republic, together with the Slovak Republic, followed the Eastern European type of reproductive behaviour, with the following features:

- A higher level of total fertility rate was maintained up to the end of the 1980s. In 1970 it was 1.93, in 1980 2.07, and in 1990 1.89 (Statistical Yearbook, 1991).
- A low age at first marriage (on average 24.5 years for men and on average 21.5 for women) (Kučera & Fialová, 1996).

- A low age at the birth of the first (22.5 years) and the second child (24.5 years). The reproductive lives of the majority of women ended at 25 years of age (Kučera & Fialová, 1996).
- A low percentage of extra-marital children (5% for a long period of time; towards the end of the 1980s it increased to 8%) (Statistical Yearbook, 1991).

Marriage had high credit in socialism. Thus, in the 1970s, 95% of single men and 97% of women (in the 1980s, 90% of men and 96% of women) entered into marriage. A high proportion of people got married after a short relationship (approximately half of first marriages were entered due to pregnancy). According to Kučera and Fialová (1996), getting married was often the first independent step in the lives of young people (high school or vocational training was chosen by their parents when they were 15. By the middle of the 1960, school graduates were employed based on billets – obligatory appointments; and later based on contacts – connections of their parents, etc.). Getting married and the birth of the first child was also necessary in order to be eligible for obtaining a company, cooperative or state flat (singles and the childless had almost no chance of obtaining an apartment). Many young families lived, at least in their first years of marriage, in a common household or flat, or house with their parents. Young people usually established their own household only several years after getting married, when they were granted their own housing (unless they divorced). The highest divorce rate was in the third or fourth year of matrimony. The average duration of marriages ending in divorce was 9–11 years[6] (Kučera & Fialová, 1996). In the countryside, entry into marriage marked the time to build a family house (relatives as well as neighbours and acquaintances assisted in the construction).

Entry into marriage was closely correlated with the type of education. The first people to get married were the graduates of special schools (special education) and young people with elementary education (10% of girls and boys had only basic education or no education at all), then the graduates of vocational training courses (50% of boys and 40% of girls) and graduates of high schools (27% of boys and 40% of girls), and only then the university graduates (13% of boys and 10% of women). Around 90% of young people in the age group 18–20 were employed. Thus, the high and frequent marriage rate is evaluated by Kučera and Fialová (1996) to be a result of limited options for other types of self-realization and of the pragmatic exploitation of the only opportunities that socialism provided to young people.

Since the birth rates had decreased substantially and the abortion rates increased during the 1960s,[7] at the beginning of the 1970s the so-called "pro-natalist" measures were adopted. These included interest-free loans for newly married couples up to 30 years of age, prolonged and financially supported maternity leave, higher child benefits, etc. After 15 years of marriage, only 2–3% of married women did not have children. More than 2/3 of married women had two children (Kučera & Fialová, 1996).

In the 1990s, marriage and fertility rates decreased substantially. In 1990, 90,953 marriages were registered, while in 2001 there were only 52,374. The lowest annual number of children born (89,774) in the post-war history of our country was in the year 1999. This model of marriage rate and matrimony remained in place until the beginning of the 1990s and then it started to diversify substantially. The average age of people getting married has increased in the last decade by more than 4 years for women (to 25.8 years) and by 3.7 years for men (to 28.2 years). The total fertility rate went down to 1.14 children per woman in 2001 (Statistical Yearbook, 2002).

Some experts (e.g. Kučera, 2000) indicate that the change in demographic behaviour of the younger generation is caused mainly by aggravated economic conditions, a real decrease in living standards and a lower level of social protection provided to families (low initial wages, high level of unemployment for school graduates, lower availability of separate housing due to rising cost, insufficient support to young families and families with children compared with the past, etc.). Other scholars (e.g. Kuchařová & Zamykalová, 2000) suggest that this change is determined by a transformation in value orientations of young people, broader opportunities for self-realization, higher employment ambitions, emancipation of women, and acceptance of alternative forms of partnerships and family cohabitation. The availability and quality of contraception also plays an important role. Kuchařová and Zamykalová (2000) distinguish approximately five models of marriage and natality behaviour:

(1) Early marriage – the first child is born shortly after the marriage, then in a relatively short period of time another child is born.
(2) Early marriage – but the children are born a long time after getting married.
(3) Later marriage – children are born shortly after marriage or before the marriage.
(4) Later marriage – childbirth postponed until later.
(5) Programmatic long-term or life-long childlessness and rejection of matrimony.

Cohabitations are more frequent than in the past, but young people consider it rather a "transitional" phase before getting married; a "first stage" before marriage (Hamplová & Pikálková, 2002) rather than a permanent form of cohabitation – an alternative to marriage, as it becomes for people divorced in the 1990s (Tuček et al., 1998).

After 1989, there is a strong indirect relationship between the educational level of a woman and her fertility (the higher the educational level achieved, the lower

Table 1.   Families and Households in the Czech Republic (%).

Type of Family and Household	1961	1970	1980	1991	2001
Complete families	74.8	71.0	66.0	62.0	54.6
Incomplete families	7.8	8.8	8.4	10.7	13.5
Multiple-member non-family households	1.4	1.1	1.4	0.4	2.0
Households of individuals	16.0	19.1	24.2	26.9	29.9

Source: Census (2001).

the number of children born) and a direct relationship between the woman's educational level and the legitimacy of the child (Hamplová et al., 2003). In spite of the fact that people with a university education tend to be the vehicles of liberal trends and new value orientations, this does not apply in the case of children born outside of marriage. In 2001, only 10% of children were born outside of marriage to university-educated women, while more than 70% were born to women with a basic education (Hamplová et al., 2003). Neither Czech demography nor sociology has provided a satisfactory explanation for this fact so far.[8]

The majority of children (80% in 1994, 73% in 2001) live in complete families with both biological parents (see Table 1). In 2001, 488,000 children lived in incomplete (monoparental) families. Most of these families were the result of divorce.[9] After divorce, 90–93% of children are placed in the custody of their mothers, with only 7–10% being placed in the custody of their fathers (Bakalář & Kovařík, 2000). Since 1998, there is a possibility of the simultaneous or alternate care of children after divorce, but the statistics do not record this information. The living standard of incomplete families is often very low. They receive the Social Conditions Allowance (designed for families with children with income lower than subsistence or slightly exceeding the subsistence level) twice as frequently as complete families (Kuchařová, 2003).

In terms of number of children, the model of the family with two children has prevailed in the Czech Republic (see Table 2).

Table 2.   Number of Children in Families (%).

Year	1 Child	2 Children	3 Children	4 and More
1961	48.2	35.8	11.2	4.8
1970	52.1	37.1	8.3	2.5
1980	36.8	49.2	11.7	2.3
1991	40.6	48.0	9.8	1.6
2001	43.4	47.4	7.7	1.5

Source: Census (2001).

Multigenerational families exist, but they are less common than in the past. The relatively low mobility of the Czech population results in adult children living quite close to their parents, enabling close contact between the generations of the family without having to share the same house or flat. Cohabitation of multiple generations within a house is more frequent in rural than in urban areas.

Role of Children in the Family

One of the main purposes of the family under socialism was to ensure the future of children. Assistance from parents was expected and was provided in terms of housing, financial support of newly married couples, assistance in looking after the children, etc. Help provided by parents to their children was not only common but also important for their "entry into life." On the other hand, children "returned" this care to their parents when they were old. The middle generation (i.e. in the ages between 40 and 55) usually took care of their old parents, as facilities taking care of the elderly did not exist in sufficient quantity and quality. Under socialism, this middle generation ("the sandwich generation") carried the burden that in advanced economies is to a large extent borne by specialised institutions. Currently, assistance is still transferred both ways, but it is less frequent and important compared with previously. The trend "to be independent of the family of origin" starts to emerge mainly in large cities (with over 100 thousand people), and it applies also to traditional childcare, which starts to be replaced by paid childminders (Maříková, 2003).

In spite of the fact that the birth rate in the Czech Republic has decreased substantially, young people do not neglect family and children in their plans. The changed social situation leads them to focus on "career" ("gaining good position at work") and on "realization of their own hobbies and interests," but marriage and children follow immediately after that and rank before options such as "travel abroad to gain experience" and "develop independent entrepreneurial activities" (Kučera, 2000).

Why do people want to have children? What value does the child represent for them? The answer to this question is neither simple nor unambiguous. Czech psychologist Matějček (1978), who dealt with this topic in the past, reached the conclusion that by having children the parents are mainly satisfying their mental needs. International comparative research – PPA (Population-related Policies Acceptance) – from 1991 (see Table 3) showed that the level of agreement in the Czech population about the symbolic value of the child (statements A and B) as well as the social value (F), with the perception of the child as source of human identity (C) or source of happiness (G), or with feelings of fulfilled life thanks to

Table 3. Values Related to "Having a Child" in the Czechoslovak Federal
Republic (1991) and in the Czech Republic (2001).

Statements	1991	2001	2001 30 Years Old and Younger Respondents
A. I like the feeling of having children around	88	83.2	71.7
B. The relationship to children is the closest relationship a person can have	89	80.7	71.0
C. It is nice to have children – they need you so much	84	80.5	73.3
D. Happy at home with children	70	72.8	61.8
E. Who was a good father/mother can be fully satisfied with their life	74	72.5	65.0
F. To have children is our responsibility towards the society	[a]	61.6	55.1
G. A person cannot be really happy without having children	74	48.1	37.8

Source: Šalamounová (2003).
[a] The data were not available; $N = 1060$; Population between 18 and 75.

children (D and E), was several times higher in the former Czechoslovakia than in the Netherlands (i.e. modern Western society) or Spain (i.e. a relatively "young" democratic state) (Rabuši, 2000). This finding is explained by the absence of other alternatives to a career than family. Also, the value of a child is relatively high, but it is significantly lower in the case of the younger generation (up to 30 years of age) because the value focus as well as the actual lives of that generation show a growing trend towards individualization.

GENDER ROLES IN THE FAMILY

In the Czech Republic, sharing the household work and family duties is still rather unequal from the point of view of gender. A majority of the population accepts the "traditional" Czech model of distinctive family roles, where the man primarily provides financial resources for the family and the woman is responsible for taking care of the family and the household. The man is considered to be the main breadwinner, in spite of the fact that in the vast majority of families, the woman participates (to a considerable extent) in providing for the family financially. Yet the housework and childcare is still, in most cases, the responsibility of the woman. If men are involved in the housework at all, their involvement is irregular and limited to certain tasks. Housework is not highly valued in Czech society and the position of housewife is one of very low prestige (Rodina, 94 – Family 1994).

A majority of women work full-time (about 90%), with duties associated with the household and children representing their "second shift." From the point of view of sharing the work in the household, men have the role of assistants rather than that of an equivalent partner, because they usually do not have any responsibility for performing housework. Men living in rural areas, who may be older and less educated, perform only the so-called men's housework (farming, common repairs in the household, necessary but less demanding craft works such as decorating the apartment). If men participate in the family and household, they are involved in bringing up children rather than in their everyday care or housework.

FAMILY PROCESSES

Rituals and Customs

A family where both parents work usually meets in the evenings and on weekends. The most important ritual of a workday is the common meal. During the week, it is at dinnertime when the parents gather with their children. On the weekend, the main common meal is lunch. If there are small children of pre-school or early school age, then the evening ritual includes putting the child to bed and often watching evening cartoons on TV and reading fairy tales. Older children often watch evening TV programs together with their parents.

In the Czech Republic, families frequently spend the weekends at cottages, away from the city environment, or they work in the garden. Parents most often do sports with children – in winter they ski, hike, ride a bike, etc. During the summer holiday they spend time at rivers or lakes or by the seaside abroad. Parents attend cultural events such as cinema, theatre, exhibitions or concerts less often with their children.

Celebrating holidays and birthdays are some of the festive rituals usually involving small children and grandparents. A party with the child's peers is usually organized separately. In the Czech Republic, the religious holidays celebrated most widely include Christmas and St. Nicholas's Day. Compared with Christmas, Easter is not perceived as such an important holiday. This is because Czech society (with the exception of Southern Moravia and Eastern Bohemia) is significantly secularized. In the majority of families, these holidays are related to rituals of a secular rather than a religious nature, although their original content was religious.[10] Most of these originally religious holidays currently have a distinctly commercial character.

Due to the current requirements for higher performance at work compared with the past, parents have less time to spend with their children, especially during the week. Children are often at home on their own and they spend a lot of time in front of the computer. The way in which free time is spent in the family is determined not only by the family's life cycle but also by the developmental stage of each family member.

FAMILY IN THE COUNTRYSIDE AND IN THE CITY: TRADITIONAL AND MODERN

In terms of life style in Czech society, it is still possible to differentiate between the towns and the countryside. This difference is also reflected in the lives of families. The family is more stable in the country than in towns, it holds more traditional morals (e.g. rejecting extramarital contacts and lack of responsibility in taking care of children), and it has an important economic function (in maintaining living standards through farming activities; there is also a high level of material support from grandparents) (Šindelářová, 1997). Compared with families in larger cities, the lives of those in the countryside (or in smaller towns) are based more on solidarity, mutual cooperation of families, and local community networks.

Although the importance of self-realization at work and having a more active life style is growing throughout society, this trend is less apparent in the countryside, which shows a tendency towards a value-orientation based on responsibility, discipline and modesty. Passive (defensive) strategies are usually applied within the family in the countryside (i.e. restriction of family expenses, economic approaches, the large volume of housework, a large number of services that are normally paid for and provided by a market saturated with local people's own unpaid work) (Sýkorová, 1999). Farming has been revived only to a minimal extent,[11] but farming for one's own consumption still endures.

As opposed to the countryside, families living in urban areas apply the opposite strategies. Active or offensive strategies of economic behaviour are focused on increasing the income from one's current job or gaining additional income from part-time employment and occasional work. Modern family behaviour is characterized by entrepreneurship as a condition of family welfare, with weaker solidarity among relatives and peers (probably due to the fact that family units are closed and independent, and, objectively, have less need of help). More emphasis is placed on work and leisure, with less on matrimony and family, than in families in the countryside. Urban families tend to hold more liberal opinions on the structure of gender relationships and on the upbringing of children. They usually focus on independence, responsibility and assertiveness in children, as opposed to the countryside, where families emphasize virtue, obedience and religious beliefs. In the countryside and in cities, families experienced less free time after 1989, and it is most frequently spent passively.

The family in the countryside may be also characterized as the traditional family, where solidarity and religion play more important roles than in an urban (modern) family, which is more open and liberal in its opinions. In spite of the fact that the traditional family type is more prevalent in the countryside and the modern family in cities, this does not mean that they are not present in the opposite environment.

CHILDREARING PRACTICES

In the Czech Republic, it is common to stay at home with children when they are small. Currently, a six-month maternity leave is available, paid with 90% of the income (if the income exceeds the average, the percentage is lower). After this period, the mother is guaranteed to return to the same work position. Also, the mother may stay at home until the child is 3 years old and receive an allowance.[12] After the end of parental leave, the employer is required to hire the woman again (but she is not entitled to return to the same position). Parental leave was introduced on 1st January 2001 for both women and men. However, men use this opportunity very sporadically (only 1% of people receiving parental allowance are men). So-called "paternal leave" (special leave for men) has not been introduced in our country.

Children are taken care of primarily by mothers. Recent research (Our Society, 2003) showed that the mother is still the dominant person in the family in terms of childcare and upbringing. It is still up to the mother to manage the regular day-to-day activities as well as to take care of a sick child or to go with the child to the doctor. Mothers more often than fathers have time for children when they need it.

The father in the contemporary family participates less than his father (comparing the generation of contemporary parents with the generation of grandparents) in "doing homework with children," "doing sports with children," "punishing children," "deciding on future career or type of studies of child"; these activities are more often than in the past shared by "both parents together." The most significant change is in disciplining the children, where the number of "punishing" fathers has decreased from 27.6 to 15.8% (Maříková, 2003). However, punishment of children is still a characteristic of the Czech family. Physical punishment is common in families and society tolerates it. Men are more tolerant of punishment than women. Women favour "mental punishment" (such as a ban on TV, going out, a ban on hobbies, etc.) rather than "physical punishment" or "more severe types of punishment" (e.g. pulling hair) (Vymětalová, 2001).

Children have a looser relationship with the father than with the mother (Možný, 1990), with whom it is possible to talk about school, friends, movies or fashion up to the time of adolescence. It is possible to talk with the father about sports and politics. The father is less interested in school than the mother and talks less with children about his work than the mother. The father commands more often than the mother, who usually asks and pleads. Children often have a worse relationship with their father than with their mother (Možný, 1990). Even though childrearing in the Czech Republic is becoming more democratic and liberal than in the past, it is still rather authoritarian, at least in some types of families or social classes, compared with other Western countries.

Children, Youth and Peers

According to some experts (e.g. Potůček, 2002), the requirements for success in the labour market undermine the stability of the family, not just in terms of its reproductive function but also in the functions of upbringing and social care. This statement is reflected in the statistics on violent crime committed by children (6–15 years old) and juveniles (15–18 years old) and the growth of aggressive behaviour in these age groups.[13] After 1989, there has been a general rise in crime, particularly youth crime (Marešová et al., 1999). From 1989 to 1998, the number of children prosecuted for crimes increased two and a half times and the number of juveniles two times. Thus, out of the total number of people investigated by police (19,373), 15% were younger than 18 (8,824 children; 10,549 juveniles).

According to an extensive survey by the Institute of Criminology and Social Prevention called "Criminology Aspects of Social Pathological Phenomena in Children" (6–15 years old):

* A majority of these children live in an incomplete family of one of the parents or is brought up by somebody other than the natural parents (grandparents, adoption, educational or reformatory institutions, etc.) and appropriate upbringing strategies are usually not applied to these children;
* mothers have extremely low levels of education (most frequently unqualified labourers);
* parents are often unemployed; they show rather negative attitudes to work;
* in Romany Gipsy families, the extremely low level of education is combined with high levels of unemployment and a social cultural handicap (poor knowledge of Czech, different life style);

- some of these children suffer from evident mental problems (high aggressiveness);
- many of the children smoke and experiment with drugs;
- children tend to have learning and behavioural difficulties at school – almost half of them go to special schools (for the educationally subnormal). They are often truant, and their relationship with the school and education is very negative;
- these children predominantly commit crimes against property.

In cases where the educational influence of parents was monitored, the parents were usually inconsistent, neglectful of the child, and they often showed lack of love or indifference. Fathers of these children punished them often (Večerka et al., 2001).

Children and adolescents with behavioural problems create peer groups (subcultures or gangs) with features of asocial behaviour where they find a certain understanding that they miss at home. These groups often lack a meaningful way of spending their free time. Danger consists in the inclination of the gang to socio-pathological or criminal activities that offer excitement and thrills as well as sources of income (gaming machines, etc.). Membership in these gangs is related to increased levels of truancy and cases where the child runs away from home.

After 1989, there was a general rise in children's aggressive behaviour (bullying at schools, etc). The influence of violence and pornography in the media, the loosening of family relationships, and the strong emphasis on material values as opposed to spiritual values are considered to be the main causes of this increase in aggression (Říčan, 1995).

Education

The determination of the number of students to be admitted for technical vocational schools, grammar schools and universities was cancelled after 1989. This was reflected in the increased interest of young people in advanced studies. The number, and partially also the structure, of students in schools changed in the 1990s. For example, in 1991, only 1/3 of the students were 18 years old, whereas they comprised more than 2/3 in 1997. Generally, the interest of young people in studying at technical secondary schools increased and was accompanied by a fall in numbers for vocational secondary school (by 20% for boys, by 18% for girls) (Statistical Yearbook of the Czech Republic, 2002).

There are more boys in grammar schools and secondary technical schools and girls can again study at specialized schools of "home economics" (Fialová et al., 2000). However, from the gender point of view, there are no significant changes at this level of education. Men and women have the same types of occupations as in the past: about 80% of women are in medical and pedagogical schools and about 70% of them are in economic schools (only slightly less than in the last decade), whereas men more frequently study at technical schools. Young people have a wider choice of various schooling facilities, which is not limited to state schools (as it used to be under socialism), but also includes private and religious schools.

There is also a much higher level of interest in university level education, resulting in an increase in university students. For example, in 1986, a total of 87,700 students studied at Czech universities (12.8% of 20–24 year old people), while in 1998, there were 145,100 students (15.9% of this age category), and in 2001, there were 200,450 university students (Statistical Yearbook of the Czech Republic, 2002).

In the 1990s, the number of universities increased and they were established in all regional centres, which improved the availability of higher education (in spite of limited accommodation for students). The interest in formerly restricted fields of university study grew (i.e. social and history sciences, philosophy and languages). There was also an increased interest in economic fields, while interest in the study of technical and agricultural fields decreased (Fialová et al., 2000). The changes to the length and scope of studies that took place in the 1990s meant that a higher proportion of young people studied, and for a longer period of time than in the past (e.g. they graduated from school approximately 2–4 years later than their parents).

RESEARCH ON FAMILY

In the 1990s, various research studies were carried out relating to family, children or young people, with the most attention being paid to the following:

- Demographic behaviour of the young population: fertility, forms of younger generation family life, analyses and forecasts of population development in the Czech Republic;
- Sociological research of families: structure and typology of families, their stratification, behaviour patterns of the Czech family, trends of family development, new forms of taking care of children in the family, aggression in the family;
- Research on youth: values and value orientations of secondary school youth, media in the life of youth, development trends in the consciousness and behaviour of Czech youth, attitude of young people towards education and their professional success, spirituality in the life of youth, social and psychological determinants of spreading violence and aggressiveness among youth;

- Research on children: children's aggressiveness, bullying in small social groups, prevention of drug addiction and other addictions.

Various institutions carry out research in the Czech Republic, particularly those within the Academy of Sciences or university departments. Projects are also carried out by ministries (particularly the Ministry of Labour and Social Affairs of the Czech Republic and the Ministry of Education, Youth and Sports of the Czech Republic) or by specialised research organisations such as the Institute of Criminology and Social Prevention.

Representative sociological surveys are most often implemented on a sample of 1,000–1,500 persons, usually by quota selection (if they apply to the entire population, then the quotas are defined by gender, age, education, size of the place of residence and possibly by other indicators). Quantitative surveys are based mainly on questionnaire investigations. Qualitative surveys use various techniques. The interview is the method most often used in qualitative sociological surveys.

In the 1990s, some international comparative research studies relating to family were implemented, such as *ISSP 1994 (Family 1994)* and *ISSP 2002 (Family and Gender)*. These were representative surveys of the Czech population of 18 years of age and older. The sample included, in both cases, more than 1,000 persons selected by quota (age, gender, education, size of the place of residence, region). Within the survey, attitudes toward marriage, gender roles, parenthood, and new forms of partner behaviour were investigated as well as the life and family cycles of respondents. Within the framework of the international project, called *Options and Limits of Family in Contemporary Europe*, an empirical investigation on *Family and Community in Central Europe* was implemented with the financial support of the Voluntary Fund of the International Year of the Family and under the technical auspices of the Bratislava International Centre for Family Studies (BICSF). The Czech Republic, Poland and Slovakia participated in this project. The survey was carried out in four municipalities in Northern Moravia region, representing communities with so-called traditional and modern family behaviour. Two pairs of municipalities with maximum differences in nationality and religion and a population ranging from 500 to 1,500 were selected. The research set was created using stratified selection. The stratums were constituted by municipalities of certain types, with higher levels of devoutness vs. a predominantly non-religious population; or with purely Czech vs. mixed nationalities.

This qualitative research was based on a study of documents, non-standardised interviews with mayors and with "experts" (chroniclers, elderly citizens). Standardized interviews were carried out in selected families covering opinions, attitudes and "family" values related to living conditions, living and family strategies, reactions to social changes and their consequences in the everyday life of the family, and reflection on their own life situation.

It would be desirable to focus future family research on the following aspects:

- The relationship between developmental trends within the family, functioning of specific types of families, and the family or social policy of the government;
- The impacts of the transformation of the society on the family, or various types of families from the point of view of their structure, family cycle, and social position (i.e. monitor mainly the strategies and patterns of behaviour in various types of families and the impact of family social status on its reproduction and upbringing of children);
- Carrying out of international comparative research on the abovementioned topics, particularly in the countries of the former socialist bloc, or countries with similar historical and cultural development over the last decades (extending and intensifying the cooperation in the field of family research particularly with the Slovak Republic, Poland and Hungary).

CONCLUSION

The processes started in 1989 by the Velvet Revolution had a significant impact not just on individuals, but particularly on families. The "steady state" of the end of the 1980s, when there were very small differences among families, was disrupted. The current differences in family income, consumption and life style are determined by the completeness/incompleteness of the family as well as by the professions of men (fathers) and women (mothers). The most significant drop in living standards over the last decade was experienced by single-parent families, labourer families and those living in the countryside. The pattern of parental behaviour – mainly the inequality in sharing work at home and care for children – is often the same as in the past. If it changes, it will be due to the pressure of economic and social transformations rather than from an "internal need" of men and women to apply gender equality in day-to-day life. In today's family, the position of the child and his/her importance in the lives of parents is changing.

The transformation of Czech society has significantly influenced the "existence" of the family. Demographic data shows that young people up to 30 years of age in most cases postpone entry into marriage and delay childbirth. This, together with a high divorce rate, has resulted in a change in the size as well as the structure of families. The average size of the family is decreasing; the ratio of the so-called complete family households to the total households is also decreasing. Thus, the future "fate" of the family as well as the form in which it will exist depends especially on the value orientation and life strategies of young people. Since the

Czech family did not go through the same stages of development as the "Western" family, its structure and the dynamics of changes currently taking place are different in several aspects.

NOTES

1. An individual had the right to work but also the duty to work and so there was officially no unemployment. The supply and demand for work was regulated by state bodies and organizations by means of a plan. Over-employment was a distinct feature of the socialist economy.

2. i.e. unavailability and filtration of information from the countries of the so-called capitalist West, but often also local information or information from other socialist countries.

3. The communist ideology used the term "convergence of classes" (workers, farmers and working intelligentsia).

4. In the 1990s, women also represented 45% of the work force.

5. The quality of some services as well as the choice improved within the framework of these measures. By 1989, these services were provided only by the state sector; now they are also provided by private entities or by commercial or non-commercial, not-for-profit organizations.

6. Seventeen percent of marriages in the sixties, 27% in the 1970s, and 36% in the 1980s ended in divorce. The increased divorce rate is ascribed to liberalisation of the Family Act, whereby consent of the partner who did not file the divorce petition is not required. Approximately 70% of divorced men and 60% of women married again within the first few years after divorce.

7. Abortions have been legal in the Czech Republic since 1957. In 1986, mini-abortions were introduced, which were rather formal, as woman had to apply for abortion and the application was evaluated by a committee that either approved or rejected it. Legalisation of abortions eliminated illicit abortions performed by people without medical training. Under socialism, abortions were used mainly by married couples. Abortions were basically an "ex post" birth control measure (contraception was difficult to get and expensive at that time) rather than a solution to extreme cases of undesirable pregnancy, which was the original purpose of abortion.

8. With respect to the fact that the mothers of the majority of these children are not just women with the lowest level of education, but also women from lower social classes living in areas with high unemployment, it may be assumed that for them the child may represent a secure income. Unemployed single women with low education levels achieve approximately the same level of income as if they worked, and this income is higher than potential unemployment benefits.

9. The high divorce rate is to a significant extent caused by the secularisation of Czech society. In 1991, 44% of the population claimed to be religious; some people probably claimed to be religious just to demonstrate distance from communism. In 2001, 32% of the population identified themselves as religious.

10. For example, on Christmas Day there is usually a rich Christmas dinner, gifts under the Christmas tree, singing of Christmas carols etc., but everything is often done without the religious content.

11. According to Šindelářová (1997), land farming requires too dramatic a change of life style and in the context of Czech society it represents a greater risk than do other industries.

12. Currently, a spouse on parental leave may have unlimited additional income while receiving a parental allowance.

13. However, this is a more complex issue than simply a problem caused by strained working activity of parents and lack of time to spend with children.

REFERENCES

Bakalář, E., & Kovařík, J. (2000). Otcové, otcovství v České republice (Father, fatherhood in the Czech Republic). *Demografie, 4,* 266–272.

Fialová, L., Hamplová, D., Kučera, M., & Vymětalová, S. (2000). *Představy mladých lidí o manželství a rodičovství (Young people's ideas about marriage and family).* Praha: SLON.

Hamplová, D., & Pikálková, S. (2002). Manželství, nesezdaná soužití a partnerský vztah (Marriage, cohabitation and partnership). In: Z. Mansfeldová & M. Tuček (Eds), *Současná česká společnost.* Praha: SoÚ AV ČR.

Hamplová, D., Rychtaříková, J., & Pikálková, S. (2003). *České ženy: Vzdělání, partnerství reprodukce a rodina (Czech women: Education, partnership, reproduction, family).* Praha: SoÚ AV ČR.

Kučera, M., & Fialová, L. (1996). *Demografické chování obyvatelstva České republiky během přeměny společnosti po roce 1989 (Demographic behaviour of Czech population in transformation).* Praha: SoÚ AV ČR. Pracovní texty.

Kučera, M. (2000). Představy o postavení sňatku a narození dětí v životní dráze mladých svobodných lidí. In: L. Fialová et al. (Eds), *Představy mladých lidí o manželství a rodičovství* (pp. 45–66). Praha: SLON.

Kuchařová, V. (2003). Demografické změny (Demographic changes). In: M. Tuček et al. (Eds), *Dynamika české společnosti* (pp. 41–53). Praha: SLON.

Kuchařová, V., & Zamykalová, L. (2000). Předpoklady sňatkového a rodinného chování mladé generace (Family behaviour of young generation). *Sociální Politika, 2,* 14–16.

Marešová, A., Kadeřábková, D., & Martinková, M. (1999). *Kriminalita v roce 1998 (Criminality in 1998).* Praha: IKSP.

Maříková, H. (2003). *Podpora využívání rodičovské dovolené muži. Závěrečná zpráva. (Support for enjoying the parentel leave by men. Final report.).* Praha: MPSV.

Matějček, Z. (1978). Hodnota dítite pro rodinu (Child as a value for family). *Demografie, 2,* 134–141.

Možný, I. (1990). Moderní rodina *(Modern family).* Brno: Blok.

Možný, I. (1991). *Proč tak snadno . . . Nìkteré rodinné důvody sametové revoluce (Why so easy . . . Some family motives of velvet revolution).* Praha: SLON.

Naše společnost 03 (Our Society 2003). (2003). Praha: CVVM.

Potůček, M. (2002). Sociální stát – vývojové trendy, ohrožení a rozvojové příležitosti do roku 2015 (Social state – trends up to 2015). www.mpsv.cz.

Rabuši, L. (2000). Hodnota dítìte (Child value). *Demografie, 4,* 286–290.

Říčan, P. (1995). *Agresivita a šikana mezi dětmi (Aggression and bullying among children).* Praha: Portál.

Rodina 94 (Family 1994). (1994). Praha: SoÚ AV ČR.

Šalamounová, P. (2003). Hodnota dítěte v české společnosti (Child value in the Czech society). Unpublished article.

Šindelářová, J. (1997). Sociologie venkova a zemědělství (*Rural sociology and sociology of agriculture*). Brno: Mendlova zemědělská a lesnická univerzita.

Statistická ročenka České republiky 1991, 2002 (*Statistical Yearbook of the Czech Republic 1991, 2002*). Praha: ČSÚ.

Statistická ročenka Československé federativní republiky 1991 (Statistical Yearbook of the Federativ Republic of Czechoslovakia 1991). Praha: ČsSÚ.

Sýkorová, D. (1999). Rodina a obec ve střední Evropě (The family and community in Central Europe). *Sociologický časopis, 2*, 207–218.

Tuček, M., Čermáková, M., Kuchařová, V., & Maříková, H. (1998). *Česká rodinav transformaci – Stratifikace, dělba rolí a hodnotové orientace* (Czech family intransformation – Stratification, family roles, family values). Praha: SoÚ AV ČR.

Večerka, K., Holas, J., Štěchová, M., & Diblíková, S. (2001). Kriminologické charakteristiky dětí s nařízenou ústavní či ochrannou výchovou (Criminological characteristics of children with court-ordered institutional and protective care). *Sociologický časopis, 1*, 89–102.

Večerník, J. (1991). Distribuční systém v socialistickém Československu: Empirická data, výkladové hypotézy (The system of distribution in socialist Czechoslovakia: Empirical data and hypotheses of explanation). *Sociologický časopis, 1*, 39–56.

Vymětalová, S. (2001). Domácí násilí: Přirozený jev? (Domestic violence: A natural phenomenon?). *Sociologický časopis, 1*, 103–121.

FAMILIES IN SLOVAKIA

Jarmila Filadelfiová

By dividing Czechoslovakia in 1993, a new state – The Slovak Republic – was created. The map of Europe was extended. Many characteristics of European countries may be applied to Slovakia. However, individual European countries are characterised by specific traits. In spite of their homogenous image, each nation preserves its customs and collective memory. Regional characteristics and traditional family and religious customs are maintained. How did social conditions and economic and political changes during a relatively short historical period influence the lives of people and families in Slovakia?

SOCIO-HISTORIC AND ECONOMIC CONTEXT

Life in Slovakia, as in most European countries, was formed under the strong influence of Christianity. It influenced the standards of society and determined general behaviour, relationships among people, and especially family life. Christianity emphasised long-term low mobility, resulting in a strong traditionalism that persists in many spheres of life today.

The location of Slovakia in the centre of Europe and its geographical diversity has greatly influenced the regional and cultural heterogeneity of its population. Many national and ethnic minorities live here. The most numerous are the Hungarian and Romany minorities, but Polish, German, Ukrainian, Ruthenian, Croatian, Bulgarian, and Bohemian ethnic groups are also represented here. In terms of religion, besides the Roman Catholics (nearly 70% of the total population), there are Protestants, Jews, Orthodox Christians and many others (Census, 2001).

Families in Eastern Europe
Contemporary Perspectives in Family Research, Volume 5, 49–68
Copyright © 2004 by Elsevier Ltd.
All rights of reproduction in any form reserved
ISSN: 1530-3535/doi:10.1016/S1530-3535(04)05004-6

Communities with about five different churches are not unusual. Ethnic and religious diversity also produces a variety of dialects, values and ways of behaviour (Botíková et al., 1997).

In the past, most of the population lived in the country. For example, in 1869, there were only 17 persons employed in industry and craft for every 100 persons working in agriculture. While Slovakia was predominantly a typical agrarian country, there were many significant towns, many of which have retained their historical character. With industrialisation (started in the 1950s), the ratio of urban to rural population has evened out, with the urban population now slightly in the majority. Recently, the urban population constituted 56% of the total population. The proportion of people engaged in agriculture has decreased more dramatically: today there are only 6 persons working in agriculture per 100 persons working in other industries. Young people have moved from the country in search of industrial work to towns with factories. Over a long period of time, the number of young people has decreased and the rural areas have "aged." Daily commuting from the country to the city, or in the case of single people and men, staying temporarily in the place of work (so-called "weekly commuting") has always been a widespread practice.

In Slovakia, the impact of industrialisation on the character of housing had two consequences. On the one hand, it led to the transformation of villages and improvement in housing conditions. Small houses without proper sanitation were replaced by large, often imposing homes with modern conveniences. People would often build their homes with their own hands, the construction of houses for sale being exceptional and having begun to occur only in the last decade.

The process of industrialisation initiated the mass production of apartments in giant housing estates on the outskirts of towns. Thus, in Slovakia today, the population dwells in cities and in the country, in family houses and in large blocks of apartments, on isolated farms in tiny hamlets and in crowded housing estates. A description of Slovak housing conditions would not be complete without a discussion of the chronic shortages that greatly influence the way the population lives. This accounts for the relatively low mobility rate and the restrictions on family life. Possession of an apartment has become a stabilising feature in the life of an individual and people move very rarely in the course of their lifetime. For members of the older generation, it is not unusual never to have moved at all. In these cases, people spend their entire lives in their parental homes. For the majority of the population, however, one change is typical – the move from the parental home to one's own house or apartment.

Currently, the Slovak Republic (SR) has 5.3 million inhabitants living in 2,653 villages and 138 towns. The territory of the SR has been divided administratively into 8 regions and 79 districts. There are 109 inhabitants per square kilometre and 1,861 inhabitants per municipality. The country has a state-socialist past, which was a political arrangement based on a non-pluralistic party system and a centrally managed, planned economy. The Slovakian social system was based on redistribution, one pillar government, and state paternalism. Since 1989, it has been reforming its economy and restructuring its political system. In July 2000, the country was invited to join the Organisation for Economic Co-operation and Development (OECD) and in May 2004 became a member of the European Union.

This transformation has produced mixed economic and social results. From an economic perspective, Slovakia is not one of the wealthier countries of the world, or even of Europe. Nowadays, the GDP (Gross Domestic Product) per capita of Slovakia is less than half the OECD average (as expressed in purchasing power parities). At the end of the 1990s, the GDP reached more than 700 billion Slovak Crowns (SKK) and GDP per capita was around US$12,000 (*National . . .*, 2000, 2001). Despite some relatively favourable economic indicators and notable progress in the political and human rights spheres, Slovakia continues to face many challenges. Attempts to stabilise and restructure the economy have not necessarily translated into social improvements. For many people, the transformation has not resulted in increased well-being; on the contrary, some social or human indicators have deteriorated (*National . . .*, 2000). The beginning of the new millennium found Slovakia with 11% of the population below the minimum subsistence level, and with a nearly 20% unemployment rate (*Statistical. . .*, 2000). For many social groups (especially the Roma population) poverty, social exclusion and marginalisation increased. The situation of women is not very favourable; they are under-represented in decision-making processes, are concentrated in lowly paid jobs, and their earnings are only 70–75% that of men. It has become clear the transformation is not only a process of privatisation and market liberalisation, and that efforts should be focused on increasing people's choices and opportunities (*National . . .*, 2000). These problems, as well as those of everyday family life should be at the centre of policy determination.

When the living conditions in the country deteriorated so much that people could barely survive (especially in Slovak villages), they were forced to emigrate to different parts of the world. The result is that about three million Slovaks live around the world, especially in the USA, Canada and Australia.

FAMILY DEMOGRAPHICS IN SLOVAKIA

Marriage

In Slovakia, approximately 90% of the adult population marry at least once in their lives. The family based on marriage has always been considered a fundamental social value. According to surveys, nearly 90% of the Slovak population considers the family to be the most important value in their lives (*European*..., 1991, 1999/2000). In contrast, only 11% consider marriage to be an outdated institution (*European*..., 1991, 1999/2000). The family based on matrimony is a culturally, religiously, and also legislatively accepted form of cohabitation.

The Family Act of 1963 regulates basic family legal relationships. The law stipulates that the minimum age for marriage is 18 years; younger persons need the permission of the court to marry. Marriage requires the consent of both the man and the woman. Marriages performed either by the church or state authorities are acceptable.

Until the mid-20th century, Slovakia was predominantly rural. During this period, customs and social status determined the way people selected partners. Couples from the same village and from families of a similar social level came together, and parents greatly influenced the mate selection process. Urban marriages were more heterogeneous, as the manner of selecting a mate changed under the impact of urbanisation and industrialisation. The personal preferences of young couples won priority. During the socialist regime, economic self-sufficiency became less important for getting married and establishing a family. At that time, social policy was supportive, especially towards young families. These supportive measures, together with a lack of sexual education and knowledge about methods for the prevention of pregnancy resulted in very young marriages.

For many decades, Slovakia experienced a combination of a high marriage rate and low age at first marriage. This reflected Christian values and the way of life of traditional rural families (Filadelfiová et al., 1996; Filadelfiová & Guráň, 1999). The crude marriage rate had remained between 7 and 10 marriages per 1,000 people. Fluctuations in certain periods were more a result of higher numbers of people of marriageable age than changes in the marriage-related behaviour or attitudes of young people in Slovakia.

Under state-socialism, several advantages linked to marriage helped keep the marriage rate high. These included the priority allocation of apartments first to families and the provision of loans to newlyweds by the state, where reductions could be made for each child born, etc. After 1990, loans for newlyweds were abolished and the shortage of apartments intensified. Therefore, starting their own household had become progressively more difficult for a large section of the young adult population (Filadelfiová, 1992, 2001a, b; Lenczová, 1998).

Since the end of the 1970s, the marriage rate has gradually declined. This trend, with the exception of the years 1990 and 1992, continued until the mid-1990s, when the rate stabilised at approximately 5 marriages per 1,000 people. During the same period, the average age at first marriage had increased from 22.5 years for women and 24 years for men in 1990 to 24.6 and 27.1 years respectively, by 2002 (Statistical Yearbook, 2002).

The decline in the marriage rate also indicated a decrease in second or successive marriages. In the past, the delay between divorce and remarriage used to be very short, especially for men. A higher rate of remarriages in men was also confirmed: 6% of new marriages were between a divorced man and single woman, while there were 2% fewer cases among divorced women and single men. Marriages of a divorcé and another divorcée represented less than 5% of the total (Vaňo, 2002).

The divorce rate in Slovakia has grown slowly over the decades. Whereas there was less than one divorce per 1,000 people in the 1970s, by the end of the 1980s it had reached 1.6 divorces (*Slovak Population . . .*, 1989–2002). After 1990, the rate dropped for three years and a similar decrease was observed again after 1996. However, these fluctuations did not reverse the overall growth tendency. In 2002, the rate was 2.04 divorces per 1,000 people.

The majority of divorces are filed by women (almost 70% in 2002). The average length of marriages ending in divorce is more than 13 years. In the past, 75% of divorces took place in families with children, but in 2002, this share dropped to 70%, which means that seven out of ten divorcing marriages had at least one dependent child (*Slovak Population. . .*, 2002). As a rule, the children stay with their mothers after divorce. Out of all single-parent families, almost 90% were headed by the mother (Filadelfiová & Cuperová, 2000; Filadelfiová, 2001a, b; Vaňo, 1999).

In Slovakia, a tendency can be detected which is the reverse of that in post-modern Europe. While in the West there is greater hesitation over entering a marriage and less on leaving it, in Slovakia it is the other way around. While people rush "headlong" into marriage, often under pressure of circumstances and surroundings (accidental pregnancy, strong conservative environment in rural areas, and so on), divorce is undertaken with greater reluctance. The low rate of divorce and the high number of divorce petitions that are withdrawn are evidence of this.

Family Structure

Besides marriage and divorce rates, natality processes have important consequences on family structure. Over the past 40 years, natality in Slovakia has been in consistent decline. Looking at developments in the birth rate throughout the 20th century, the current period is the third to show a decline. The first occurred in the years 1925–1940, when the crude birth rate dropped from 35.3 to 22.8 live

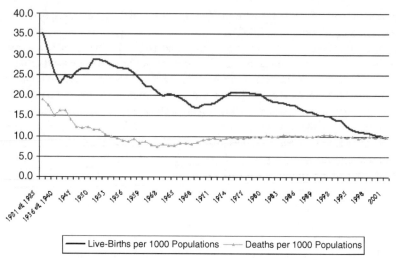

Fig. 1.   Crude Birth and Death Rates in Slovakia (per 1,000 People). *Source:* Stav a pohyb
obyvateľstva v SR. Bratislava, ŠÚ SR.

births per 1,000 people. The second was in the years 1952–1968 (a decrease to
a level of 17 live births) and the third and current period began in 1976 (which
reached 9.5 live-births in 2002) (see Fig. 1).

In the past, the birth rate in Slovakia had its own specific features. A typical
aspect was the low age of women bearing their first child – one of the lowest in
Europe – and the high ratio of brides already pregnant at the time of marriage
(almost 50%) (Filadelfiová, 1995; Filadelfiová & Guráň, 1992). After giving birth
to the first child, a second or third usually followed quite soon. Families with higher
numbers of children were less usual and mostly occurred among Roma women.

Among the positive trends in reproductive behaviour since 1989 has been the
gradual increase in the mean age of mothers at childbirth, from 21 years in the
1980s to 24.1 years at the birth of the first child in 2002 (Filadelfiová, 2001; Vaňo,
2002). There is also a trend of the birth rate shifting to older ages. In women over
25, the decline in natality has progressively slowed in the last five years, and the
latest data even indicate moderate growth.

The main reason for the declining birth rate seems to be the postponing of
parenthood until a later date and age. Other reasons for the birth rate declining
are: (a) a worsening of conditions for starting a family, such as rising prices
of consumer goods and household expenditures, abolishment of both loans for
newlyweds and subsidies on foodstuffs and other items for children, a decline in
housing construction, minimum opportunities for allocation of state or community

apartments; (b) differentiation of young people's life strategies and orientations –
new opportunities for self-fulfilment arising for young people, marriage no longer
being the only route to independence from parents; (c) young people now being
able to travel, study and work abroad, an opportunity which thousands of them
have taken advantage of. According to 1997 data, approximately 5,000 girls were
working as *au pairs* in the United Kingdom alone (*Slovak Au-pairs . . .*, 1998).
Another survey of young girls and women found that more than 60% of them
would like to work abroad for a certain period of time. Their main motivation
included an interest in improving their foreign language proficiency and economic
advantages (*Názory. . .*, 2000, 2003).

During the 1980s, the overall decline in the birth rate and in the births of a
third or more children led to the emergence of the two-children-family model (see
Table 1).

The rate of extra-marital births increased from 1.6 per 1,000 people in 1950
to 2 in 2002. The percentage of children born out of wedlock in the overall
number of children born in a given year increased from 5.4% in 1950 to 21.6%
in 2002 (Statistical Yearbook, 2002). This means that almost every fifth child in
Slovakia is born out of wedlock (Filadelfiová, 2000, 2001; Vaňo, 2002). The high
incidence of extra-marital births has been observed in both young and very young
mothers (20% of mothers are younger than 18 years old; 13.2% of them have
subsequent childbirths). On average, women less than 19 years old give birth to
40% of all these children (Džambazovič, 2001; Filadelfiová, 2001). Women with
elementary education or vocational school education represent the majority (80%)
(Džambazovič, 2001; Filadelfiová, 2001a, b).

Aside from the demographic factors, a high level of diversity arises through
cultural factors, especially those of nationality and religion. The highest number
of out-of-wedlock children are born to Roma mothers. Yearly, as much as 45% of

Table 1. Child Birth Order.

Year	For 100 Live-Births by Order (in%)				
	1	2	3	4	5+
1980	38.7	36.4	15.8	5.2	3.9
1985	38.9	36.2	15.9	5.4	3.6
1990	40.2	36.5	15.0	5.1	3.2
1995	41.6	35.2	13.8	5.2	4.2
2000	44.0	34.1	12.0	4.7	5.2
2001	42.6	35.0	12.2	4.7	5.5
2002	43.3	34.8	12.0	4.6	5.3

Source: Slovak Population and its Fluctuation (1980–2002). Bratislava: Statistical Office of the SR.

all children born to Roma mothers were born out of wedlock. This considerable proportion of extra-marital births among Roma ethnics stems from their attitudes toward marriage. The couple gets married, but the wedding is only a Roma ceremony, since the bride is often far from being of age according to our legal system. The partners then live together and have children, but they only get married officially when they reach the age of 18, or they continue in their unofficial relationship. This is evidenced by an increasing number of out-of-wedlock childbirths (Džambazovič, 2000, 2001; Filadelfiová, 2001a, b; Lenczová, 1998a, b, c; *Národná . . .*, 2000).

Considered as a general demographic development, the abortion rate decreased in Slovakia after 1989. In the past, frequent recourse to medical intervention to terminate unwanted pregnancies was one of the most negative aspects of demographic development. Termination of the pregnancy became a substitute for contraception and many women went through repeated terminations. Even women with higher levels of education were inadequately informed about family planning methods and did little to prevent pregnancies.

Abortions in Slovakia have been registered since 1958, i.e. one year after the adoption of the so-called Termination Act. Legislation and changing moral attitudes under the Communist Party regime, coupled with a lack of public awareness programmes and contraceptives and an absence of sex education, led to a rapid increase in the number of abortions. From 13 abortions per 100 births in 1958, pregnancy terminations increased over the following thirty years to 61 per 100 live births in 1988. In absolute numbers, this represented a growth from 12,383 terminations to 51,000. The gross abortion rate grew sevenfold: from 1.6 to 11.3 abortions per 1,000 people (*Slovak Population. . .*, 1989). Since 1989, the overall abortion rate, as well as the percentage of pregnancy terminations, has been steadily and rapidly decreasing. This reversal in the abortion rate is quite unique in the countries of the former Eastern Bloc (Filadelfiová & Guráň, 1997; Filadelfiová, 2000; Vaňo, 1999).

In Slovakia, family planning was at a very low level in the past. Prevention of further pregnancy was perceived by most of the Slovak population as a matter concerning women, while the use of contraception was not very widespread. During the 1990s, the use of pregnancy prevention grew significantly. The ratio of women using hormonal contraception increased by more than five times (more than 13% of women of fertile age). However, compared with other countries, especially in the West, but also in the Czech Republic or Hungary, this was a very small percentage (Filadelfiová, 2000; Kliment, 1998, 2001).

The decrease in birth rates, extension of life expectancy, increase in divorce rates, the growing number of children born out of wedlock, the growth of migration, and many other development trends decreased the population size. Changes in reproductive behaviour are also reflected in the overall structure of households (*Analýza . . .*, 1997; *Demographic . . .*, 1997; Filadelfiová & Guráň, 1997a, b, 1999; Vaňo, 1999).

In terms of household composition, in the early 1990s, family households (75%) were the main type of family households being held by two-parent families (see Table 2). However, there has been a recent decrease in this trend, with the share of families now being mainly in favour of households of individual persons. Along with the ageing of the population and a subsequent increase in the number of elderly individuals living on their own, this was caused by a decrease in marriage rates and a growth in the divorce rates. Whenever the divorce rate grows and the marriage rate drops, there is a proportional increase in one-parent families. These reasons, together with a decrease in the birth rate, are reflected in a gradual elimination of the difference between the number of families without children and those with children. The prevalence of families with children – so characteristic in the past – has gradually been disappearing.

Thus, the overall structure of households is becoming much more varied. Over the last 40 years, the prevalence of two-parent families based on wedlock with two or more children and an active support network of wider family (once more than 80%) has become a thing of the past. The current trends are: a decrease in the number of two-parent families, an increase in one-parent families, and a gradual increase in the number of childless families. In terms of family structure during the 1990s, two-parent families with two children represented more than one-quarter. The proportion of families with more children went down from 13 to 10%, and

Table 2. Structure of Households in Slovakia.

Type of Household	1961	1970	1980	1991	2001
Common budgetary households (CBH) (in thous.)	–	1267	1585	1778	1900
Number of members of CBH					
1	–	–	18.1	20.9	26.3
2	–	–	21.7	22.9	21.5
3	–	–	18.8	18.1	17.9
4	–	–	23.3	23.4	20.8
5	–	–	11.2	9.9	8.3
6+	–	–	6.9	4.8	5.2
Average number of household members	3.5	3.4	3.0	2.9	2.6
Two-parents families	81.2	78.5	70.6	67.7	56.4
One-parent families	8.4	8.6	8.2	10.4	11.9
Households of singles	9.3	11.9	19.8	21.8	30.0
Other non-family households	1.1	1.0	1.4	0.4	1.7

Source: Informative Reports of the Statistical Office. (29.10.2002), http://www.statistics.sk.

one-child families from 19% to just below 18% (Filadelfiová & Guráň, 1997; Filadelfiová, 2000).

Changes in the household structure of the traditional Slovak family have been confirmed by sociological researches and demographic data. Many of these changes are similar to those in Western countries, but it is possible to detect several differences. Among these are the ten-year time lag in the onset of these changes in Slovakia, and their differing rapidity and intensity. The reasons for the changes in the family are also different. While in Western countries the changes generally reflected the process of individualisation, in Slovakia external pressure was in the past the dominant initiator of changes in the family. This included the measures and ideology of communism, which shaped forty years of Slovakia's most recent history. Its effect was manifest in the reduced scope for independent decision-making, in the restriction of the possibility of mobility, and in isolationism. In the economic sphere, it was felt especially in the low-income level, necessitating the earning of two incomes in order to provide for the family. The result of these external pressures was the homogenisation of the life paths of the population; that is, the unification of the lives of different groups under one predominant model.

The 1990s were characterised by a growth in differentiation, a gradual nuclearisation, and a shrinking of households. The smaller the Slovak family grew horizontally, that is, the fewer members it had within one generation, the more it grew vertically: the great-grandparental generation expanded. As the phenomenon of early parenthood is repeated over several generations within a family, today there are more families with three or four generations. Currently, people often become grandparents at the age of forty-five, when they are fully capable of economic activity. Consequently, sibling ties start to become weaker, which, in further generations will signify the narrowing of the extended family.

The number of family members drops not only as a result of the reduced number of children. Families are also losing their adult members through divorce. This process, however, has not yet reached significant proportions, although public opinion sometimes regards it as being catastrophic.

The changing structure of the Slovak family necessitates the transformations in its function. Coherent and integrated family policies are necessary to secure a balance between the legal, social and economic aspects of families, as well as helping them fulfil their role in ensuring a dignified life.

FAMILY PROCESSES

Under the socialist regime, it was impossible for a single person to acquire an apartment. Before marriage, up to 83% of young people lived in their parents' home (Filadelfiová, 1992). The majority of young people did not experience a stage of independent existence. Some negative consequences brought about by this pattern include insufficient socialisation abilities, low independence, and an "imitation" of parental behaviour and traditional values.

After marriage, 80% of newlyweds spent a one- to five-year period of living with the family of the bride or groom (Filadelfiová, 1992; Možný, 1991; Vereš, 1990). During this time of waiting for an apartment of their own or for the construction of a house, the birth of the first, and – not infrequently – the second child often occurred. In Slovakia, it has become common practice for the start of married and family life to take place "under the roof" of the parental home. Moreover, this was a very early start, without economic or social maturity or independence. Independence in economic and residential terms has ceased to be a precondition for the founding of a family. Research studies indicate that more than 90% of young couples have been more or less dependent on material aid from parents (Filadelfiová, 1992; Vereš, 1990). Contributing to this is the fact that in Slovak culture it has become the norm for parents to feel responsibility for a child and an obligation to look after the child even when it has matured and entered into marriage (*European . . .*, 1991, 1999).

The beginning of sexual life and the establishment of relations with a partner in Slovakia differ from patterns in the majority of European countries. The period of courtship does not last long and young people rarely live together before marriage. Weddings in Slovakia have been big and joyful; in villages more than 100 people are often invited. Various district customs and habits connected with weddings are preserved in many locations (Botíková et al., 1997; Potočárová, 1999). Nowadays, these grandiose weddings and the traditional way of establishing relations have declined due to the economic situation of many families, as well as the changing attitudes of young people.

Relationships among relatives remain important, and strong mutual contact is maintained with uncles, aunts, nephews and nieces, and cousins. Each natural event is used for a family meeting (Bodnárová & Filadelfiová, 2003; Botíková et al., 1997): a christening, funeral, or wedding is a good reason for meeting relatives, for mutual giving of presents or assistance.

WOMEN AND MEN IN FAMILIES

Girls tend to be more interested in and have a more traditional attitude towards marriage. Boys seem to be more "modern" in their attitude – more often than girls they state that they would like to live with a partner out of wedlock. After the marriage occurs, however, this proportion quickly reverses. Under the pressure of daily cares, the more "progressively"-minded boys become more conservative husbands, and the more traditionally-minded girls become wives demanding equal relations and the sharing of household chores (Bútorová, 1996; *European. . .*, 1999/2000).

In Slovak families, domestic chores and childcare remain largely on the shoulders of women. These duties are taken on after the birth of a child more or less freely and spontaneously during the time of maternity leave, which may last for up to three years. Problems arising from excessive chores and childcare emerge when the woman returns to work. They affect most marriages, as the employment rate of married mothers is unusually high in Slovakia; almost 90%, and, moreover, full-time. Women do not enter the labour force merely from economic necessity, but increasingly to meet their need for self-fulfilment. This trend reflects the educational level of women, which is higher than that of men in Slovakia. Out of 100 women thirty years or younger, 44 have taken school leaving exams, whereas of 100 men of the same age, only 33 have done so.

In spite of these conditions, most husbands are still reluctant to take on their share of the care of the children and the household. A lack of adequate services and the rising cost of paid childcare place the married couple in a difficult situation to cope in the future. Conjugal relations in Slovakia are only at the very start of shifting from the traditionally patriarchal model to the modern pattern of equality (Bútorová, 1996; Bútorová et al., 2002).

CHILDREN

The high level of employment of women has had a decisive impact on the situation of children in Slovakia. Because the family requires two incomes to meet its needs, married mothers practically have no choice but to join the workforce no later than the child's third year (usually even earlier). For the majority of children, the first period of life takes place not only in the family but also in pre-school facilities. From early childhood they become accustomed to a certain stereotype dictated by a regime of childcare centres and nursery schools, and likewise to the fact that the basic habits they acquire come not only from their parents, but also from "aunts outside the family." Fortunately, these are nursery and kindergarten teachers, who often play a positive role in the child's development in cases of family breakdown.

Children reach school age when they are six years old. The duration of mandatory school attendance has changed over the years. Presently, basic schooling extends for nine years. Education continues beyond this at four-year schools, with a general curriculum (gymnasia) or with a trade orientation (industrial), or in a three-year preparation for jobs at apprentice schools. Successful completion of secondary school constitutes a first, but not a sufficient condition for study in universities. The applicant must undergo intensive interviews, and because the interest in studying is much greater than the available number of places, the result is often disappointment and disillusion. Places at economics and law faculties, as well as medical and art schools, are in the greatest demand. University education lasts five to six years, according to the field, and in the past, all expenses were met from the state budget. Today, part of the cost is assumed by the family.

Classes in primary schools last for eight hours daily followed by after-school programs for small children who cannot go straight home (they remain at school with a trained care provider). Children have the option of attending one of the extensive networks of basic art schools, which offer training of a high professional standard. The older children remain at home by themselves after lunch until their parents arrive home from work.

Though parents generally express a high appreciation of children, in reality they spend little time with their children, since often both parents are out at work. Time spent together is limited in most families to a few hours in evenings and on weekends. Exposure to the latest mass media reduces this time even further. In many respects, children are idolised in Slovakia. With the reduced number of children in a family, the amount of attention given to each has increased. Considering the parents' current lack of free time, however, this attention is frequently expressed only materially. Parents want their children to have the most modern baby carriages, the most modern clothes, the newest types of toys, and so on. All these things are quite expensive for those earning the average wage. Often it is here that the assistance of the grandparents and relatives is welcome. Children from families without this broader support are often disadvantaged. With the growing wage differences, the child population is also becoming differentiated, with an increase in the number of children whose parents "can't keep up" (Filadelfiová & Guráň, 1997a, b, 1999).

RESEARCH ON THE FAMILY

The main question arising in public discussions of family policy in the last decade has been how to change the family support system to better adapt to contemporary conditions. Three major themes appear in publications dealing with family: the decreasing trend in natality, the increasing proportion of families with children among social groups most affected by poverty, and increasing unemployment, which has serious effects on families with children.

Many publications relate to demographic developments (e.g. *Analýza...*, 1997; Bodnárová & Piscová, 1995; *Demographic...*, 1997; Lenczová, 1998;

Filadelfiová, 2000, 2001; Vaňo, 1999; *Yes to Family*, 2000). Discussions focus on pro-natalist viewpoints and the erosion of family values. Economists and social scientists with a liberal orientation put special emphasis on the fact that the level of welfare expenditures is too high in relation to the economic development of the country. They have suggested a radical reform of the welfare system that contains better-targeted benefits and lower expenditures (Daneková & Riháková, 2000; Rybárová, 1993; Valná, 1996). Others scholars understand the family support system from the social-democrat viewpoint, criticising the changes in the welfare system and asking for strengthening of the democratic rights of citizens and strict control of political power (Bodnárová, 1999; Kvapilová, 2000, 2001; Radičová, 1998a, b; Vašečka, 1998; Woleková, 1995, 1998; Woleková & Radičová, 2000).

Other studies deal with cash benefits as a family support system (Bednárik, 1996; Bednárik & Valná, 1998; Bodnárová and Hrabovská, 1996; Filipová, 1996; Kopecká & Filipová, 1998; Valná, 2000). Two major perspectives exist: the first proposes the extension of tax allowances for families with children; the second gives priority to the reintroduction of direct cash benefits and the universal child-allowance system. Another frequent issue centres on the family support system in general and concentrates on the impact of benefits on poverty, their effects on reproductive behaviour, and the shift of responsibility from the state towards families (*Analýza. . .*, 1997; Bednárik, 1993; Džambazovič, 2000; Konečný, 1999; Lenczová, 1997, 1998; Reuterová et al., 2000). The increasing of unemployment rates raises the question of preventing social exclusion of families (Bednárik & Valná, 1993; Bodnárová, 2001; Radičová, 1998a).

Some of these topics were analysed in comparison with other European countries. Many comparisons were done by sociological or economic institutes within the Slovak Academy of Sciences (Bodnárová & Piscová, 1995; Filadelfiová & Guráň, 1992), the Bratislava International Centre for Family Studies (Bodnárová et al., 2001a,b; Filadelfiová & Cuperová, 2000; Filadelfiová, 2000), the Institute for Public Affairs (Bútorová, 1996, 2002; Filadelfiová, 2001), or by the Social Policy Analysis Centre (Radičová, 1997, 1998a, b). However, a complex evaluation of specific programs from the point of view of their impact on families is still rare. Further analyses are needed to determine the relationship between changes in social protection and family support systems on the one hand, and changes in the family on the other.

POLICIES AND PROGRAMS SUPPORTING FAMILIES

Before 1989, the family support system in Slovakia was extensive and based on high state budget expenditures. In the period of liberal economic reforms, which was characterised by serious economic difficulties (decreasing wages, high level of unemployment, etc.), different types of family policies were adopted by government. The family support system existent before 1989 was revised repeatedly and supplemented by new elements.

Slovakia has had an explicit family policy since 1996, and policy-makers have also previously declared their support for the family. The country has been trying to change the paradigm, moving away from the collectivist interpretation of the family. However, it is not always clearly defined (no consensus within society has been reached) which interpretation to lean towards: conservative, liberal, or feminist. The resulting family policy mostly represents a mix of elements from various paradigms. The problem of so-called "pendulum swings" has also emerged: a sweeping shift from one paradigm to another, not always, but mostly, related to a change of government.

In 1996, the Slovak Government approved *Conception of Governmental Family Policy* (*Conception . . .*, 1996), where the government declared its responsibility for maintaining democratic policies that guarantee a legal, economic, and institutional framework for the well-being of families. Its main principle is that families are autonomous units, unique sources for the satisfaction of the needs of their members, and that the role of the State is to intervene only in cases when families fail. The *Conception* declared among its objectives democratisation, autonomy, guaranteeing the independence of families, and being a primary support for families with children. However, it also declared a preference for "a family based on a marriage" (a formulation which represents a traditional notion of family). In contrast, in a majority of family policies in Europe, the definition of family as based on "an arrangement according to the particular wish of the parents" prevails.

Slovakia has established basic measures related to the care of children and their upbringing such as maternity leave, parental leave, family allowances, and so on. It has been trying to achieve efficient distribution of responsibility and resources among individuals, families, the state, and other entities (municipalities, companies, NGOs, churches). A small segment of family policy is aimed at reconciliation of professional and parenting functions. So far, little has been done to support sex education, education for family and marriage, promoting awareness of domestic violence, etc. There is neither time nor resources left for this kind of prevention policy (Konečný, 1999; Reuterová, 1999; Reuterová et al., 2000).

In recent years, a shift towards a more systematic approach can be discerned. In relation to the association of Slovakia with the European Union, attention has been paid to the development of a common European policy. However, an integrated and coherent family policy has not yet been achieved; such goals can only be secured if they are accepted by all governments' administrative sectors (a cross-sectoral approach). However, the reality is that social and family policies are considered to be a matter for the social affairs ministry. This results in frequent conflict between individual ministries, in particular between the Ministry of Social Affairs and the Ministry of Finance. Decisions of the government, especially in the economic sphere, are not sufficiently – if at all – co-ordinated with the adopted *Conception of governmental family policy*. The cross-sectoral character of family policy therefore becomes a mere formality: it is declared in the *Conception*, but is not taken into consideration when decisions are being implemented (Bodnárová & Filadelfiová, 2001; Filadelfiová, 1998). The development of new systems for social assistance to families has been non-systematic, controversial and fragmented. During various stages, governmental family policy and the attitudes of the public, or a significant part of it, have also been in contradiction – for instance, on gender equality and domestic violence issues.

Currently, the approach to these issues has become much more realistic and professional through use of the knowledge accumulated during research. International recommendations are also considered when searching for solutions. Slovakia has signed the majority of documents and conventions of European/international legislation. However, the fact that many politicians and political strategists are not familiar with the content of international documents is a problem. Apart from insufficient expertise, difficulties arise from the assertion of certain values by some political groups that are contrary to those contained in the international documents (Bodnárová et al., 2001b). There is a lack of policies responding to the demographic trends or providing equal opportunities for men and women. These policies are absent in particular at the implementation level. Although they appear conceptually (*National . . .*, 1997), they are not present in practice.

CONCLUSION

The last few years have been politically, economically, and socially challenging for Slovakia. Changes have occurred at all levels, affecting the individual, the family, and the society. The events that have taken place since 1989 cannot be understood as "simple" modifications to a political and economic system. Their impact is much more extensive. Slovak society has just embarked on a dramatic process of structural and socio-cultural change. There are some values that can unite people all over the world, and there are also some that divide them or even set them at loggerheads. Respect for the family can certainly be included in the first group. Indeed, there is perhaps no nation that would not regard the family as crucially important to the life of the individual and of the whole of society. Slovakia is no exception. Many social turning points of the past century have left their mark on the character of the contemporary Slovak family; thus it is, in some respects, somewhat exceptional in comparison with the rest of Europe. Indeed, people in their 80s have experienced several social systems and several different countries without even having to cross the threshold of their own home. These people were born into families in dynastic Austria-Hungary; they founded their own families in the first Czechoslovak Republic; and they raised their children in wartime independent "puppet-state" Slovakia. Their grandchildren have been born in the second independent democratic Slovakia. Many of the paradoxes in contemporary life in Slovakia derive from the winding path the society has travelled.

REFERENCES

Analýza poklesu pôrodnosti a návrh opatrení potrebných pre stabilizovanie a podporu populačného vývoja na Slovensku. (Analysis of Decline in Natality and Proposals of Measures Needed for Stabilisation and Support of Demographic Development in Slovakia.) (1997). Bratislava: MPSVR SR (Ministry for Labor, Social Affairs and Family).

Áno pre rodinu (Yes to Family) (2000). Zborník príspevkov z konferencie. Bratislava: Christian Democratic Movement.

Bednárik, R. (1993). *Situácia a aktuálne problémy rodiny na Slovensku. (Situation and current problems of families in Slovakia)*. Bratislava: VUPSVR (Research Institute for Labor, Social Affairs and Family).

Bednárik, R. (1996). *Obraz vnímania opatrení štátnej rodinnej politiky v rodinách na Slovensku. (Perception of governmental family policies among families in Slovakia)*. Bratislava: VUPSVR.

Bednárik, R., & Valná, S. (1993). *Podmienky života rodín s nezamestnaným členom. (Life conditions of families with an unemployed member)*. Bratislava: VUPSVR.

Bednárik, R., & Valná, S. (1998). *Analýza príjmovej situácie domácností Slovenskej republiky v r. 1992 a v roku 1996. (Household income analysis in 1992 and 1996)*. Bratislava: VUPSVR.

Bodnárová, B. (1999). Sociálna politika. (Social policy.) In: G. Mesežnikov & M. Kollár (Ed.), *Slovensko 1999. (Slovakia 1999. A Global Report on Status of Society)* (pp. 170–182). Bratislava: IVO.

Bodnárová, B. (2001). *Nezamestnanosť a jej dôsledky pre rodinu. (Unemployment and its impact on family)*. Reprint No. 3. Bratislava: BICFS.

Bodnárová, B., Botezatu, S. I., Filadelfiová, J., Guráň, P., Rudan, Z., Stankūnienė, V., & Starinskaya, T. N. (2001a). *Reflections of recent demographic conditions on family and social policies in CEE countries – Belarus, Hungary, Lithuania, Romania, Slovakia*. National Reports. Bratislava: BICFS.

Bodnárová, B., & Filadelfiová, J. (2001). Demografický vývoj vz. rodinná a sociálna politika: príklad krajín strednej a východnej Európy (Demographic development and family and social policy: Case of selected CEE countries). *Mozaika rodiny, 1*, 7–32.

Bodnárová, B., & Filadelfiová, J. (2003). Slovakia. In: J. J. Ponzetti, Jr. (Ed.), *International Encyclopedia of Marriage and Family* (2nd ed., Vol. 4). New York: Thomson Gale.

Bodnárová, B., Filadelfiová, J., & Guráň, P. (2001b). *Reflections of recent demographic conditions on family and social policies in CEE countries*. Final Report Part II. Bratislava: BICFS.

Bodnárová, B., & Hrabovská, A. (1996). Finančné príjmy ako predpoklad ekonomickej situácie rodiny v období prechodu k trhovému hospodárstvu. (Income as a precondition of economic situation of families in transition period to a market economy). *Sociológia, 28*(2), 147–158.

Bodnárová, B., & Piscová, M. (1995). Society, law, family. In: M. Piscová (Ed.), *Family in Slovakia in Figures and Commentaries* (pp. 78–84). Bratislava: Institute of Sociology, Slovak Academy of Sciences.

Botíková, M., Švecová, S., & Jakubíková, S. (1997). *Tradície Slovenskej rodiny. (Traditions of the Slovak family).* Bratislava: Veda.

Bútorová, Z. (Ed.). (1996). *She and he in Slovakia: Gender issues in public opinion.* Bratislava: IVO.

Bútorová, Z., Filadelfiová, J., Gyárfášová, O., Cviková, J., & Farkašová, K. (2002). Women, men and equal opportunities. In: M. Kollár & G. Mesežnikov (Eds), *Slovakia 2002: A Global Report on the State of Society* (Vol. II, pp. 333–346). Bratislava: IVO.

Conception of Governmental Family Policy (1996). Bratislava: Úrad vlády SR.

Daneková, Z., & Riháková, M. (2000). *Zmeny v cenách bývania v roku 1999–2000, ich dopady na štruktúru výdavkov a zaťaženosť rozpočtov domácností.*(Changes in housing prices in 1999–2000, impact on structure of household expenditures and household budget). Bratislava: VUPSVR.

Demografická situácia na Slovensku (1997). Zborník príspevkov z diskusie organizovanej Konferenciou biskupov Slovenska. (*Demographic Situation in Slovakia. A Collection of Contributions to a Discussion Organised by the Conference of Slovak Bishops*). Bratiaslava: SKCH, KBS.

Džambazovič, R. (2000). Poverty of the Roma. In: L. Vagač (Ed.), *National Human Development Report: Slovak Republic 2000* (pp. 95–108). Bratislava: UNDP, CED.

Džambazovič, R. (2001). *Premeny rómskej rodiny. (Changes of Roma family).* Reprint No. 2, Bratislava: BICFS.

European Values Survey (1991, 1999/2000). Bratislava: Tiburg University, Institute of Sociology, SAS.

Filadelfiová, J. (1992). Problém spoloèného bývania rodín na Slovensku. (Co-residence of parents and adult children in Slovakia). *Sociológia, 24*(2), 555–570.

Filadelfiová, J. (1995). Natality processes in Slovakia. In: M. Piscová (Ed.), *Family in Slovakia in Figures and Comentaries* (pp. 7–33). Bratislava: Institute of Sociology, SAS.

Filadelfiová, J. (1998). Rodina a rodinná politika (Family and family policy). In: G. Mesežnikov (Ed.), *Voľby 1998: Analýza volebných programov politických strán a hnutí* (pp. 113–126). Bratislava: IVO.

Filadelfiová, J. (2000). *Basic characteristics of demographic development in the selected CEE countries.* Final Report Part I. Bratislava: BICFS.

Filadelfiová, J. (2001a). Rodina 90. rokov na Slovensku (Slovak family in the 90s). In: Ľ. Kráľová (Ed.), *Rodina v spoloèenských premenách Slovenska* (pp. 11–41). Prešov: FF PU.

Filadelfiová, J. (2001b). Demographic development in Slovakia. In: G. Mesežnikov & M. Kollár (Eds), *Slovakia 2001. A Global Report on Status of Society* (pp. 320–348). Bratislava: IVO.

Filadelfiová, J., & Cuperová, K. (2000). *Diversity of the demographic development in Europe.* Bratislava: BICFS.

Filadelfiová, J. & Guráň, P. (1992). Paradoxy rodiny: mýty, pravdy, pochybnosti (Paradoxes of family: Myth(s), truth(s), doubt). In: P. Guráň (Ed.), *Slovensko a systémové zmeny v spoloènosti. (Slovakia and System's Changes in Society)* (pp. 5–18). Bratislava: Institute of Sociology, SAS.

Filadelfiová, J., & Guráň, P. (1997a). Aká si rodina? (What are you, family?). *Mozaika rodiny, 3*, Bratislava: BICFS.

Filadelfiová, J., & Guráň, P. (1997b). *Demographic trends and family in European postcommunistic countries*. Bratislava: BICFS.

Filadelfiová, J., & Guráň, P. (1999). *The possibilities and limits of family in today's Europe*. Final Research Report. Bratislava: BICFS.

Filadelfiová, J., Guráň, P., & Ritomský, A. (1996). Tradičné vs. moderné: Zmeny a život súčasných rodín. (Traditional vs. modern: Changes and life of contemporary families). *Sociológia, 29*(1), 5–20.

Filipová, J. (1996). *Analýza príjmovej situácie domácností SR. (Household income analysis in Slovakia)*. Bratislava: VUPSVR.

Kliment, M. (1998). *Analýza problémov v oblasti reprodukčného zdravia v SR. (Analysis of reproductive health problems in the SR)*. Bratislava: SSPRVR.

Kliment, M. (2000–2001). The basic treaty between the Slovak Republic and the Holy See from the viewpoint of sexual and reproductive rights and health. *Aspekt* No. 2/2000–1/2001.

Konečný, S. (1999). *Analýza aktivít neštátnych subjektov poskytujúcich sociálne služby. (Analysis of NGOs activities in the field of social services)*. Bratislava: VUPSVR.

Kopecká, J., & Filipová, J. (1998). *Sociálno-ekonomická situácia mladých rodín s nezaopatrenými deťmi (Socio-economic situation of young families with dependent children)*. Bratislava: VUPSVR.

Kvapilová, E. (2000). Rôznorodosť rodinných foriem – výzva pre sociálnu politiku. (Diversity of family forms – Social policy challenge). *Sociológia, 32*(5), 435–448.

Kvapilová, E. (2001). Rod, rodina a sociálny štát: Príspevok feminizmu k obohateniu teórie sociálneho štátu. (Gender, family and welfare state: Contribution of feminist authors to extension of mainstream theories of welfare state). *Mozaika rodiny, 1,* 2–6.

Lenczová, T. (1997). *Rodina a verejná sféra. (Family and public sphere)*. Bratislava: VUPSVR.

Lenczová, T. (1998a). *Štát v službách rodiny. (The state at service to family)*. Bratislava: VUPSVR.

Lenczová, T. (1998b). *Možnosti a bariéry integrácie Rómov v spoločnosti na Slovensku. (Possibilities and barriers of integration of the Romany ethnic group into mainstream society in Slovakia)*. Bratislava: VUPSVR.

Lenczová, T. (1998c). *Postavenie viacdetných rodín v demografickom vývoji na Slovensku (Situation of large size families in demographic development in Slovakia)*. Bratislava: VUPSVR.

Možný, I. (1991). *Proč tak snadno . . . (Why so easy . . .)*. Praha: SLON.

Národná správa o ľudskom rozvoji: Slovensko 2000 (National Human Development Report: Slovak Republic 2000.) (2000). Bratislava: UNDP, CED.

Národná správa o ľudskom rozvoji: Slovensko 2001 (National Human Development Report: Slovak Republic 2001.) (2001). Bratislava: UNDP, CED.

National Action Plan for Women in Slovakia. (1997). Bratislava: Úrad vlády SR.

Názory a postoje mladých žien na Slovensku na prácu v zahraničí (Opinions and Attitudes of Young Women in Slovakia to the Work in Abroat.) (2000, 2003). Bratislava: BICFS, IOM.

Potočárová, M. (1999). Hodnoty slovenskej rodiny. (Values of the Slovak family). *Pedagogická revue*, 204–213.

Radičová, I. (Ed.) (1997). *Vieme čo odmietame a vieme čo chceme? (Do we know what we are refusing and what we want?)*. Bratislava: S.P.A.C.E.

Radičová, I. (1998a). Zabezpečenie v nezamestnanosti. (Social security in case of unemployment.) In: I. Radičová, H. Woleková & J. Nemec (Eds), *Zdravie, práca, dôchodok* (pp. 139–179). Bratislava: S.P.A.C.E. & Centrum pre zdravotnú politiku a stratégie.

68 JARMILA FILADELFIOVÁ

Radičová, I. (1998b). Systém sociálnej ochrany v SR. (Social protection system in the SR.) In: I. Radičová, H. Woleková & J. Nemec (Eds), *Zdravie, práca, dôchodok* (pp. 9–39). Bratislava: S.P.A.C.E. & Centrum pre zdravotnú politiku a stratégie.

Reuterová, E. (1999). *Problematika služieb na podporu rodinných funkcií v rodinách podnikateľov (Services to support family functions in entrepreneurial families)*. Bratislava: VUPSVR.

Reuterová, M., Arvayová, R., & Bednárik, R. (2000). *Vývoj služieb alebo iných foriem pomoci rodine v pôsobnosti obcí, cenová dostupnosť (Development of services or other forms of community aid for families, price affordability)*. Bratislava: VUPSVR.

Rybárová, S. (1993). *Analýza sociálno-ekonomických podmienok mladých rodín (Analysis of socio-economic of young families)*. Bratislava: VUPSVR.

Slovak Au-pairs in the United Kingdom. Research Report. (1998). Bratislava: BICFS.

Stav a pohyb obyvateľstva (Slovak Population and its Fluctuation). (1980–2002). Bratislava: Statistical Office of the SR.

Statistical Yearbooks of the Slovak Republic. (1993–2002). Bratislava: Statistical Office of the SR.

Valná, S. (1996). Sociologický prieskum názorov domácností SR na výšku výdavkových položiek vstupujúcich do životného minima (Household opinion poll on the level of expenditures that constitute minimum subsistence). Bratislava: VUPSVR.

Valná, S. (2000). *Sociálno-ekonomická situácia rodín s deťmi pripravujúcimi sa na povolanie – úèasť štátu na ich riešení (Socio-economic situation of families with children preparing for jobs – Involmenmt of the state)*. Bratislava: VUPSVR.

Vaňo, B. (1999). *Populaèný vývoj v Slovenskej republike (Demographic development in the Slovak Republic)*. Bratislava: INFOSTAT, VDC.

Vaňo, B. (2002). *Populačný vývoj v Slovenskej republike. (Demographic development in the Slovak Republic)*. Bratislava: INFOSTAT, VDC.

Vašečka, I. (1998). Transformácia systému sociálnej starostlivosti na systém sociálnej pomoci v podmienkach Slovenska v rokoch 1990–1996 (Transformation of social security system to social assistence in Slovakia between 1990–1996). In: I. Radičová (Ed.), *Sociálna politika na Slovensku* (pp. 55–82). Bratislava: S.P.A.C.E.

Vereš, P. (1990). Mladá manželství po pěti letech (Young couples after five years). *Demografie*, *1*, 45–56.

Woleková, H. (1995). Social security and legal protection of children. In: Z. Alnerová (Ed.), *Situation Analysis. Children – Slovakia's Future* (pp. 36–48). Bratislava: Slovak Committee of UNICEF.

Woleková, H. (1998). Štátna sociálna podpora (State social support). In: I. Radičová (Ed.), *Sociálna politika na Slovensku* (pp. 55–82). Bratislava: S.P.A.C.E.

Woleková, H., & Radičová, I. (2000). Sociálna politika (Social policy). In: G. Mesežnikov & M. Kollár (Eds), *Slovensko 2000. Súhrnná správa o spoločnosti* (pp. 607–623). Bratislava: IVO.

THE POLISH FAMILY: ALWAYS AN INSTITUTION?

Anna Titkow and Danuta Duch

SOCIO-HISTORIC AND ECONOMIC CONTEXT

In the 19th and at the beginning of the 20th century, the role and character of the Polish family was prescribed by specific political conditions. Because of the repressions against Poles (especially in the parts of Poland which were under Prussian and Russian occupation) and the lack of a national education system and other specific social institutions, the family took over some functions that, under normal conditions, would have been fulfilled by these institutions (Bojar, 1991). This occurred over the past 120 years, after the loss of nationhood in 1795. It is assumed that next to the Church, the family played the deciding role in the transmission of many values and skills that are necessary for sustaining national identity. "Poland became a family" (Łoziński, 1958) not only because "occupants did not manage to control the Polish home" but also because, after 1945, the family was the basic reference group for Polish society.

The second historical feature relevant to the Polish family is the fact that while in 1931 72% of Polish citizens lived in rural areas only 46% did so in 1972 (Turowski, 1975). The cohesion of the rural family was based predominantly on its productive function, a stable marriage and children's dependency on their father's wealth. Despite the transferring of many of its functions to wider groups and institutions, during the 1970s the importance of the family as an institution was still observed. However, great progress in satisfying the needs of every day life has curtailed many of the functions of the family (Szpakowska, 2002).

Families in Eastern Europe
Contemporary Perspectives in Family Research, Volume 5, 69–85
© 2004 Published by Elsevier Ltd.
ISSN: 1530-3535/doi:10.1016/S1530-3535(04)05005-8

Changes in the socio-political system after 1989 demanded from the family mobilization of its strengths and its material and psychological resources. Economic problems (e.g. high unemployment) (National Census, 2002), crisis of social institutions (i.e. public health system), political parties backing off from various warranties and social benefits, and anomy of values made the family a capital link of great importance. It has been the only relatively stable element, and a point of reference in the vacuum of the transformation. For several years the family has been an "overstrained shock absorber of changes" (Domański et al., 1993). Polish families can be understood as a form of adaptive mechanism in times when the society experienced a vivid dissonance between the world of cultural scripts and the possibilities of their realization.

Difficult economic and housing conditions do not allow many Polish families to establish their own family households; 12% live in two-family households and less than 1% in three and more family households (Demographic Yearbook of Poland, 2002). The high level of unemployment in Poland, low incomes, and low unemployment benefits create conditions whereby many families live in poverty.

The threat of poverty is the greatest for the younger generation and multi-children families. Thirty-five percent of families with one child live below the social minimum, as well as 50% of families with two children, 67.5% with three children, 84.5% with four and more children, as well as 55% of single mothers (Nowakowska, 2000). In 1999, every 10th Polish family was not able to purchase the necessary school books (which are very expensive) for their children. Every fifth family did not send the children for additional, paid courses. In the opinion of 30% of families, that year was worse than the previous one when it came to satisfying the needs related to children's education. It has been estimated that in recent years around 34% of children have gone to orphanages because of their parents' level of poverty (Nowakowska, 2000). Poverty affects average working families whose income oscillates around the minimum wage. For example, a couple of young teachers with a child make approximately 1,400 zlotys (about US$350), when the social minimum for this type of family is 1,750 zl (about US$438) (Instytut Pracy i Spraw Socjalnych, 2003). They can be classified as poor and are called the working poor (Mateja, 2003).

DEMOGRAPHIC CHARACTERISTICS
OF THE POLISH FAMILY

Decrease in the Number of Marriages

Since 1981, there has been a decrease in the ratio of new marriages per 1,000 people, especially for the youngest groups, from 108 women and 96 men (20–24 years old) in 1980, to 63 women and 45 men (20–24 years old) in 2001 (Demographic Yearbook of Poland, 2002). This lower ratio of marriages in the youngest group is not compensated for by growth in higher age groups (28 women and 52 men (25–29 years old) out of 1,000 married in 1980, and 33 women and 45 men married in 2001) (Demographic Yearbook of Poland, 2002). This shows not only the tendency to delay marriage, but also a reduced willingness to get married, which "seems to be a result of a change in youth's approach to start and build a family, reflecting attitudes created under conditions of significant economic and housing problems" (Rządowa Komisja Ludnościowa, 1998).

Growing Numbers of Divorces

Between the mid-1980s and mid-1990s, the divorce ratio in Poland was systematically dropping, but since 1994 the number of divorces has started to grow. Still, Poland has quite a low divorce ratio compared to other countries. People living in the cities get divorced more often than those living in rural areas: for every 1,000 marriages, 281 marriages in the cities and 80 in rural areas end in divorce. In most cases the courts decide the divorce without noting a guilty party. Among various reasons for divorces, the first is unmatched character, followed by adultery and alcoholism. Women are filing for divorce twice as often as men, and among such cases only 34% are designating a guilty partner. In cases of men filing for divorce, personal guilt is noted in 27% of the cases.

Approximately 40% of divorced people remarry. In 1988, 12% and in 1995, 11% of marriages involved at least one previously married partner. Divorced women remarry less often than divorced men. Until the 1970s, a growing number of divorced couples had small children; in 1951, they constituted 39% of divorces, in 1970, 63% and nowadays, 64% of all divorcing couples (Demographic Yearbook of Poland, 2002). As a result of divorces, there were 28,763 single parent families encompassing 42,000 children. In the majority of the cases (65%), child custody was given to mothers; in 30% of cases to both parents; and in only 4% of cases was the father given custody rights.

Separation

In 2001, through the influence of strong Polish Catholic circles, the institution of separation was introduced into law. In 2000, courts approved 1,340 separations, and in 2001, 2,345 legal decisions involved a couple's separation. As with divorces, more cases were the result of the wife's petition (75%) than the husband's (17%). In 2001, unanimous petition of both persons was filed in 8% of cases. For every

1,000 marriages there were 12 separations, and people living in cities used this opportunity five times more often than people living in rural areas (Demographic Yearbook of Poland, 2002).

Fertility Rate

After a growth in the number of births during 1970s, the fertility rate decreased from 2.33 in 1985 to 1.29 in 2001 (Demographic Yearbook of Poland, 2002). This trend has not been affected by a change in the 1993 law, which drastically limited the legal options for abortion. The decrease in the number of births was caused not only by the smaller number of women of reproductive age, but also by the fact that there were fewer births.

Extramarital Births

Before World War II, extramarital births in Poland were estimated to comprise 6% of all births. Women who had extramarital children were socially stigmatized as fallen, immoral, sinful, and loose. Such children, too, were stigmatized. Until 1939, the law forbade determining fatherhood and demanding financial help for the mother and child. It is not surprising then, that children of extramarital births were commonly abandoned, sent to orphanages, and in some cases murdered (Pietkiewicz, 2003). After World War II, the rate of extramarital births decreased and stabilized for a quarter of a century at a level of 4–5%. Lax socialist morality removed the stigma of sin from single mothers with children, but the change in public opinion was not as quick. Even today, some unwed pregnant women are rejected by their families, and the abandoning of children as well as cases of the murder of new-borns is increasing.

The decline in extramarital births after the war was influenced by a change in the law that allowed for the possibility of determining fatherhood and awarding alimony. In this situation, fathers of extramarital children were often convinced to get married by the couple's parents. It was also important that in 1956 abortion was legalized. In circumstances where marriage was impossible, this was an emergency option. The low ratio of extramarital births (5%) lasted until the mid-1980s, in spite of the fact that the socialist state took special care of single mothers.

The end of the 1980s saw a gradual increase in extramarital births, but from the beginning of the 1990s, this growth became more noticeable. In 1996, the ratio of extramarital births exceeded 10%, and in 2001 it reached 13.1% (Demographic Yearbook of Poland, 2002). Among single mothers, 86.7% are never married,

10.9% are divorced, and 2.3% are widows. A woman's decision to have a child is increasingly unrelated to marrying the child's father (Pietkiewicz, 2003).

A phenomenon that is increasingly visible in Poland is the growing number of single mothers who give birth to children of different partners. Such patterns of behavior are related to enclaves of poverty, hopelessness, unemployment, and alcoholism, conditions under which the degradation of family and social ties can be observed. These situations are increasingly visible in Poland. One fifth of single mothers in Poland live on social welfare, alimonies, social help, gifts, etc. (Pietkiewicz, 2003).

Family Structure

The changes in the marital status of Poles show that proportionally fewer stay married. In 1988, 62.8% of women 15 years and older were married, and only 55.6% in 2002 (67.8%, 60.3% of men were married, respectively) (Demographic Year of Poland, 2002; National Census, 2002, Preliminary Results, GUS). In recent years, the proportion of people who have never been married grew from 19% in 1988 to 23.7% in 2002 among women, and from 27.1 to 32.5% among men (National Census, 2002, Preliminary Results, GUS).

From 1988 to 1995, there was a decrease in the number of families with children (61.8 to 59.6%) and a growth in the number of childless marriages (22.8 to 23.6%). Meanwhile, the ratio of single mothers grew from 13.7 to 15% and for fathers from 1.7 to 1.8%. Every sixth family raising children in Poland is not a 2-parent nuclear family. Most often the mother is the only breadwinner and, much more rarely, the father. Among single mothers, the largest proportion had children while they were married, 40% of them were left by their husbands, and 30% divorced (Pietkiewicz, 2003). Polish sociologists stress that single-mother families are very diverse (Rymsza, 2001). A typology of single motherhood was developed based on the following variables: education, marital status, vocational activity (or lack of it), number and age of children in family, sharing household with a third party (or parties), and the level of received welfare (Ciecielag, 2001). Accordingly, four types of single motherhood were distinguished: *unintentional, by choice, circumstantial,* and *not-really-single* single motherhood (Ciecielag, 2001).

In Poland there are no specific statistics concerning remarried families that would describe their demographic characteristics. There are, however, data that can be used as a source of information about the phenomenon of reconstructed families indicating that the number of remarriages grew from 12% in 1960, to 12.5% in 1989, to 14.5% in 1990 (Kwak, 1994).

Cohabitation

Every year, almost 10,000 people, usually large city inhabitants, make the decision to live together with no intention to formalize their relationships. These are not only relationships of young people treating living together as a stage preceding marriage. These are also people who have experienced an unsuccessful marriage and who do not want to repeat that experience. Some people choose not to get married for ideological reasons. For others, such as homosexuals, it is not a matter of choice – they cannot legally get married.

The government is unfriendly towards informal relationships. The rights of spouses are admitted only to those who have formalized their relationships. According to Polish law, a person can be either married or single – no other option is possible. In social practice, decrees, acts, regulations, etc. do take the realities into consideration. For example, the Social Welfare Law defines a family as "people living and managing a household together." Social Welfare employees do not care about the civil status of their clients – they work with all types of families. Most banks enable a joint credit account not just for spouses, but for other relationships as well.

Information describing how common cohabitation is in Poland is based on estimates. In 1978, there were 95,000 unmarried couples living together, while now there are around 225,000 (1.9% of all couples). These couples manage their households jointly and have children (Skwiecińska et al., 2002; National Census, 2002, Preliminary Results, GUS). The formal civil status of cohabiting people varies significantly. Most of these couples are formed by people who have never married (69,000 in 2002) and divorcees (31,400) (National Census, 2002, Preliminary Results, GUS).

In 2002, a Member of Parliament from the Left Wing Alliance, Joanna Sosnowska, declared that she was working on a draft bill on cohabitation that would give unmarried couples similar rights to married couples. The new law was intended to regulate legal and financial matters of people living together without marriage including housing, insurance, taxation, and inheritance but excluding adoption. The declaration draft bill aroused disputes on the frontiers of tolerance, especially as the law was designed to consider not only heterosexual couples but homosexuals as well. Catholic Church representatives characterized the idea as an "assault on marriage and family" (Środa, 2002). Despite political disputes and the unsure fate of the proposed bill, Polish society tends to be moving toward greater approval of cohabitation. The ambivalence towards homosexual relations remains, however, unchanged. While 70% of Poles consider homosexual relations inadmissible, 58% support homosexuals' property rights (Skwiecińska et al., 2002).

FAMILY DYNAMICS

Sociological research has shown that Poles place a successful marriage and personal life at the top of their value hierarchy (Dobrowolska, 1975; Nowak, 1979). A successful personal life is the most important factor for over 3/4 of respondents (Titkow et al., 1999). Second place is occupied by another "family" value – having and raising children. Seventy-one percent of Poles value this as important, and it surpassed good material condition, which in the 1970s and 1980s was perceived as the second most important goal in life (see Table 1).

In the consciousness of Poles, marriage is strongly related to having children. Planned childlessness is not appreciated and it is commonly expected that married people are going to have offspring. A decision not to have offspring was valued negatively by 52% of Poles and 33% valued it as rather not right. Only 6% of respondents positively valued the decision to stay childless (Titkow et al., 1999). Women and men equally disapproved of planned childlessness. Data from 1998 are similar to those from 1979 and 1989 (see Table 2). A conviction that marriage should result in offspring is still common. The preferences show clearly that marriage means the achievement of higher economic status and having children – these are understood as the attributes of family as an institution.

Family Customs

In Poland, family ties are reinforced on a daily basis. Research shows that 72% of adults visit their parents at least once a week (CBOS, 2000). In 83% of homes dinner is prepared every day. In 69% of households all inhabitants eat a meal together at least once a day. Celebrating holidays strengthens the feeling of community.

Table 1. Poles' Values (Means).

What is Important in Life?	0 – Extremely Unimportant 10 – Extremely Important		η
	Women	Men	
1. Family	9.83 (1)	9.64 (1)	0.11
2. Friends	8.13 (2)	8.03 (3)	–
3. Leisure time	7.47 (5)	7.58 (4)	–
4. Politics	3.45 (6)	4.25 (6)	0.15
5. Work	7.92 (3)	8.31 (2)	0.08
6. Religion	7.64 (4)	6.65 (5)	0.17
7. Voluntary organizations	3.19 (7)	3.45 (7)	0.05

Source: European Social Survey, Round 1 2002/2003; significance $p < 0.01$.

Table 2. Types of Marriage (Procreation Attitudes Perspective).

Types of Marriage	% (Rank)		
	1979 r.[a]	1989 r.[b]	1998 r.[c]
Mary and Andrew first want to gain suitable living and dwelling conditions and only then will decide to have a child	45,9 (1)	40,8 (1)	41,0 (1)
Rational model *Ann and Robert* in the first years of their marriage want to enjoy each other's company and then will decide to have a child	16,4 (3)	21,3 (3)	12,9 (3)
Ludic model *Eve and Paul* have interesting jobs and like their professional activities, therefore, first of all, they want to have same professional achievements and only then will decide to have a child	7,5 (4)	5,4 (4)	8,5 (4)
Self–fulfillment oriented model *Barbara and Michael* regard having and rearing children as one of the most important goals in marriage, so they intend to have right away	30,2 (2)	32,5 (2)	29,4 (2)
Traditional model Undecided	–	–	8,2 (5)

[a] Titkow (1984).
[b] Duch (1998).
[c] Titkow et al. (1999).

For example, 96% of respondents claim that in their houses, family ceremonies at Easter or Christmas are prepared jointly (Titkow et al., 2002).

Almost 60% of Poles admit that their houses are managed similarly to those of their parents (Titkow et al., 2002). The same percentage claim that in their houses, there are discussions about the family history. Most Poles possess knowledge of family events covering at least the previous generation, and 5% know of events from their grandparents' childhood. Only 21% admit a lack of knowledge about family events that took place before their lives (CBOS, 2000).

GENDER ROLES

Answers to the question "in what role did you see yourself entering an adult life?" offer the possibility to map women's opinions considering their place in society. In the last years of socialism, when "an ideological equity of genders" dominated,

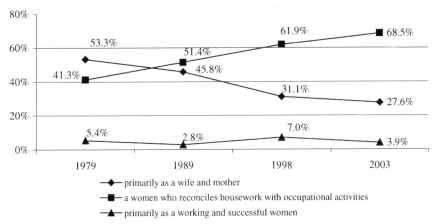

Fig. 1. Woman's Place in Society (Women' Opinion). *Sources*: Titkow (1984); Duch (1998); Titkow et al. (1999); see Note 1.

more than half of women (53.3%) had seen themselves first of all in the roles of wives and mothers (Titkow, 1984). Even though after 1980 the role of wife and mother as an operating life-goal was strongly advocated, the percentage of women envisioning themselves in this role declined to 45.8% in 1989 (Duch, 1998) and to 27.6% in 2003 (Titkow et al., 1999, 2003). College-educated women see themselves functioning both in the private and public spheres.

Women's perception of family and professional life is different from men's (see Fig. 1 and Table 3). Women are less likely to see the traditional division of roles between couples as good for the family and that a woman's career has a negative influence on the "quality" of her motherhood. However, both women and men share the opinion that a wife who has a small child should resign from work outside the home for the child's wellbeing.

The conviction that "it is much better for the family when a man makes money and a woman takes care of the house" is declining in Polish society (see Table 3). In 1992, this opinion was accepted almost equally by women (83.6%) and men (86.8%). In 2003, 67.4% of women and 76.6% of men agreed that this traditional division of roles was a good one (Cichomski et al., 1999).[1] The higher education women had, the more often they opposed the traditional division of roles. On the other hand, men embraced traditional division of roles regardless of their education level.

Women and men show significant differences in their views of the prestige of women's roles. Polish men value women's traditional roles highly, indicating that in both working professionally and home-caring, women are shown similar societal

Table 3.   Family Life Models (w%)[a]

Statements		Strongly Agree	Agree	Disagree	Strongly Disagree	Hard to Say	$V_{cramera}$
It's better for a family	W	32.9	34.5	19.4	8.4	4.8	
when man cares about	M	43.6	33	13.8	4.3	5.2	0.14
money and woman							
cares about household							
and children							
It is not good for the baby	W	27.2	31.5	24.4	14	2.9	–
when the mother works	M	31.4	31.8	22.3	9.7	4.8	
Working mother can	W	33	31.5	22.1	11.2	2.2	0.15
provide to her children	M	24	28.5	28.2	13.2	6.2	
the same feeling of							
warmth and security as							
an unworking mother							
Wife would prefer	W	8.8	18.2	38.3	23.1	11.6	0.13
securing her husband	M	9.4	23.6	37.4	14.5	15.1	
professional career							
rather then focus on							
making a career herself							
Husband would treat his	W	39.4	43.1	6.8	1.7	9.1	–
wife's career on the	M	39	40.6	10	2.6	7.8	
same way as his own							

Source: see Note 1.
[a] Significance $p < 0.01$.

esteem. Almost 60% of women and only 37% of men agree that working women enjoy greater social esteem in our society than non-working women (Budrowska et al., 2003). The differences regarding the prestige of women's roles are independent of levels of education.

Regardless of having a job or working at home, women still perform activities such as cooking, clothes washing, ironing, and dishwashing. The traditional division of roles is strongly supported by the opinions of women themselves. In a CBOS report (CBOS, 1993), 68% of women agreed that "men are responsible for the material well being of the family" and 74% admitted that "home duties such as cooking, washing and cleaning are natural duties of a woman." In 2002 (Titkow et al., 2002), a conviction that men were responsible for the material well being of the family rose among women (up to 80%), while the feeling that home duties belonged to women fell to 64%.

Research conducted by CBOS (1993, 1997) indicated that women's professional activity modifies the traditional division of roles in the family: husbands and children become more and more partners of their wives and mothers in performing at least some household duties, although tasks such as laundering, ironing, or general cleaning are still traditionally women's domain. Women with the highest social and material status receive the most help with housework. Women receive some help with household tasks from their daughters, less often from sons (CBOS, 1993, 1997).

Changes in the division of home duties occur very slowly. According to the Central Statistical Office research on home budgets of time, in 1996 women spent on average 4 hours 50 minutes a day performing household work, while the men worked at home for 2 hours 36 minutes (see Table 4). Men spent on average 5 hours 31 minutes per day on their free time activities, which was almost an hour

Table 4. Time Budget and Gender in 1996.

Type of Duties	Women	Men
Work		
Average time (hours)[a]	6	7.28
Frequency (percentage of working people)	28.8	44.5
Education		
Average time (hours)[a]	5.06	5.09
Frequency (percentage of studying people)	20	17.9
Housekeeping		
Average time (hours)[a]	4.5	2.36
Frequency (percentage of doing housework)	93.5	80.1
Cooking		
Average time (hours)[a]	2.2	0.52
Frequency (percentage of cooking)	86.5	44.1
Cleaning		
Average time (hours)[a]	1.04	0.58
Frequency (percentage of cleaning)	77.9	48.4
Shopping and using services		
Average time (hours)[a]	0.48	0.55
Frequency (percentage of shopping and using services)	44	23.6
Care about adults		
Average time (hours)[a]	0.57	1
Frequency (percentage of caring about adults)	3.4	0.9
Care about children		
Average time (in hours)[a]	1.47	1.19
Frequency (percentage of caring about children)	32.9	20.2

Source: GUS (1999, p. 108).
[a] Time in hours and minutes.

longer then women. Also, men spent 31 minutes more than women on sports (GUS, 1999).

The most recent research, *Women 2002/2003*, shows that household duties continue to be dominated by women. Engagement in this kind of activity was declared by 66.6% of women (in 2000 – 72.5%) and raising children by 31.2% (in 2000 – 36.9%). Simultaneously, a vast majority of these women (87.4%) admit that: *I would like that in my marriage/relationship duties related to keeping a household and raising children were shared by both man and woman* (ARC, 2003).

Attempts to evaluate the work conducted in the household were undertaken in Poland in the 1970s and 1980s (Szczerbińska, 1986). Mikuta (2001) found that the average time spent on household duties was 5.5 hours per day in the cities and 6.5 in rural areas. Monetary values of particular activities (based on average hourly rates in 25 occupations) representing the functions performed in households were evaluated. It was found that the value of home work was comparable to the value of the average monthly income in the national economy. Accordingly, it would have thus increased the value of GDP by around 23% (Mikuta, 2001).

PARENTING STYLES

In the 1990s, the approach to parenting styles was liberalized. An idea that relations between parents and children should be easy and characterized by a partnership approach became popular. Research showed that parents were increasingly opposed to physical punishment for children (46%) (see Fig. 2; Duch, 1998; Titkow et al., 1999, 2002). Still, every fourth respondent admitted that they "slapped the child hard" within the last year, including 12% who admitted having done it in the last month (CBOS, 1995).

In Polish families, everyday care and education of children is primarily in the domain of women. Three quarters of mothers help their children with their homework at least a few times a week; more than a half find time to play with them; and 80% talk to their children a few times a week about their problems, concerns, experiences, colleagues, etc. At the same time, 15% of mothers and 37% of fathers declare a complete lack of time to help their children with homework; 14% of mothers and 20% of fathers never have time to play with their children; and 3% of mothers and 15% of fathers have almost no time to talk to their children about their concerns (CBOS, 1995).

Most families focus the education of their children on school duties; for example, 80% of parents, regardless of their place of residence or education level, would like their children to achieve a college degree (Niezgoda, 2003). Additional activities to

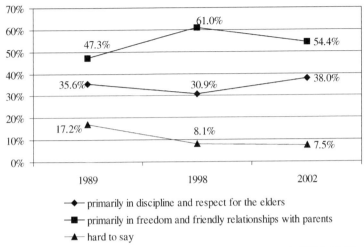

Fig. 2. Parenting Styles. *Sources*: Duch (1998); Titkow et al. (1999, 2002).

develop skills and talents are provided to children by parents with a higher level of education as well as by richer parents. This contributes to an increase in educational inequalities among children. There is a clear category of "dear children" which are part (primarily) of single child families. They are children who are taken care of and educated by the highest quality of babysitters, in kindergartens and private schools. They are commonly referred to as "children who are condemned to success." Their parents invest in their upbringing in order that they might become successful and escape poverty. They want their offspring to have "a better and easier life" than they had (Niezgoda, 2003).

The children and youth from the former State Farms have reduced employment opportunities in the area, have lower levels of education, struggle to achieve self-sufficiency and lack assertiveness. Their goals are dominated by establishing a family and employment security. Therefore, 40% of people living in these areas chose a state-owned business as a dream workplace, settling for a minimalist model of life aspirations (Sikora, 2001).

FAMILY WELFARE POLICIES

In the 1990s, the state social policy towards the family was shaped by three factors (Balcerzak-Paradowska et al., 2003). First, a change in the system of family welfare was initiated as a result of budget expenditure cuts. The Polish

Government accepted a program that relaxed the level of income to family welfare. The limited resources were to be directed towards those who needed them the most.

Secondly, social politics were altered by changing political ideologies. Between 1970 and 2001, AWS (Solidarity Election Committee), the largest party in the parliament and the party most strongly related to the Catholic Church, introduced programs to support multi-children families and longer parental leave. In 2000, the period of parental leave was increased from 16 to 20 weeks after birth, and, in 2001, to 26 weeks. Families received higher family welfare payments for the third and each subsequent child. In 2002, under a new government created by the Left Wing Alliance (SLD), parental leave was reduced to 16 weeks for the first child and 18 for each one that followed. The income level for the provision of social aid was also lowered.

Thirdly, family welfare policies were influenced by a desire for membership in the European Union, which has created external pressures to eliminate gender inequalities in all social programs, including social welfare. The level of welfare for women and men who were taking care of children was brought to parity, a right to parental care aid was introduced in 1995, and a right to parental nurture aid a year later. Also, laws that prohibited fathers from using this aid were eliminated. This was accompanied by a reduction in benefits of 20% because the difference in men and women's income had increased the state budget expenditures.

In contrast to family welfare, maternal benefits were not changed very much. Through all this time, it remained a benefit paid by the social security fund, although the period of payment was changing. The right to take maternal leave was extended to fathers. There are no data to show how often men use this privilege and stayed home to take care of children. The experiences of the Czech Republic and Hungary, which had introduced similar changes in providing such benefits, revealed that fathers' parental leave occurred in less than 1% of cases (Balcerzak-Paradowska et al., 2003). In Poland, the state budget also finances other benefits such as family benefits, alimony funds, and welfare.

At the end of the 1990s, a series of consequences of these changes were noticeable. There was a sharp decrease in the family benefits share of GDP. The number of people benefiting from social welfare had been growing until 1998 and then it declined. This was caused by growing problems in the sphere of public finances and a decreasing amount of money spent for social welfare by national and local governments. According to estimates, the demand for welfare grew because the number of people whose income qualified them to receive benefits and the number of unemployed who lost the right to benefits rose (Balcerzak-Paradowska et al., 2003).

CONCLUSION

Statistical data show that the Polish family, in spite of the transformations it has been experiencing, still fulfills – although in a more limited scope – the function of a shock absorber of the dangers and challenges from the society. The stabilizing functions of the family are based mainly on the strong traditional power of its cultural status in Polish social life and dominance of its material-cultural ties over psychological ones. The results of the 2002 European Social Survey have confirmed Polish sociologists' doubts concerning the quality and the role of psychological ties in Polish families (Bojar, 1991; Titkow, 1993).

NOTE

1. Data concerning the year 2003 are taken from the second part of the research "Szklany sufit: bariery *i* ograniczenia karier kobiet" ["Glass ceiling: barriers and limits of woman's careers"] by B. Budrowska, D. Duch and A. Titkow, Institute of Public Affair (ISP) (2003). The research was conducted by CBOS using a quantitative methodology.

ACKNOWLEDGMENTS

The translation of this chapter by Mirosław Bieniecki was supported by grant KBN No. 5 H02E 028 20 "Nieodpłatna praca kobiet i jej społeczno-kulturowy kontekst" [Unpaid women's work and its socio-cultural context].

REFERENCES

ARC Rynek i Opinia (2003). *Kobiety 2002/2003 (Women 2002/2003)*. Warszawa.

Balcerzak-Paradowska, B., Chłoń-Domińczak, A., Fultz, E., Kotowska, I. E., Olejniczuk-Merta, A., Steinhilbe, S., Topińska, I., & Wójcicka, I. (2003). *Kobiety i mężczyźni w reformie systemu zabezpieczenia społecznego w Polsce (The gender dimensions of the social security reform in Poland)*. Warszawa: Instytut Badań nad Gospodarką Rynkową.

Bojar, H. (1991). Rodzina i życie rodzinne *(Family and family life)*. In: M. Marody (Ed.), *Społeczeństwo polskie u progu zmiany systemowej* (pp. 28–66). Londyn: "ANEKS".

Budrowska, B., Duch, D., & Titkow, A., (2003). *Szklany sufit. Bariery i ograniczenia karier polskich kobiet (Glass ceiling. Barriers and limitations women's career)*. Research Report, Warszawa: Instytut Spraw Publicznych.

CBOS (Public Opinion Research Center) (1993). *Tradycyjny czy partnerski model rodziny (Traditional or modern family model)*. Research Newsletter.

CBOS (Public Opinion Research Center) (1995). *Wychowanie i opieka nad dziećmi w polskich rodzinach (Child rearing and parental care in Polish families)*. Research Newsletter.

84 ANNA TITKOW AND DANUTA DUCH

CBOS (Public Opinion Research Center) (1997). *Kobiety o podziale obowiązków domowych w rodzinie (Women's opinions about division of housework)*. Research Newsletter.

CBOS (Public Opinion Research Center) (2000). *Dzieje rodziny w naszej pamięci (Our memories of family history)*. Research Newsletter.

Cichomski, B., Morawski, P., Zieliński, M., & Jerzyński, T. (1999). *Polski Generalny Sondaż Społeczny 1992–1997 (Polish social survey)*. Warszawa: Uniwersytet Warszawski.

Ciecielag, J. (2001). Kategorie samotnych matek. Analiza statystyczna. *(Type of single mothers. Statistical analysis).* In: M. Rymsza (Ed.), *Samotne macierzyństwo i polityka społeczna* (pp. 123–133). Warszawa: Instytut Spraw Publicznych.

Demographic Yearbook of Poland (2002). Warsaw: Central Statistical Office.

Dobrowolska, D. (1975). Wartości związane z życiem rodzinnym (Family values). In· J. Komorowska (Ed.), *Przemiany rodziny polskiej* (pp. 260–278).

Domański, H., Firkowska-Mankiewicz, A., Janicka, K., & Titkow, A. (1993). Społeczeństwo bez reguł (Society without rules). In: A. Rychard & M. Fedorowicz (Eds), *Społeczeństwo w transformacji* (pp. 143–169). Warszawa: Instytut Filozofii i Socjologii Polskiej Akademii Nauk.

Duch, D. (1998). *Małżeństwo, seks, prokreacja (Marriage, sex, procreation)*. Warszawa: Wydawnictwo IFiS PAN.

European Social Survey (2002). Round 1 2002/2003; www.europeansocialsurvey.org.

GUS (Central Statistical Office) (1999). Badanie budżetu czasu (Time budget research). Warszawa.

Instytut Pracy i Spraw Socjalnych (Institute of Work and Social Welfare) (2003). www:ipiss.com.pl.

Kwak, A. (1994). *Rodzina i jej przemiany (Family in the process of transformations)*. Warszawa: Uniwersytet Warszawski.

Łoziński, Wl. (1958). *Życie polskie w dawnych wiekach (Polish life in a former centuries)*. Kraków: Wydawnictwo Literackie.

Mateja, A. (2003). Polska bomba geriatryczna (Polish geriatric bomb). *Tygodnik Powszechny, 31*, 4.

Mikuta, B. (2001). *Studia nad wartością pracy domowej w mieście i na wsi (The value of household work in the town and in the country)*. Unpublished doctoral dissertation. Warszawa: Szkoła Główna Gospodarstwa Wiejskiego.

National Census (2002). Preliminary results, GUS: www.stat.gov.pl.

Niezgoda, A. (2003). Raport. Dzieci skazane na sukces (Report. Children sentenced to success). *Polityka, 38*, 3–10.

Nowak, S. (1979). Przekonania i odczucia współczesnych (Beliefs and feelings our contemporaries). In: M. Roztworowski (Ed.), *Polaków portret własny* (pp. 122–144). Kraków: Wydawnictwo Literackie.

Nowakowska, E. (2000). Gorsze dzieci. Raport: nie wyrasta się z biedy i nieszczęścia (Worse children. No way to go out from poverty and misery). *Polityka, 9*, 3–8.

Pietkiewicz, B. (2003). Nieślubne dzieci. Raport: Pożegnanie z bękartem (Illegimate children. Report: Farewell to a bastard). *Polityka*, 3–8.

Rymsza, M. (2001). *Samotne macierzyństwo i polityka społeczna (Single motherhood and social policy)*. Warszawa: Instytut Spraw Publicznych.

Rządowa Komisja Ludnościowa (Governmental Population Commission) (1998). *Raport: Sytuacja demograficzna Polski (Report: Demographic situation of Poland)*. Warszawa.

Sikora, E. (2001). Młodzież o swej sytuacji, planach, dążeniach życiowych i zawodowych (Youth and their situation, plans and aspirations). In: Z. Kawczyńska-Butrym (Ed.), *Mieszkańcy osiedli byłych pegeerów o swojej sytuacji życiowej*. Olsztyn: Uniwersytet Warmińsko-Mazurski.

Skwiecińska, O., Skipietrow, N., Więcka, A. (2002). Konkubinat nas podzieli. (Cohabitation divide us), *Nesweek, 24.02.02*, 74–80.

Środa, M. (2002). Konkubinat. Na kocią łapę (Cohabitation. Cat's life). In: *Wysokie obcasy*. 09.03.2002.

Szczerbinska, L. (1986). Wartość pracy gospodarstw domowych (The value of household work). In: *Z prac Zakładu Badań Statystyczno-Ekonomicznych, Szkoła Główna Gospodarstwa Wiejskiego* (pp.162–180). Warszawa.

Szpakowska, M. (2002). Lecz kiedy jej nie ma samotnyś jak pies (Without family you are lonely as a dog). *Res Publica, 12*, 23–27.

Titkow, A. (1984). *Child and Values*. Warszawa: The Institute of Philosophy and Sociology PAN.

Titkow, A. (1993). *Stres i życie społeczne. Polskie doświadczenia (Social stress. Polish experience)*. Warszawa: Panstwowy Instytut Wydawniczy.

Titkow, A. (Ed.) (2003). *Szklany sufit. Bariery i ograniczenia karier kobiet (Glass ceiling. Barriers and limitations women's career)*. Warszawa: Instytut Spraw Publicznych.

Titkow, A., Budrowska, B., & Duch-Krzystoszek, D. (2002). *Nieodpłatna praca kobiet i jej społeczno-kulturowy kontekst (Unpaid women's work and its socio-cultural context)*. Report Grant KBN 5 H02E 028 20.

Titkow, A., Duch-Krzystoszek, D., & Dukaczewska-Nałęcz, A. (1999). *Społeczna i kulturowa tożsamość kobiet. Raport z badania (Gender identity of Polish women)*. Warszawa: Research Report Grant KBN 1 H02E 067 10.

Turowski, J. (1975). Struktura i funkcje rodziny a teoria rodziny nuklearnej (Family structure, family functions and nuclear family theory). In: J. Komorowska (Ed.), *Przemiany rodziny polskiej* (pp. 242–259). Warszawa: Instytut Wydawniczy CRZZ.

CHANGES IN FAMILY LIFE COURSES IN SLOVENIA

Mirjana Ule

FAMILY LIFE STRUCTURES IN SLOVENIA

Among the social changes that cause distress today, the most important are those involving partnerships, relations, family life, and parenthood. In contemporary society, it is difficult to speak of the family within a traditional framework. Like elsewhere in Europe, people in Slovenia are confronted with new challenges and risks. They are living in a country that appears to be relatively successful and stable, at least within the East European context. Furthermore, Slovenia offers an individualized social and cultural climate that has been gaining ground, and providing new options. However, there are risks involved. It is no longer possible to lean on past sources of security and reliance (e.g. values, systems of social security). Young people and their parents are compelled to make choices not only earlier, but also from a better informed position. This means that individuals are forced to shift responsibility for their own lives, almost from the period of childhood.

Data concerning family structure and family life courses in Slovenia show that in this area, the population is conspicuously European in character. This delineation includes factors such as type and size of families, fertility, marriages and divorces, co-habitation, and common law marriages place Slovenia within the European statistical averages (Statistical Yearbook, 2002). Moreover, developmental trends in the area of family life do not essentially differ from predominant European trends. However, this does not imply that family life has been heading towards

Families in Eastern Europe
Contemporary Perspectives in Family Research, Volume 5, 87–101
Copyright © 2004 by Elsevier Ltd.
All rights of reproduction in any form reserved
ISSN: 1530-3535/doi:10.1016/S1530-3535(04)05006-X

Table 1. Family Demographics in Slovenia.

	1985–1989 (Mean)	1990–1994 (Mean)	1995	1999	2000	2001
Number of marriages	10,102	8,630	8,245	7,716	7,201	6,935
Number of out-of wedlock births	5,344	5,571	5,657	6,203	Not available	Not available
Age at marriage (mean)						
Women	23.8	26.1	26.9	28.1	28.4	28.8
Men	26.6	29.4	30.1	31.3	31.4	31.8
Women at child birth (mean age)	25.7	26.5	27.2	28.1	28.3	28.5
Fertility rate	–	–	1.29	1.21	1.26	1.21

Source: Statistical Yearbook of the Republic of Slovenia (2002).

uniformity. The overall picture, resulting from the developmental trends in Slovenian family life includes:

(1) A strong pluralization of family formations and lifestyles. The traditional family (i.e. a married couple with children), accounts for only one third of all the family types in Slovenia.

(2) Formalized marriage has been losing its social status and significance. Increasing numbers of people, primarily young couples, opt for partnership or other types of family union. The general trend in the 1990s saw a decline in the number of marriages (see Table 1) (Statistical Yearbook, 2002).

(3) Increasing numbers of children are born to unmarried couples living in partnership unions, i.e. more than 30%. (see Table 1) (Statistical Yearbook, 2002).

(4) The number of divorces has risen. On average, one in four marriages in Slovenia ends in divorce (Statistical Yearbook, 2002).

(5) There has been an increase in the number of single-parent families. According to the available statistical data (Statistical Yearbook, 2002), single mother families are predominant in this group, accounting for 18.5% of all families. Research shows that the living circumstances of single-parent families are the most difficult compared to those of other family types (Rener, 2003).

(6) Reconstituted families, where at least one parent sets up a new family, have become more common. Around 30% of children in Slovenia today do not live with both biological parents (Ule & Rener, 2003).

(7) The area that has undergone the most important changes is the transition stage. This is the time when young people leave their family of origin and establish their own families, and fertility patterns. An increasing number of

young people continue to live with their parents in a unique, semi-dependent style.

The definition now widely known as LAT (Living Apart Together) characterizes the new "semi-family life" of young people. It denotes a pattern in which young people live with their partners, but also continue to live with their families. Unfortunately, there is a lack of precise data on the LAT phase of life among young adults in Slovenia. The available data indicates a trend towards a higher marriage age for both women and men, and an increase in the average age at the birth of the first child (see Table 1) (Statistical Yearbook, 2002).

Of all of the changes affecting family life, it appears that the shifts in patterns related to the transition stage have attracted the most attention. This is the stage at which a young person leaves their family of origin and sets up his/her own family. It is the passage to this stage that is being increasingly postponed. This phenomenon is known as a late transition to parenthood and is common throughout Europe. On average, young people in North European countries leave their parents' homes in their early twenties (Cook & Furstenberg, 2001). In contrast, young adults in Southern Europe live with their parents until their early thirties. Thus, between 1989 and 1998, the percentage of young people aged 25–29 still living with their parents increased from 45 to 70% (Giuliano, 2002). This increase is also occurring in Northern Europe.

In Southern Europe, a "strong" family continues to be the cultural norm. This is apparent in the prolonged stay of children with their parents, as well as the fact that children care for their aging parents. This focus on kinship and vertical relationships between generations is a result of the strong Catholic influence. It is also a remnant of Muslim traditions that are characterized by community life patterns and networks of relatives. In contrast, Germanic traditions and the Protestant culture have contributed towards the development of a comparatively "weak" family system in Northern Europe. This is a result of the importance of values such as individualism and generational independence. In these societies, children gain independence from their parents at a faster rate than their Southern European peers. Moreover, parents rely less on their children's support in their old age (Iacovou, 1998).

There are some Southern European countries that are characterized by a late transition to parenthood. For example in Italy and Greece, living with parents for a prolonged period appears to be a matter of choice. In contrast, the data for Slovenia shows that extended residence with parents results from a lack of choice. Research on young people conducted in the 1990s by the Center for Social Psychology (Ule et al., 2000; Ule & Kuhar, 2002) revealed that the transition from the family of orientation to the family of procreation takes place at a later stage. The reasons stated by young people in this study were both objective and subjective. The former included factors such as prolonged schooling, difficulties with finding jobs and attaining economic independence, and housing problems. The latter reasons included the comfort and cheapness of living at home, a high level of freedom and autonomy at home, friendly relations with parents, material and emotional security.

The gradual increase in the age at which young people leave school, enter the labor market, leave the home of their parents, establish a stable, affectionate relationship and start their own home, has triggered a whole series of life course changes. No particular step in this process is necessarily a prerequisite for the next step. However, it appears that all of the above events must have taken place before young people make the decision to have a child. This is indicated by data on the average age at which Slovenian women have their first child. That is, in 2001 it was 2.8 years higher than in the late 1980s (see Table 1) (Statistical Yearbook, 2002).

Fertility has been steadily declining in all European countries (World Resources Institute, 2003). In 2003, Albania was the only country in Europe to have a fertility rate higher than 2 children (World Resources Institute, 2003). In all other countries, on average women gave birth to fewer than 2 children. It is interesting to note that fertility in Europe is lower in the East than in the West and lower in the South than in the North (Giuliano, 2002).

Declining fertility rates are not only a result of parents making a deliberate decision to have fewer children, but are also due to the postponement of the first child. This frequently results in a lower number of subsequent births. Analysis of birth cohorts in several European countries shows that the percentage of childless families increases with each sequential cohort. Among Western Europeans born between the mid to late 1960s, the percentage of childless families was already 20% and has steadily increased (Frejka & Calot, 2001). In other words, a childless lifestyle has become firmly established in Western Europe, along with the alternative of deliberately choosing single parenthood (Scanzoni, 1995). In Eastern Europe, however, these changes only began to occur after the collapse of socialist governments in the 1990s. This period saw a drastic decline in fertility rates, as well as a significant increase in single or childless partnerships.

In comparison to other post-socialist countries in Eastern Europe, Slovenia is an exception in terms of its reproductive patterns. Elsewhere, a conspicuous decline and postponement of marriages and births, coupled with a rise in common law marriages and out-of-wedlock births, occurred in the early 1990s, following shifts in the economic and political system. However in Slovenia, these demographic changes had been steadily occurring since the 1980s. At the beginning of this decade, fertility in Slovenia was higher than two children per woman. By the mid

1980s, it had fallen to 1.7 children and by 2000 it had fallen even further to 1.2 children (see Table 1) (Statistical Yearbook, 2002).

Nearly the entire cohort of women born in the first half of the 1960s had given birth to at least one child by 1995 (Obersnel et al., 2001). While a similar trend is apparent among the cohort born in the second half of the 1960s, this group included 20% of educated women who had not had a child between 30–34 years of age. In 1995, 85% of women with an elementary education and 80% of those with secondary school education (25–29 years old) had had a child. This was compared to 30% of women with high school or university education. A comparative study of European countries (Frejka & Calot, 2001) also concluded that the "basic general trend of rising proportions of childless women" is undoubtedly present in Slovenia. This proportion is expected to rise in the cohort born in the 1970s. The decline in the number of births is not expected to be reversed in the near future.

FAMILY POLICIES IN POST-SOCIALIST COUNTRIES INCLUDING SLOVENIA

Changes in family structure and orientations reveal shifts in life courses and, inevitably, changes in the institutions that regulate these transitions. During the 1990s, the life experiences of people living in Western and Eastern Europe changed as part of the transition to a post-modern society. The intense processes of globalization and individualization underlined this shift. Some of these changes were also related to circumstances that transcend national borders, e.g. the restructuring of the labor market, as characterized by the demand for a new, specialized, flexible and educated workforce. In addition, measures arose from social policies, which prolonged the dependence of young people on their families of origin. While these changes occurred throughout Europe, they have had a particular effect on the post-socialist countries of Eastern Europe.

In addition to the movement towards modernity, Eastern European countries also embarked on the transition from a planned society, to one based on the values and movements of the market. The socialist society had been disintegrating for several decades, even before the fall of the system in the early 1990s. While this disintegration created room for a market-based social order, it is still chaotic in the majority of East European countries. One trait shared by all the former socialist countries was the fact that it was the family that shouldered the greatest burden. That is, they took responsibility for the maintenance of social cohesion in the period of transition. Today's young people are much more financially and emotionally dependent on family than the previous generation.

There are many distressing consequences of post-socialism, which include the collapse of the labor market and the resulting mass unemployment, inequality of income and new forms of poverty. Additionally, there has been a renaissance of neo-liberal understandings of the market's role in which focus is placed on individual initiative, self-trust, and a more pronounced feeling of responsibility for one's own life. The changes that are characteristic of the transition processes lead to inevitable changes in the structure of private and family lives. In post-socialism, all Eastern European countries have experienced significant demographic changes. That is, the number of marriages decreased and couples began to delay having children. This resulted in a sharp decline in fertility. The present low fertility rate is historically unprecedented in times of peace. The childless lifestyle has rapidly gained in popularity. Before the transition, nearly all women in Eastern Europe had had at least one child by the end of their fertility period, with most families having two children born a few years apart. What is more, marriage was a universal trend.

An important cause of new demographic trends in Eastern Europe is related to various economic problems associated with the transition from socialism. These problems have increased the direct cost of having children. The delay in childbearing was influenced, both directly and indirectly, by the changes in employment, housing and social policies. The abolishment of mandatory employment resulted in a higher rate of unemployment. In all post-socialist countries, this measure particularly affected women, as nearly all of them had been employed until then.

Family policy was an important element of the elaborate system of social policies that had characterized the former socialist countries. Initially, the goals of such policies were the mitigation of poverty and the promotion of social and economic equality. Later, another goal was added to these, i.e. population growth. Preoccupation with this goal was engrossing in Romania, leading to strict, mandatory measures to boost fertility (Philipov, 2001). Hungary and Czechoslovakia practiced various generous social policies that encouraged couples to have as many children as possible (Philipov, 2001). In Poland and the former Yugoslavia, the nature of demographic trends eliminated the need for additional state intervention (Hakim, 2003). Thus, at the beginning of the transition period, all Eastern European countries had carefully deliberated family policies. These included effective implementation tools such as a long, paid maternity leave, child-care leave and child allowances. While long parental leave is still in place even after the transition, payments have been curbed.

In post-socialist countries, the role of family policies and accompanying measures has a greater importance than in other European countries. The citizens of these countries are accustomed to comprehensive state intervention. Public opinion surveys show that people expect the same level of state support as they received in the past (Philipov, 2001). However, the necessity of creating conditions that encourage individual responsibility has been overlooked. Instead of advancing initiatives that promote self-sufficiency, the current trend seems to favor an increase in state aid to families.

Slovenia has always been an exception, economically and culturally, even before the transition period. The rise in the cost of bringing up children in post-socialism only affected the less prosperous segments of the population. In fact, Slovenia actually managed to make economic adjustments without experiencing a great recession. It is also exceptional among post-socialist countries in terms of its high rate of female participation in the labor market. After the political changes, the participation of women did not fall, compared to that of men. This is in stark contrast to other former Soviet bloc countries where women's employment fell by 20–25% between 1985 and 1997 (UNECE, 2000). All indicators classify Slovenia as non-typical among the former socialist countries. It is positioned as an intermediate point between the West and the East. It has successfully combined the positive sides of socialism (full employment, egalitarianism, social justice) and the positive sides of western welfare states (relative material prosperity, democracy).

Slovenia is also different in that it has continued to maintain a relatively generous family policy, even in the post-socialist period. This generosity is evident in the fact that it has the longest, fully paid parental leave in Europe. While wages for parental leave are also 100% reimbursed in Bulgaria, Poland, Estonia, Lithuania, and Latvia, the duration of the leave is shorter than in Slovenia, where it lasts for 12 months (Stropnik, 2001). Mothers are eligible to three-month's leave, while the remaining nine months can be used by the mother or the father. Both can choose between either a full 260-day leave for childcare, or a partial 520-day leave combined with part-time work. The option of paternal leave was introduced in Slovenia in 1977, three years after it was first introduced in Sweden. The payment, which is covered by medical insurance during absence from work, amounts to 100% of the average salary during the 12 months preceding the leave.

Thus, parental leave in Slovenia is relatively long and generous. As such it allows parents to have as many children as they desire and to balance parental and career responsibilities. Some Eastern European countries offer those parents who renounce paid employment a special payment aimed at enabling them to take care of their small child. In the Czech Republic, this aid is provided until the child reaches the age of 4; in Slovakia and Hungary, until the age of 3, and in Poland until the age of 2 (Kocourkova, 2001). In this instance, Slovenia is the least generous of all post-socialist countries. However, this condition can be explained by the fact that for most families the amount of income lost during the prolonged absence from work is too high, despite reimbursements. Therefore, according to public opinion surveys, people are not interested in this option.

In 2001, Slovenia passed a law on parental care and family income that instituted rather generous family payments. These included parental allowance, financial aid at the birth of a child, child allowance, large-family allowance, childcare allowance, and partial compensation for lost income. Pre-school childcare is also relatively well organized and there is a choice of either public or private kindergartens. The state provides generous funding for pre-school care in public kindergartens, with the size of the subsidy dependant on the income bracket. The average subsidy per child in 1998 amounted to approximately 69% of the full price of a place in the kindergarten program. Despite such a relatively generous family policy, the demographic trends in Slovenia have not changed (i.e. the birth-rate is declining, the average age of women when they have their first child is increasing, and the number of families who choose lifestyles without children is on the rise). There are numerous reasons for this phenomenon.

THE FAMILY AS A PLANNING PROJECT

Young people in post-socialist countries are confronted with risks that were unknown to their parents' generation. The majority of changes (e.g. unemployment and the insecure job market, tight competition for positions, the disintegration of former social security systems) occurred within a relatively short period of time. Thus, the references that once ensured a more or less reliable and predictable transition to adulthood have become uncertain and obscured. The increasing uncertainty of the transition to adulthood, dubbed by some authors as "the ontological void" (Giddens, 1991), is a common denominator for all youth across contemporary Europe. The individualized nature of life has forced people to see themselves as the center of their plans and to reflexively construct their biographies. This influences partnership relations as well as decisions about forming a family and having children. Although personal choices remain highly structured and collectively determined, they are perceived as individual and therefore solutions are sought in private and isolated ways.

These appear to be the main reasons for the radical changes in the attitude towards privacy and family life in Slovenia (Rener & Švab, 1998; Toš, 1999). Public opinion surveys, as well as studies of youth in the 1990s indicate an inclination towards privacy and the family (Ule, 1998). Along with friendship, the family has become the most important value for young people. The higher significance attached to privacy and the family has also been attributed to at least two other macro-social factors. Firstly, the influence of traditional structural constraints (e.g. class, ethnicity, race, sexual orientation) has recently decreased. However at the same time, social inequality within basic institutions or agencies that cut across the traditional class structure of society has increased. Young people belonging to different social classes do not have access to equal quantities and types of resources, options, and opportunities. This comes despite the fact that the outcomes of their journeys to adulthood are now more dependent on their position within and support from the sub-systems (institutions, agencies).

Social inequalities (social inclusion/exclusion) have shifted away from inter-class towards intra-class differentiation. While this does not mean that class differences are no longer significant, it does mean that the factors underlying differentiation within classes, particularly with regard to family support, have been reinforced. The emotional support and social network of families play a decisive role in helping the individual face the increased competitiveness for places in (prestigious) schools and access to (suitable) jobs.

There is another important reason for the increasing significance of privacy. That is, there has been an even more intense deconstruction of the welfare state and a conspicuous re-allocation of costs and responsibilities from the state (and its social policies) to parents. Other significant conclusions drawn from empirical research are as follows (Ule & Kuhar, 2002):

- A shift from the ethical and educational family model to an emotional and supportive one. The traditional distribution of rigid generational and gender roles implying heteronomous rules coming from "the top" has become inefficient.
- Models of communication within the family have changed. Parents and children define and re-define their roles on a daily basis. Family life is characterized by intense work on relations involving mutual negotiations and agreements. A high level of tolerance and the allowance of individual autonomy characterize this type of "work intense" family.
- The role of parents in the life of young people has become more significant. The mother, in particular, has more influence on both the instrumental and emotional levels. Mothers are increasingly assuming the role of the therapist who mitigates distress and conflicts caused by the outside world.

The attitude towards family life in Slovenia is particularly ambivalent. On the one hand, young people are delaying establishing their own families, so the proportion of unmarried, childless individuals is on the rise. On the other hand, surveys indicate that individuals, including young people, attach great significance to private family life (Miheljak et al., 2002; Ule et al., 2000). The study entitled Youth 2000 (Miheljak et al., 2002), conducted with a sample of 1,800 young people between the ages of 22 and 33, included the questions "Will you have children?" and "How many children would you like to have?" In response, 99.5% asserted that they would like to have children. Furthermore, more than half stated that the ideal number of children was 2 and for 29.2%, the ideal number was 3 (Ule

& Kuhar, 2002). The inconsistency between these results and the demographic indicators and low fertility rate in Slovenia, led to focus groups and interviews being set up to analyze this gap between publicly expressed opinion and actual behavior. The sample included three types of participants: individuals aged 23–33 years, couples living in partnership unions, and young families with children (Ule & Kuhar, 2003). The analysis yielded some surprising facts:

- The high level of support for family life demonstrated in public opinion surveys is partially a result of the idealization of the family in Slovenia. This comes primarily from the Roman Catholic Church, in which a pro-family attitude is seen as desirable.
- While young people want to have a family, their decision is dependent on many other factors. Thus, it is not spontaneous and cannot be taken for granted.
- The decision to start a family is a carefully planned step dependent on both subjective and objective conditions.
- The most important objective conditions are economic in character. They include employment, financial security, basic housing, the possibility of combining work, career and family life, and the availability of child-care.
- The basic subjective conditions concern maturity, the quality of personal life, good partnership relations, and readiness to accept responsibility for a family and children.
- Some respondents highlighted the fact that young people today are no longer willing to make sacrifices or to take on (extra) responsibilities.
- Many respondents from the 22 to 33 age bracket openly admitted that they did not feel sufficiently mature for parenthood.
- In the course of their answers, quite a number of respondents referred to their family history, i.e. their parents' narratives.

New generations of young people in Slovenia have to choose between the advantages of family life and those of single life. According to the respondents, the advantages of family life include social integration, social and emotional support (having company, having someone to share your life with), and economic support. People seek intimacy within the family through safe and loving relations. In the opinion of the respondents, these qualities were the essential subjective conditions leading to the decision to have children. One trend that primarily occurred among female students and educated young women was the acceptability of single parenthood. The main advantages of single life are freedom and autonomy. The respondents also assessed the important elements regarding quality of life and attributed the decline in fertility to several factors:

- Economic factors (insufficient or uncertain income as a consequence of the economic crisis and unemployment, high costs of child-care, low possibility of a resolution to the housing problem, difficulties in balancing professional life/career with family life).
- Quality of life (a tendency towards a more comfortable life, desire for independence and personal development, career, self-fulfillment).
- New risks and uncertainties (fear of the future, unstable partnerships, greater responsibility and more demanding tasks related to the process of growing-up, schooling, children's education, negative experience in parents' family).
- Huge responsibility and demands of parenthood (this is related to high aspirations concerning children. That is, young people want to be responsible parents, so they postpone the birth of their children until they can provide all the conditions necessary for exemplary parenthood).

Interviews with young families showed that those with children are in a worse economic situation and have greater housing problems than other groups (Ule & Kuhar, 2002). The majority referred to the costs of having a child primarily in financial terms, although the time and energy required for children and the obligations involved were also mentioned.

The research showed that most of the individuals who already have children enjoy parenthood (Ule & Kuhar, 2002). While independent single young adults attach the greatest value to freedom, young adults with children value family life the most and couples without children are satisfied with their intermediate position. It seems that the transition from one phase to another is accompanied by a change in the personal hierarchy of values.

The research also confirmed the norm of responsible parenthood. Parents want to devote as much attention as possible to their children, and to provide them with a quality life and material resources (Ule & Kuhar, 2002). Ensuring a suitable education, as well as help in professional and everyday life, requires a great deal of resources and places strain on the parents. Virtually all respondents agreed that children deserve the best options and maximum investment possible. The research also confirmed a phenomenon that has been present in Slovenia for some centuries now. That is, there is an exceptionally strong ideological conviction that the mother has to be extremely self-sacrificing in her attitude toward her children (Ule & Kuhar, 2002). Due to this strong obligation towards their children, the harmonization of professional and family duties causes emotional distress for some women. As a result, young women, primarily educated ones are often faced with the irresolvable dilemma of choosing between a career and a family. Until recently, women resolved this dilemma by shouldering a double burden. However today, young women see this as a dilemma to which the solution is increasingly difficult.

Many of the respondents, especially students and highly educated individuals, referred to the difficulties experienced by young people when balancing their professional and family lives (Ule & Kuhar, 2002). Young women in particular highlighted the importance of self-sacrifice and competitiveness in the workplace. They felt that it is impossible to balance these issues with the complexity of tasks required by parenthood. The changing labor market and increased uncertainty also influence the concerns of young people in terms of balancing work and family. One reason for this is the high career standards, parenthood responsibilities, quality of life, and comfort set by young people in Slovenia.

IN SEARCH OF NEW FAMILY LIFESTYLES

The modernization process, which in Slovenia was accompanied by the shocks of the transition, has affected young people through the institutions to which they are subjected in everyday life. These include the family environment, school and leisure activities. Modern societies constantly produce risks such as unemployment, social exclusion, impoverishment, and ecological threats, and Slovenian society is no exception. What is more, these social risks are unevenly distributed. Individualized life compels people to see themselves as the center of their own life plans and to reflexively construct their own biographies. Employment and the work place have ceased to be the arena of serious social conflicts. Instead, these are mainly associated with the fear of unemployment. Young people are first to feel the consequences of these changes and are forced to confront risks that were virtually unknown to their parents' generation. As the majority of changes occurred within a relatively short period of time, they have become uncertain and vague.

Modern European societies such as Slovenia support early mental and behavioral adjustments. However, the conditions in which these happen remain contradictory. That is, prolonged schooling and prolonged economic dependence stand in stark contrast to pressures to make early choices and accept the related responsibilities. Similarly, challenges posed by the outside world are also contradictory. Due to the accessibility of multiculturalism and global internationalism through information technology and the media, young people are well informed about new cultures and lifestyles. This certainly broadens their horizons and modernizes young people, freeing them from the constraints of tradition. Negatively, it also causes new kinds of distress and uncertainty.

Along with prolonged schooling, the period in which young people are dependant on their family of origin has also extended. This process is believed to be particularly manifest in Slovenia. It has been suggested (e.g. Heinz, 1997) that despite prolonged economic dependence, social and emotional ties between parents and children are becoming weaker. This is due to the increasingly strong influence of peer groups and the mass media. However, research on youth in Slovenia has not confirmed this impression. Family support protects young people from social vulnerability (Ule et al., 2000). The influence of the immediate environments in which young people live is undoubtedly becoming stronger, while the influence of structural determinants may be weaker.

In today's world, forming a family no longer represents self-assertion of the individual as a mature person or citizen. In the course of modern life there are no longer any automatic transitions or strong incentives to begin a new phase. For example, a wedding has ceased to exist as a social ritual through which young people declare their adulthood. Many people experience the phase of forming a family as a loss of freedom rather than a profitable decision (in the past, marriage meant gaining freedom). Therefore, it is not surprising that young couples postpone leaving the freedom of the metaphorical playground. According to research (Ule & Kuhar, 2003), young people in Slovenia today no longer perceive the family as a task or destiny that should be accepted for the sake of the nation, country, or as part of ethical norms. Instead, the family is primarily an institution that functions as a personal support network. In the eyes of young people, formalized marriage has also lost its previous status and significance.

Late parenthood is directly related to an increasing need for individual planning of a personal life course and autonomous decision-making. This desire has become a real possibility. The current generation of women has more freedom and opportunities than their mothers had. They view education, work and career as means of preserving their independence. These are all important components of identity. On the other hand, for modern women the role of mother is an emotional one, rather than a mission. The decision to postpone parenthood is a result of negotiating relationships. More and more individuals are testing their relationships before they commit themselves to parenthood (Beck & Beck-Gernsheim, 1990). Research indicates that this strategy is also a unique protective mechanism against unsuccessful relationships (Ule & Kuhar, 2002, 2003). Parenthood is no longer perceived as an obligation or as a destiny. Instead, it has become a carefully deliberated decision. The weakening of traditional ties has tipped the balance of family relations in favor of greater equality between generations and genders. Serious conflicts between young people and their parents have been replaced with a rich, almost playful testing of limits in which young people set the pace.

Individualization of risks means that the situations that once called for collective or political action are now interpreted as scenarios that can only be solved by the person involved. The combination of the pressure to accept individual responsibility (which is a mechanism of disciplining), and the realistic experience of helplessness, has resulted in the perceived omnipresence of risks and dangers. Uncertainty and doubts have pervaded all aspects of life. Additionally, self-identities have become fluid and subject to continual reinterpretations. Life has become a reflexive project that demands incessant modifications to personal biographies in accordance with ever changing possibilities and risks.

REFERENCES

Beck, U., & Beck-Gernsheim, E. (1990). *Das ganz normale Chaos der Liebe*. Frankfurt/M: Suhrkamp.
Cook, T. D., & Furstenberg, F. F. (2001). Juggling school, work, and family: The transition to adulthood in Italy, Sweden, Germany, and the U.S. Child, Adolescent and Family Studies Working Papers. WP 01–01. IPR Publications. http://www.northwestern.edu/ipr/publications/papers/juggling.pdf (accessed on 10.5.2003).
Frejka, T., & Calot, G. (2001). The postponement of births of low births in low fertility countries: An overview. Paper presented at the IUSSP Working Group on Low Fertility meeting on International Perspectives on Low Fertility: Trends, Theories, and Policies. Tokyo, March 21–23, 2001. (accessed on 10.5.2003) http://demography.anu.edu.au/Publications/ConferencePapers/IUSSP2001/Program.html.
Giddens, A. (1991). *Modernity and self-identity: Self and society in the late modern age*. Stanford: Stanford University Press.
Giuliano, P. (2002). *The Peter Pan paradox: Why Mediterranean youth stay at home, do not marry, do not have children (and may not work)*. www.iies.su.se/seminars/giulianopaola_paper1.pdf (accessed on 10.10. 2003).
Hakim, C. (2003). Competing family models, competing social policies. *Family Matters, 64*, 52–61.
Heinz, W. R. (1997). Status passages, social risks and the life course: A conceptual framework. In: W. R. Heinz (Ed.), *Theoretical Advances in Life Course Research* (pp. 9–22). Weinheim: Deutscher Studien Verlag.
Iacovou, M. (1998). Young people in Europe: Two models of household formation. Working Paper. Institute for Social and Economic Research, University of Essex.
Kocourkova, J. (2001). Comparing population policies in the Czech Republic, Slovakia, Poland and Hungary in the 1990s. Paper presented at the European Population Conference, Helsinki, 7–9 June, 2001: http://www.vaestoliitto.fi/toimintayksikot/vaestontutkimuslaitos/eapskonferenssi/Papers/Theme%20G/Kocourkova.pdf (last accessed on September 10. 2003).
Miheljak, V., Rener, T., Ule, M., Mencin, M., Tivadar, B., & Kuhar, M. (2002). *Mladina 2000. Slovenska mladina na prehodu v tretje tisočletje (Youth 2000, Slovenian Youth in transition in third Milenium)*. Aristej: Ljubljana & Maribor.
Obersnel Kveder, D., Kožuh Novak, M., Černič Istenič, M., Šircelj, V., Vehovar, V., & Rojnik, B. (2001). *Fertility and family surveys in countries of the ECE region. Standard country report. Slovenia*. New York & Geneva: United Nations.
Philipov, D. (2001). Low fertility in Central and Eastern Europe: Culture or economy? Paper presented at the IUSSP Working Group on Low Fertility meeting on International Perspectives on Low Fertility: Trends, Theories, and Policies. Tokyo, March 21–23, 2001. http://demography.anu.edu.au/Publications/ConferencePapers/IUSSP2001/Program.html (1. 10. 2003).
Rener, T., & Švab, A. (1998). Family status. In: M. Ule (Ed.), *Youth in Slovenia – New Perspectives from the Nineties* (pp. 41–67). Ljubljana: Republic of Slovenia Youth Department.

Scanzoni, J. (1995). *Contemporary families and relationships.* New York: McGraw-Hill.

Statistični letopis Republike Slovenije 2003 (Statistical Yearbook of the Republic of Slovenia 2002, 2003). Ljubljana: Statistical department of Slovenia.

Stropnik, N. (2001). Preferences in Slovenia vs. reality in Europe: The case of parental leave and child benefit. Paper presented at the European Population Conference, Helsinki, 7–9 June, 2001. http://www.vaestoliitto.fi/toimintayksikot/vaestontutkimuslaitos/eapskonferenssi/Papers/Theme%20G/stropnik.pdf (5. 10. 2002).

Toš, N. (1999): *Vrednote v prehodu II, Slovensko javno mnenje 1990–1998 (Vaules in transition, Slovenian Public Opinion 1990–1998).* University of Ljubljana: Faculty of Social Sciences.

Ule, M. (Ed.) (1998). *Youth in Slovenia: New perspectives from the nineties.* Ljubljana: Ministry of Education and Sport, Youth Department.

Ule, M., & Kuhar, M. (2002). *Ekonomsko socialni položaj mladih družin (The economic and social position of young families).* Report. University of Ljubljana: Faculty of Social Sciences.

Ule, M., & Kuhar, M. (2003). *Mladina, družina, starševstvo.spremembe življenjskih potekov in družinskih struktur v Sloveniji (Youth, family, parenthood: Changes in family structures and family life courses in Slovenia).* Ljubljana: Faculty Press.

Ule, M., & Rener, T. (2003). *Tipi družin in socialne mreže (Family types and social networks in Slovenia).* Report. University of Ljubljana: Faculty of Social Sciences.

Ule, M., Rener, T., Mencin, M., & Tivadar, B. (2000). *Socialna ranljivost mladih (Social vulnerability of young people).* Aristej: Ljubljana & Maribor.

UNECE (2000). Fertility decline in the transition economies, 1989–1998: Economic and social factors revisited. *Economic Survey of Europe, 1,* 189–208.

World Resources Institute (2003). *Earth trends: The environmental information portal.* http://earthtrends.wri.org/text/POP/variables/369.htm (12. 9. 2003).

FAMILIES IN THE REPUBLIC OF MACEDONIA

Divna Lakinska-Popovska and Suzana Bornarova

SOCIO-HISTORIC AND ECONOMIC CONTEXT

Historic and Political Context of the Country

The Republic of Macedonia is a small country on the Balkan Peninsula, comprising 25,713 square kilometers and a population of two million. For 45 years it functioned as one of the six constituent republics of the Yugoslav Federation. It was declared an independent and sovereign state in 1991. The new Constitution established the Republic not only as independent and sovereign, but also as a civil and democratic nation-state. This guaranteed complete equality and coexistence of the Macedonian people with the Albanian, Turkish, Vlach, Romany and other minorities living in the country. It also initiated the process of recognition by other states throughout the world, as well as the establishment of diplomatic relations. Macedonia was accepted as a member of the United Nations in 1993 and is currently involved in a large number of European and International associations.

The transition from a centralized to a more decentralized state has not been without its share of problems. The state is now, governed by the rules of the market, pluralistic in its party system, and is characterized by greater involvement of all sectors of the country's civil society in the building of the nation and its social welfare. A different set of challenges has been inherited from the country's former dependence on the central government of Yugoslavia. Among them are a lack of experience in policy analysis, strategic thinking, and development of national legislation. Policy and legislative development following independence

Families in Eastern Europe
Contemporary Perspectives in Family Research, Volume 5, 103–119
© 2004 Published by Elsevier Ltd.
ISSN: 1530-3535/doi:10.1016/S1530-3535(04)05007-1

has often failed to address specific needs and circumstances of the country. What is more, it has relied heavily on the national legislation of Yugoslavia. In light of its own conditions and international developments, Macedonia needs to reassess policies, as well as institutional, professional and community practices.

While new laws aimed at greater self-management and self-reliance of communities and population groups are being developed, their transformation into practice has remained weak. Under the Government's strategy for local development, the former division into 24 municipalities has been reduced to 115 new municipalities conferring certain rights and obligations for their own development. Local governments are gradually preparing for their new roles. They are faced with the challenge of building new institutional structures and adopting new approaches and regulations for social development.

Despite the unfavorable circumstances and serious difficulties encountered, the process of transition towards the new political system of pluralistic democracy has seen considerable progress. The fundamental principles of the political system, established and guaranteed by the Constitution, include: (1) citizens' sovereignty; (2) human and civil freedoms and rights; (3) national equality and co-existence with the national minorities; (4) rule of law; (5) political pluralism and free democratic elections; (6) a division of powers; and (7) local government (National Development Strategy for Macedonia, 1997).

Social Forces

Sustainable social development at national and local levels calls for social organizations, activities and new sources of funding that complement state resources. Closely associated with sustainability is the self-organizing and self-managing capacity of population groups (with their specific needs and interests), and of local communities. Organized groups, institutions and local communities need to sustain and advance their development and welfare in an open, democratic, free market and decentralized society. To achieve this they must learn to negotiate their way through the labyrinth of societal norms, divergent interests, resources and organizational patterns. They must also learn to manage and resolve the inevitable social conflicts that arise from the competing claims made on limited resources. In this context, the country is especially vulnerable. The prevailing circumstances encourage inter-ethnic tensions and conflicts within families, and other social relationships. Without monitoring and mitigation strategies by competent social professionals, as well as adequate social policies and programs, this situation clearly puts the peace and stability of the country at risk.

Many years under a centralized administration and authoritarian control have suppressed individual initiative and innovative capacities. The absence of such strategies is especially felt in the profound changes in the country's economic and social systems. Along with privatization and decentralization comes the need to upgrade management and organizational skills. It also calls for the adoption of new people-centered strategies that can foster innovation and achievement. Knowledge of contemporary concepts of organizational development, motivation theory, conflict resolution, and client relationships needs to be acquired and transferred to the work place.

As benefits and subsidies are being scaled down by a market and cost dominated system, many entitlements, services and institutions are being threatened. These include the childcare support system, health services, unemployment benefits, pension plans, housing subsidies, institutions of care and educational services (e.g. universities). In terms of the ethnic minorities, while the freedom to organize has been granted, they are faced with a general increase in intolerance resulting in ethnic tensions.

Economic Conditions

Until the middle of the 20th century, Macedonia was a typical agricultural country. In the second half of the century, a process of rapid industrialization and urbanization occurred. Migration of the rural population was then redirected to the towns, in particular to the capital city of Skopje, which reached a population of more than half a million. This process was typical for the whole period of socialism, up until the breakdown of the former Yugoslavia.

After Macedonia's independence, rapid transition of the economic system took place with all its characteristic features. This included a spontaneous restructuring of the industry, privatization of public capital, liberalization of markets, etc. At the same time there was a drastic decline in industrial production, in levels of construction and in tourism, an appearance of the gray economy, a fall in the standard of living, extremely high unemployment, etc. Since 1996, prospects have improved, economic policies have relaxed, monetary stability has been achieved, and small businesses have developed. However, these positive elements have been offset by increased social stratification (National Development Strategy for Macedonia, 1997).

Additionally, the high degree of liberalization of foreign trade, which was a condition for cooperation with the IMF (International Monetary Found), created an abundance of negative effects. As a result, in 1995 Macedonia experienced a significant decrease in its overall production and GDP (Gross Domestic Product)

(GPD reached 70% of the 1990 value). This led to a decline in wages and an increase in unemployment. Thus, the number of relatively poor people increased, and their opportunities for purchasing food, and access to good quality education fell. Additionally, construction of infrastructure and protection of the environment declined. There were also public health consequences, such as a significant increase in morbidity (National Human Development Report, 2001).

Moreover, an armed crisis hit Macedonia in 2000. This was initially due to the spillover from the Kosovo conflict on its territory, but was followed by a consequent two-year armed conflict within its borders. This worsened the already heavily burdened economic and social life of the population, and adversely affected the endeavors and prospects for improving socio-economic development.

The Impact of the Socio-Political and Economic Context on Family Life

The position of the family in general is determined by the wider social, political and economic conditions. Thus, given the above conditions, it is obvious that the Macedonian family system encountered similar problems. Apart from those typically attributable to the transition process, there are a number of other issues that prevailed long before the transition and contributed to the overall deterioration of living conditions. Among these are the low level of economic development, urban over-population, economic emigration, the need for emancipation of women (particularly of women from minority ethnic groups), and backward cultural practices. These factors are also responsible for the slow pace of reforms and the low acceptance of required changes in attitudes and behaviors. In summary, the cumulative effect of the problems arising from underdevelopment and the socially stressful process of transition has had a dramatic impact on family lives.

In the early years of post-socialism, along with the economic and political struggles, there was an emergence of social problems that directly affected family life. There had been a fall in living standards and as a consequence of greater unemployment, there was an increase in social insecurity. In 1995 the unemployment rate was 37.7% (National Development Strategy for Macedonia, 1997, p. 144). Furthermore, the reduction and irregular payment of wages brought many other problems for families. These included limitations in health care, reductions in pension and disability insurance, a decrease in the number of child allowance beneficiaries, and difficulties in the domain of education and payment for facilities that had previously been free of charge. In summary, the social position of the Macedonian family deteriorated due to the low level of economic development, the increased number of pension beneficiaries (due to the aging population), and low income.

Some of the major changes in Macedonian family life parallel the processes of industrialization and urbanization. The positive changes include the development of the nuclear instead of the patriarchal family; democratic and egalitarian rather than authoritarian family relations; a dynamic instead of passive dedication to family life and work; improvement in the quality available health care; the family as a consumer instead of a production unit. The negative changes include fewer employment possibilities and thus reduced chances to provide for the family's needs; problems related to caring for children and the elderly due to the underdevelopment of special facilities; the expense related to access to higher quality education and health care; lack of time to devote to family relations; the increase in prices in contrast to the irregular payment of wages, resulting in family costs shortages and widening of the gap between living expenses and wages. While this modern life style is common among Macedonian families, the country has not given up its traditional family values. Therefore, even in nuclear families, the values of closeness, support and communication are strongly maintained and treasured.

FAMILY PATTERNS IN MACEDONIA

In parallel with the societal development in R. Macedonia, marriage as an institution has been enriched through the addition of valuable components. Apart from its biological component, marriage has become a community of two persons from opposite sexes who share emotional, ethical, economic and psychological dimensions. The family as an institution comprises both parents and their children. The extended family may include three generations and close relatives.

The emergence of the nuclear family has lead to a stronger differentiation between married couples and their wider families. Relations with extended, and sometimes closer family members, is gradually decreasing. In short, marital relations have gained importance and are becoming stronger, while relations with relatives are losing their place within the family value system. Often, onerous economic and existential conditions do not allow a married couple to establish an independent life. Thus, it is common for couples to live with their parents within the extended family unit. The low standard of living in Macedonia restricts the capacity of married couples to establish their own households. Until there are improvements in the economic sphere, this situation will continue (Matilov, 2002).

Along with the continued weakening of ties between married couples and their extended families, there has also been a gradual rise in the number of married couples without children, and single parent families. During socialism, there was a greater chance of finding employment, obtaining credit for housing and furniture, and accessing free health care and education. These factors facilitated the decision to enter marriage.

Unlike previous eras when parental authority was strong and decisions about marriages required parental consent, approval and choice, today's economic conditions enable young couples to alter this context. Given the transition and the market economy, there is an increased feeling of insecurity concerning the future. This in turn influences the decision about whether to enter or postpone marriage. Marriages of interest (to obtain economic advantage) have become increasingly common. The rise in the age of people at the time of their first marriage is a change from the past when people married young. While this is true for Macedonian ethnics, early marriages are still common among Albanian or Roma ethnics.

In the last few decades, families with children were most prevalent. However, a tendency for a decreased family size has emerged (Matilov, 2002). As shown by the statistical index, the possibilities for childbirth have dropped from 2.5 to 1. The number of childless marriages is also growing. Intensified professional and working obligations have resulted in the postponement of childbirth and work and career are being given priority over starting a family.

Family Structure

Statistical information indicates that in 2002 there were 7.1 marriages per 1,000 people in R. Macedonia. The number of marriages has decreased, and divorce has increased. In 1991, the number of divorces per 1,000 marriages was 32.4, while in 2002 this rose to 90.2 (Macedonia in Figures, 2003).

Of the marriages that took place in 2002, for 93.9% it was the first for women, and for 91.8% it was the first marriage for men. Thus, men enter into second marriages more often than women. In 2002, the highest number of marriages was performed for women aged 20–24 (44.1%), and for men aged 25–29 (38%). The highest number of divorces was among women aged 25–30 (22.2%) and for men aged 30–34 (24.2%) (State Statistical Office, 2003).

According to data on marriages in Macedonia (see Table 1), married people are at the head of the majority of households. The number of couples in pre-marital (consensual units), is relatively small.

There are currently 564,296 households in R. Macedonia, each with an average of 3.6 members (MIA, 2003). A major change in recent decades has been the decrease in the size of families. There has been a steady decline in large families and in households composed of several families living together (Census, 1994). At the same time, the number of nuclear families has risen.

Table 1.   Head of the Households (Gender and Marital Status).

Gender of the Head of the Household	Total Number of Households	Marital Status of the Head of the Household					
		Single	Married	Widowed	Divorced	Unknown	Consensual Unit
Male	420,550	10,863	387,154	17,912	2,543	2,078	481
Female	81,413	5,489	19,653	48,151	7,335	785	110
Total	501,963	16,352	406,807	66,063	9,878	2,863	591

Source: The 1994 Census of Population, Households, Dwellings and Agricultural Holdings in R. Macedonia, Statistical Office of the R. Macedonia, Skopje, December 1997.

Families are bigger in rural areas than in the cities. This is due to the unequal strength of the family transformation processes. The average number of family members decreased from 5.3 in the 1950s to 3.8 in 1994 (3.5 in the cities and 4 or higher in rural areas) (the last available census data) (Statistical Yearbook, 1995).

While Table 2 shows that in R. Macedonia the majority of families have children, the number of families without children must not be disregarded. Of the married couples with children, the majority has 2 children, followed by families with only one child. The number of single-parent families is insignificant and it is considerably lower than the average number typical in developed countries (Census, 1994).

As Macedonia is a multi-ethnic country, the process of change within family structures differs among the groups. Namely, the changes in family structure are most evident among families of Macedonian nationality. In Albanian families, greater efforts are made towards strengthening the traditional family structure (Matilov, 2002).

Nowadays there are increasing numbers of single and non-family, multimember households (composed of relatives such as brothers or sisters, or people who are not relatives but share the household), especially in urban areas. Most numerous are nuclear families, confirming the idea that the nuclear family is becoming more common (this is more typical for Macedonian families than for Albanian families, which are often family groups composed of several smaller families that share the household).

GENDER ROLES IN THE FAMILY

In the patriarchal family, women are subordinate to men and bear the burden of all family responsibilities in relation to children, as well as household maintenance. In the contemporary family, the division of labor has changed. As a result, women

Table 2. Family Structure and Number of Children.

Type of the Family	Number of Families	Children in Families	Number of Children					
			Without Children	1 Child	2 Children	3 Children	4 Children	5 and More Children
Total number of families	539,555	788,920	132,088	138,059	196,770	47,988	15,389	9,261
Married couples without children	132,088	–	132,088	–	–	–	–	–
Married couples with children	355,825	700,927	–	110,097	181,133	42,921	13,502	8,172
Mothers with children	41,435	72,084	–	21,899	12,490	4,426	1,661	959
Fathers with children	10,207	15,909	–	6,063	3,147	641	226	130

Source: The 1994 Census of Population, Households, Dwellings and Agricultural Holdings in R. Macedonia, Statistical Office of the R. Macedonia, Skopje, December 1997.

are increasingly employed outside the home. What is more, there is a tendency towards symmetrical sharing of household responsibilities, and the strict division of domestic work along gender lines has diminished. In contemporary Macedonian families, men are becoming engaged in domestic work, which heretofore had been considered the responsibility of women. Although still in its elementary phase, the process of equalization of family relations is evident. Furthermore, the authority of men is decreasing, while a synchronic type of authority, in which the sexes equally participate in family decision-making, is growing. In terms of parent-child relations, it is evident that children's opinions are increasingly respected and that their authority within the family has strengthened.

There are several core factors that have caused changes in the position of women in the family. These include their emancipation, increased economic independence as a result of employment outside the home, and changes in family structures resulting from shifts in their reproductive behavior. The issue of female participation in family planning deserves particular attention. Unlike the past, women's voices are now heard when it comes to childbirth and family size. In general, the reproductive behavior of women is determined by factors such as education, socio-professional status, residential area (rural/urban), and ethnicity. In Macedonia, rural women with lower levels of education show the highest natality. Ethnicity is also a dominant factor when it comes to reproductive behavior. For example, unlike Macedonian women, women with Albanian or Roma ethnic backgrounds dedicate the largest part of their lives to childbirth and rearing. Also, the number of children is twice or three times higher for Albanian or Roma women, than for Macedonians. A smaller number of children reduces the traditional subordinated position of women in the family and represents a huge step towards their further emancipation. This signals the beginning of the end for male domination in the patriarchal family. This has been replaced by a new family system based on human and democratic relations in which women, in terms of their rights and obligations, are increasingly equal to men. However, there are still some factors that are slowing down the process of equality within the family. For example, the sustainment of the traditional ideology that has been rigidly passed from generation to generation, and seeks to maintain the male dominance of family authority.

FAMILY TRADITIONS

Macedonia contains multiple ethnic and religious communities. According to the 2002 Census, in R. Macedonia there were 2,022,547 people (64.18% Macedonians, 25.17% Albanians, 3.85% Turks, 2.66% Roma, 1.78% Serbs, 0.84% Bosnians,

0.48% Vlachs, and 1.04% other ethnic groups) (MIA, 2003). In terms of religious affiliation, the 1994 Census indicates that 66.6% of people are Christian Orthodox, 30% are Muslim, 0.5% are Catholics and 2.8% other affiliations or atheists. The percentage of the population in Macedonia of Muslim religion comprises not only Albanians but also Turks, Roma people and Macedonians. Until recently, a large group of atheists existed in Macedonian society, and there are categories of citizens that report no active religious involvement (Cacanovska, 2002).

The Macedonian population is basically defined as Orthodox. The Albanian population is mainly Muslim, with a small number of Catholics. The increased number of Albanians in Macedonia resulted from their massive emigration from Kosovo. This process has intensified since 1970 when, during the existence of the former Yugoslavia, there was pressure from Serbia on the Albanian population.

Role of Religion on Family Life

The transition following the socialist period in Macedonia allowed the revitalization of religion. The new period rejected the constraints of the socialist society, and as a result, religious affiliations and feelings were no longer forbidden. Thus, long suppressed and hidden religious feelings came to the surface and religious communities could operate openly. In general terms, religious topics gained greater visibility and a more significant function in the new society, compared to the past (Matilov & Cacanovska, 2001). However, as a result of the long-lasting socialist period in which families and children lived without religious influences and beliefs, their resurgence is only slowly being accepted. Therefore, religious practices are often considered as an experience rather than as a true religious conviction. As a result, religion has become a normal part of family life. Priests and other religious leaders are also in the process of reorganization of their work, especially in the domain of social services.

CHILDREARING PRACTICES

Changes in the contemporary family have also affected the roles of children. Life in the market economy, in which rationalistic living styles prevail, has produced some resistance to having more children. This is contributing to the decrease in the number of births (natality rate). The increase in nuclear families and reduction in family size has changed the position of children within the family. The smaller number of births increases the importance of each child, and not just as extra working hands, which was typical for patriarchal families. With the diminishing need to obey to the father's authority, the position of children in the contemporary family has significantly improved.

The fact that nuclear families have fewer children means that they are given more attention, and more quality time is spent on their upbringing and socialization. Due to the fact that contemporary families in Macedonia usually have two offspring or less, the children have become the center of family life and the focus of parental dedication. The children's right to make choices, and respect for their preferences is something that they may fully enjoy, unlike children in the past who were completely subordinate to their parents.

By becoming aware of their own position and role in the family and wider society, today's youth are characterized by a stronger desire to achieve independence. This was an aspiration that was restrained by the patriarchal values and norms of the traditional family. The younger generation bases its own behavior less on parental authority, or the economic and cultural characteristics of the family, and more on their own abilities. Children are increasingly independent, especially when it comes to making decisions about their education and their future or professional orientation. However, they rely on their parents' advice when it comes to complex decisions, which they are unable to make themselves.

The processes of industrialization and urbanization, which produced changes in family roles and functions, had a particular effect on the parent-child relationship. Although parental authority is still present in decision-making, the children's authority is accepted. The dynamic life of the nuclear family allows less time for the rearing and education of children, functions that are gradually transferred to other societal institutions. These institutions have become family partners in rearing and educating the young). The belief that children should be treated in an authoritarian manner with strict obedience to their parents has almost been abandoned. Parents are increasingly adopting the view that children should have a certain degree of liberty and independence, along with the respect of their parents. This reflects the democratization of family relations based on the principle of equality among all family members.

Childrearing in Macedonian families is still primarily a female obligation. The lesser involvement of men represents a residue of traditionalism. Women still bear the heaviest burden in terms of bringing up their children. Fathers only perform this function in rare cases, especially when it comes to care of the smallest children. The possibility for a greater paternal role is present, but acceptance is hampered by the fact that the role is traditionally marked as that of the mother.

Family structure, educational levels, and ethnic background also determine the changes in the upbringing of children. In nuclear families, the equalization of roles is more apparent than among those with more complex structures. In terms of education, the higher the educational level of the father, the more democratized are family relations (Matilov, 2002). Ethnic background also has an impact on childrearing attitudes. In Macedonian families there are more progressive changes in family relations, while Albanian families are more conservative, maintaining patriarchal family relations.

Peer Relations

Macedonians are hospitable and sociable, and this is reflected in relationships between the younger generation and their peers. In practice, close relations are established between children at an early age. Pre-school children share the company of their peers both within kindergartens and in the neighborhood. This is specifically the case in rural areas where neighborhood relations are stronger, families are more open to each other, and visiting practices have been maintained. In urban areas, family life does not always allow close contact between children and their peers. However, the practice of maintaining peer relations, exchanging visits, and neighborhood gatherings are still quite common.

School aged children are also in contact with peers while at school and during extra-curricular activities. Due to the low employment opportunities, continuation of their education, and financial constraints, young people are dependent on their parents. Therefore, young people live with their parents until they get married, and often settle with their newly formed families in the parents' home. Additionally, they start going out at night at an early age. Their nightlife consists of visiting coffee bars, Internet cafes, concerts, and discotheques, while less time is devoted to sports activities and cultural events. Few attempts are made to orient Macedonian youth towards more productive activities and constructive use of their free time. This results in young people staying out late at night (often until 2 or 3 in the morning), which paves the way to involvement in different deviations and substance abuses. The State recently initiated some interventions, among which are the legal constraints on sales of tobacco and alcohol to juveniles, and limitations on opening hours for coffee bars. The effects of these legislative measures have not been felt yet, but the hope is that eventually the young will start pursuing activities that will benefit not only them personally, but also society as a whole.

When it comes to the love life of young people, long-lasting relationships are common practice. Couples meet in secondary school and often stay together for years. After completion of their education, they often contact their peers from abroad in search of opportunities to leave Macedonia and find employment.

Education

Education has always been given high priority in Macedonia. This is illustrated by the volume of public resources set aside for education, both in comparison to developed countries and those of the region. Macedonia allocated circa 6.5% of its GDP to education in 1995 (National Development Strategy for Macedonia, 1997, p. 105). However, the question of whether these resources are enough to yield the expected educational outcomes remains to be seen.

Pre-school education is a stage of key importance in the intellectual, emotional and social development of children. Despite this, it suffers from a lack of teaching material and from the utilization of methods incompatible with individual development. There is a need to make certain essential changes in the content, procedure and methodologies. Kindergartens in Macedonia are predominantly state-owned, while private initiatives in pre-school education are only beginning to emerge. Within the elementary sector (primary education compulsory by law) some positive trends can be observed. These include wide age-coverage, equal treatment of girls and boys, the teaching of ethnic minorities in their native language, provision of qualified teaching staff, textbooks, ancillary literature, and visual aids. New syllabuses and curricula are bringing significant improvements to this basic segment of education. Although the initiatives towards modernization of the education system are still in the introductory phase, they are essential for meeting future needs. While the system of secondary education has been marked by certain reforms, some problems remain. These concern the unsatisfactory regionalization of the school network, a widespread diversification of professions, a relatively low level of modern educational equipment, a delay in updating teaching methodology, etc.

Within the higher education system, there is an explicit need to follow contemporary trends and the positive experiences of developed countries. The updating of curricula and syllabuses, creation of space for competitiveness among higher education institutions, and the upgrade of educational techniques and technology are some of the advantageous changes. A trend that is dominant in the area of rearing and educating children in R. Macedonia is the institutionalization of family functions. This means that in the contemporary family, some functions are gradually being transferred to the societal institutions.

In terms of the educational responsibility of the family, this function has been fully transferred to the wider society. Although schooling is free of charge, education of children is still expensive. As a result of having to pay state or private allowances, although higher education is legally opened to everybody, it is accessible only to those students who can afford it. Student who obtain the highest scores at entry exams enter higher education without taxes.

RESEARCH ON THE FAMILY

During the last decade, social research focusing on families increased in Macedonia. Some of the issues examined were the relations between the family and society (Janev, 1998), social security of the family (Matilov, 1992; Ristevki, 1999; Trajkovski, 1998), the impact of global changes (Arsovska-Nestorovska, 1998) and socio-economic factors on families (Matilov, 1993; Nikolovski, 1999). Additionally, analyses were conducted on family development, roles, and relationships (Matilov, 1994a, b; 1995), as well as on family benefits (Lakinska-Popovska, 1999) and family violence (ECF, 2000). Research projects also dealt with issues relating to ethnic minorities, such as the vulnerability of Roma children and their families (Lakinska-Popovska, 2000a, b). This research focused on exploring social, educational, health, communal and living conditions of Roma families, and resulted in a report containing recommendations for improving the lives of the Roma ethnics. Projects in the domain of the ethnic identity of the Macedonian population have also been carried out (Beshka, 2002; Simonovska, 2002).

FAMILY POLICIES AND PROGRAMS

The concept of family benefits in the Republic of Macedonia refers to a set of public policy measures. These regulate benefits relative to children, such as all forms of income support for raising and educating children (birth benefit, parental leave, educational grants, child allowance, and pension for orphans). These benefits may be in the form of either cash benefits or services.

(a) *Birth Benefit*. Assistance for the first-born child used to be given in a form of baby-package. With the recent changes, the assistance for the first-born is given only in cash, to the amount of 3,000 denars (50 Euros). This right is accorded to the mother, the father or the child's guardian.

(b) *Parental Leave*. According to Health Care Law (1996), the following persons are considered to be family members: marital partners and children born in or out of wedlock, stepchildren, and adopted children. The insured parent shall be provided income replacement during temporary work inability resulting from care of a sick child up to the age of 3, care of a sick family member older than 3 years of age (30 days), and compulsory presence of the parent with a child up to 3 years of age during hospitalization (30 days) (Extract from Article 18).

(c) *Child allowance* is granted to cover part of the expenses for a child's rearing and education. The right to child allowance belongs to one of the parents, until the child reaches 15 years of age (amount: 500 denars or 8 Euro) (State Statistical Office, 2003). Until recently, child allowance was offered to children at school (until the age of 26). This allowance is granted for the first three children and its beneficiaries are most commonly families with one employed parent.

(d) *Special child allowance to protect handicapped children* is granted for those with different degrees of mental and/or physical impediments to development. The amount of the special allowance for persons from 0 to 26 years of age is 2.920 denars (48 Euros) (State Statistical Office, 2003).

(e) *Benefits for protection of neglected, abandoned and children without parents in foster families* are reserved for school-aged children. Currently, in the Republic of Macedonia there are 85 families offering foster family care to 180 children. Foster parents receive 5,000 denars (83 Euros) per month, per child.

(f) *Social Protection during unemployment* provides compensation; preparation for employment and counseling on professional orientation; health protection, pension and disability insurance; remuneration for travel; employment of disabled persons.

(g) *The Pension and Disability Insurance System* is based on the pay as you go (PAYG) principle. In the next several years, capitalization of the Pension Fund is expected, and dividends will start to be paid out on priority shares that were transferred to the Fund in the process of privatization.

CONCLUSION

Currently, the Republic of Macedonia is undergoing a process of transition from a mono-party to a plural political system; from a planned economy to a market economy; from a centralized government to a decentralized local government. This transition affects the standard of living and family structure. Apart from the struggles typically attributed to the transition process, there are a number of problems associated with urban overpopulation and economic emigration. All of these tendencies have changed family life in the Republic of Macedonia, including trends towards mostly nuclear (two-generation) families, democratic and egalitarian family relations, increased dynamic of family life and equality of family members, along with decreased employment possibilities and under-developed child and elderly care services. Compared to the past, young people postpone marriages (and thus childbirth) to a later age (with the exception of Albanian and Roma populations). The fact that nuclear families have fewer children means that each child is given more attention and thus more resources can be used for their education. In terms of gender roles, Macedonian women are increasingly employed outside the home. However, women still bear major burdens concerned with performing domestic duties. Families in general are not deeply religious, although they attend religious events and holidays with a high level of social organization.

ACKNOWLEDGMENTS

The team engaged for the preparation of this Contribution on Families in R. Macedonia wishes to sincerely thank the following institutions that provided us with an extensive support and required information and data without which this Contribution would not have been possible:

- Institute for Sociological, Political and Juridical Research, Skopje;
- Institute for Social Work and Social Policy, Faculty of Philosophy, Skopje;
- National Centre for Training in Social Development (NCTSD), Skopje;
- State Statistical Office, Skopje;
- United Nations Development Program (UNDP), Skopje.

REFERENCES

Arsovska-Nestorovska, K. (1998). *The influence of global societal change on the social position of the family*. Sociological Sciences, Skopje.

Beshka, V. (2002). *Ethic identity of Macedonians and Albanians in Republic of Macedonia, and possibilities for creating a civil-oriented identity*. Projects (1990–2001). Institute for Sociological, Political and Juridical Research, Skopje.

Cacanovska, R. (2002). *The process of de-secularization in Macedonian society, in New Balkan politics*. An Academic Quarterly Journal of Politics, Institute of Sociological, Political and Legal Research. Skopje: SEE University Tetovo.

1994 Census of Population, Households, Dwellings and Agricultural Holdings in the Republic of Macedonia – Households and Families (1997). Book VIII, Final results. Statistical Office of the Republic of Macedonia, Skopje.

ECE – Association for emancipation, solidarity and equality of women (2000). *The family violence*. Report from conducted field research, Skopje.

Janev, G. (1998). *The relation between the family and the society*. Sociological Sciences, Skopje.

Lakinska-Popovska, D. (1999). *National survey of Republic of Macedonia, family benefits*. Monitoring the Development of Social Protection Reform in the CEES, Part 2.

Lakinska-Popovska, D. (2000a). *Vulnerability of Roma children in the dispersed Roma communities in Skopje*. National Center for Training in Social Development, supported by UNICEF and World Bank, Skopje.

Lakinska-Popovska, D. (2000b). *Vulnerability of Roma children in the municipality of Shuto Orizari.* National Center for Training in Social Development, supported by UNICEF and World Bank, Skopje.

Macedonia in Figures (2003). State Statistical Office of R. Macedonia, Skopje.

Matilov, N. (1992). *Social security of the family in Macedonia, from aspect of its institutionalization.* Dialog, Skopje.

Matilov, N. (1993). *The changes in socio-economical base of the family in Macedonia.* Annual of the Institute for Sociological, Political and Juridical Research, Skopje.

Matilov, N. (1994a). *The family authority of contemporary family in Macedonia.* Annual of the Institute for Sociological, Political and Juridical Research, Skopje.

Matilov, N. (1994b). *The changes of the family relations in urban environment in Macedonia from the aspect of family roles structure.* Dialog, Skopje.

Matilov, N. (1995). *The development phases of the family in Macedonia.* Annual of the Institute for Sociological, Political and Juridical Research, Skopje.

Matilov, N. (2002). *Sociology of marriage and family.* Institute for Sociological, Political and Legal Research, Skopje. (*Sociologija na brakot i semejstvoto.* Insitut za socioloski i politicko pravni istrazuvanja, Skopje).

Matilov, N., & Cacanovska, R. (2001). *Problems of the family and the religiosity of the population, in socioeconomic structure and problems of the population in R. Macedonia.* Institute for Sociological, Political and Legal Research, Skopje. (*Problemi na semejstvoto i religioznosta na naselenieto,* vo *Socio-ekonomska struktura i problemi na naselenieto vo Republika Makedonija.* Skopje).

MIA (2003). vesti@mia.com.mk, 01.12.2003; 15:20:25.

National Development Strategy for Macedonia (1997). Macedonian Academy of Sciences and Arts, Skopje.

National Human Development Report (2001). United Nations Development Programme, Skopje.

Nikolovski, T. (1999). *Socio-economic position of the family-case study Zelenikovo.* Sociological Sciences, Skopje.

Ristevki, V. (1999). *Social security as a factor for family stability (case study).* Sociological Sciences, Skopje.

Simonovska, E. (2002). *National and religious distance of the population in the R. Macedonia.* Projects (1990–2001). Institute for Sociological, Political and Juridical Research, Skopje.

State Statistical Office (2003). *Population.* Public Information 2.1.3.11, 29 April 2003. (Drzaven zavod za statistika (2003). *Naselenie,* Soopstenie 2.1.3.11., 29 April 2003).

Statistical Yearbook (1995). (Statisticki godisnik, 1995).

Trajkovski, D. (1998). *Family and social protection in the Republic of Macedonia.* Annual of the Institute for Sociological, Political and Juridical Research, Skopje.

THE HUNGARIAN FAMILY

Olga Tóth

SOCIO-HISTORIC AND ECONOMIC CONTEXT

Hungary is situated in east central Europe with an area of 93 thousand square kilometers and a population of 10.2 million. Its Gross Domestic Product (GDP) per capita was 5,669 Euro in 2001 (Statistical Yearbook, 2001). Ninety-seven percent of the country's population is Hungarian. The ethnic minorities, comprising 3% of the population, are German, Slovak and Romanian. The minority with the highest population, and of a peculiar status, is the Gypsies. Their proportion of the population of Hungary is estimated at 5–6% (Hablicsek, 2000). Gypsies are linguistically divided, with 70% speaking Hungarian as their maternal language. Their recognition as a separate ethnic group is currently a matter of political debate.

Until the 1990s, Hungary was regarded as a sending country, with the number of people emigrating from the country higher than the number of immigrants. The emigration rate was especially high at the time of the 1956 revolution. Since the 1990s, Hungary has become a receiving country. At the time of the Romanian revolution in 1989–1990, the number of people moving to Hungary was around 33–37 thousand a year (Demographic Yearbook, 1990). By the end of the 1990s, this number had settled at 13 to 18 thousand. People of Hungarian ethnicity from Romania represent the highest number of immigrants arriving today. There are also refugees from Asia and Africa. Despite these immigrants, the population of Hungary at the beginning of the 21st century is essentially homogeneous.

Hungary participated in World War I as part of the Austro-Hungarian Monarchy and in 1918 it became an independent republic. The Trianon Treaty closing World War I reduced Hungary's territory by two thirds, to its current size. Thus,

Families in Eastern Europe
Contemporary Perspectives in Family Research, Volume 5, 121–139
Copyright © 2004 by Elsevier Ltd.
All rights of reproduction in any form reserved
ISSN: 1530-3535/doi:10.1016/S1530-3535(04)05008-3

the population decreased from 18.2 million to 7.6 million. The majority of the population living in the lost areas was of non-Hungarian ethnicity although a third of Hungarians, i.e. 3 million people, were also placed under foreign sovereignty. The terms of the Trianon Treaty created a difficult economic situation in the country, since a significant proportion of its industrial, transport and trade potential was now situated outside its borders. Furthermore, the large numbers of Hungarians who lived outside the Hungarian borders were separated from their families, which meant that the Trianon decision caused a trauma for a significant proportion of the population that continues today. During the period between the two World Wars, political discourse was centered exclusively on the desire to revise the borders.

After World War II, Hungary was occupied by Soviet forces. Democratic elections were held in 1945, but from 1947 the country gradually shifted towards the Soviet political system. The absolute rule of the Communist Party (Hungarian Workers' Party) started in 1949, at the same time as other countries in the area. In 1956, a revolution broke out that demanded free elections, the departure of the Soviet troops and a democratic political system. The revolution was suppressed by Soviet reinforcement troops and János Kádár was appointed as the leader of the reformed Communist Party.

From the mid-1960s the communist system gradually relaxed, and the country reached a form of social compromise. The economic reforms introduced in 1968 meant an unambiguous opening towards certain features of the capitalist economy, within the bonds of the socialist planned economy. In addition, political and ideological pressure also decreased and Hungary became the most open country within the Eastern bloc. As a result of the 1968 economic reforms and of the country's opening up towards the Western market economy, the standard of living for Hungarian citizens gradually increased. However, people had to pay the price of the significantly increased workload. After a full day's work in the public (state) sector, everyone whose qualifications or circumstances allowed it, went on to work in the so-called second economy. These second jobs varied from agricultural production, construction work, overtime at the state-controlled workplace, etc. For example, in 1981 private farms, which accounted for 11.9% of all farmland, provided 32.8% of total agricultural production. For some kinds of produce (vegetables, grapes, meat, etc.), this proportion floated between 50 and 80% (Romsics, 1999). Although concrete blocks of housing (housing estates) were regarded as a characteristic symbol of the socialist regime, 64% of housing was actually built by the workforce from the private sector even in the prime of the regime, between 1961 and 1980 (Vajda & Farkas, 1990). In the 1970s and 1980s, three quarters of families had a subsidiary source of income from the second economy.

These practices have established an attitude that distinguishes Hungarian society from other countries that have undergone a change in regime. Its people have learnt that self-exploitative work, at least in the short term, brings tangible economic advantages. Also, that the extended family is an economic community in which members work for each other, and finally, that marriage brings important economic advantages, as well as emotional security. A characteristic division of labor between the sexes also emerged in some Hungarian families. While men were more likely to possess skills that were useful in the second economy, women became responsible for managing the family, and representing the family in the outside world. This work division proved to be useful and adaptable after the regime change (Szalai, 1991).

The collapse of the socialist regime in Hungary occurred in 1989, and in 1990 free elections were held. A democratic political system and a market economy began to emerge. At the 2003 referendum, 84% of the nation supported the country's entry into the European Union (EU). The President signed the treaty and the country became a member of in May 2004.

HUNGARIAN FAMILY DEMOGRAPHICS

Research documents the importance of family in Hungarian society. The family represents the main source of solidarity, mutual help, and emotional and financial support. The ideal family is represented by a married couple raising two children, with close connections to other relatives. However, there is a significant difference between demographic behavior and this ideal family formation. That is, couples have fewer children then they have planned; there are very few extended families; there is a high rate of divorce and the number of marriages is decreasing. Thus, the Hungarian family is undergoing considerable change.

Family Structure

The Hungarian population has historically been classified as a "non-European" marriage type (Hajnal, 1965). This type is characterized by early marriages, a relatively small proportion of single adults, a high level of marital fertility and a relatively high number of extended households. Deviations from this are found both among regions, and over periods of time (Andorka & Balázs-Kovács, 1986; Wrigley & Schofield, 1981). Marriage patterns started to show significant variability as early as the beginning of 20th century. Entry into a first marriage for middle-class men living in towns established financial security. Extended families

Table 1. Entry into Marriage.

Years	Entry into Marriage			
	N	Per 1000 Inhabitants	Per 1000 Single Males 15 Years and Older	Per 1000 Single Females 15 Years and Older
1948–1949	102,765	11.2	88.8	66.6
1950–1959	98,235	10.2	93.2	69.3
1960–1969	89,523	8.8	84.2	61.6
1970–1979	97,097	9.2	80.4	61.4
1980–1989	72,854	6.9	58.0	43.5
1990	66,405	6.4	47.4	35.9
1995	53,463	5.2	33.5	25.8
2001	43,583	4.3	24.4	18.9

Sources: Történeti Statisztikai Idosorok, 1867–1992. I. kötet Népesség-népmozgalom, KSH Budapest, 1992; Volumes of Demographic Yearbook.

were present only in some regions of the country and the nuclear family was universal (celibacy was not common). Marital fertility has been decreasing, but is still high compared to the Western European standard.

Demographics of young Hungarians today are very similar to those found in Western Europe. The 2001 Census indicates that of the 3,837 households in Hungary, 71% were family households, 26% one-person households and 3% were the extended type. Typically, a young married couple starts life together in one of the parents' home. Fifty-six percent of the one-person households included a widowed person. The 2001 Census indicated that 18% of females over 15 years were widows and 4% of men over 15 years were widowers. In many cases, becoming a widow causes the surviving family to drop below the poverty line, especially in the case of older women (Spéder, 2002). Young, single persons who have never been married, occupy 11% of one-person households. This social group is a relatively new phenomenon in Hungarian society, but it is attracting media and public interest.

Marriage

Today, compared to the annual average of 100,000 in 1948–1949, the number of marriages has decreased to less than 43,000 (see Table 1). At the beginning of the 1950s, the number of marriages was high partly because of postponed marriages due to the War, and partly because of traditional marital patterns. The radical economic and social changes of the 1950s also increased the number of marriages. The impact of social mobility, transformation of the social structure that accompanied the employment of women in large numbers, large-scale geographical mobility, and the transformation of mate selection norms also influenced the marriage rate. Compared to the past, there was more freedom in the selection of a partner, in that young people could choose their spouse from a much broader social and geographical circle. All these factors contributed to the boom in marriages that lasted until about the middle of the 1950s.

By the mid-1970s, there was a peak in the number of marriages. Groups born in the 1950s reached the age where they could get married. This was accompanied by a lowering of the age of entry into marriage. Marriages at early ages and in a large number were stimulated by population policy measures that encouraged people to have children. It is important to stress that apartments were only available to those who were married and had earners in the family. During this time, the most important passage to becoming an adult was marriage (Róbert & Tóth, 1984). Thus, financial and ideological pressure urged young people to marry early (Tóth & Róbert, 1994).

From the mid-1970s onwards, the number of marriages started to decrease and by 1980 there was a marriage deficit, as every year more marriages were dissolved than initiated. In 2001, the number of marriages per thousand non-married males aged 15 or older was only 24.4 (in contrast with 80 in the 1970s). For females it was only 18.9, in contrast with 61.4 in the 1970s. With minor fluctuations, the number of divorces stabilized at around 24,000 a year in the 1990s and this level remained into the early 2000s (Demographic Yearbook, 1970–2001).

The trend of early entry into marriage, and the current low rate of marriage can be explained by the combined effect of several factors. The first is the age at the first marriage, which in Hungary was traditionally expected to be in the early twenties for both males and females. In the 1970s, on average males contracted their first marriage at the age of 23.7 and females at the age of 21. Today these ages are 27.8 years for males and 25.2 years for females (Demographic Yearbook, 1970, 2001). The increase in the age of first matrimony parallels the increasing educational level of the younger generation, especially for women. Between 1990 and 2001 the number of students in tertiary education tripled and 55% were females. The other explanation is the changing economy, with a high level of unemployment amongst young people. Due to their lack of financial independence, many remain at their parents' home in the status of child.

The decreasing number of people who remarry has also contributed to the low marriage rate. By the end of the 1990s, the number of remarriages had decreased significantly. In about 2% of all new marriages each year, at least one of the parties is widowed (see Table 2). The ratio of new marriages where one of the parties is divorced is about 20% (Demographic Yearbook, 2001). Widowed persons now choose cohabitation or life without a steady partner instead of getting married.

Table 2.   Ratio of First Entries into Marriage and Remarriage.

| Year | Number of Marriages per 1000 Inhabitants | | | | | |
| | Males | | | Females | | |
	Single	Divorced	Widow	Single	Divorced	Widow
1950–59	92.5	272.3	45.1	114.8	114.8	10.9
1960–69	81.8	211.8	33.8	105.7	94.1	6.2
1970–79	83.0	128.9	22.6	115.6	70.8	4.3
1980–89	62.0	73.3	14.6	91.0	46.8	3.0
1990	53.3	46.4	10.3	74.8	32.4	2.1
1995	37.1	33.0	7.5	49.9	22.4	1.6
2001	25.4	30.2	4.7	33.4	19.9	0.9

Sources: Történeti Statisztikai Idosorok, 1867–1992. I. kötet Népesség-népmozgalom, KSH Budapest, 1992; Volumes of Demographic Yearbook.

The main reason for this choice is related to social policy. That is, somebody who is eligible for the widow's pension loses it after remarrying. This means a considerable financial risk for elderly people. In Hungary up until the 1970s, a significant percentage of divorced people remarried. Marriage was highly valued and social policy measures encouraged remarriage. While in the 1970s there were 73.3 marriages per 1,000 divorced men, in 2001 there were only 30.2. The number of marriages per 1,000 divorced women decreased from 46.8 in the 1970s, to 19.9 in 2001 (Demographic Yearbook, 1970–2001).

Cohabitation

Along with the postponement of first marriages and the decreasing number of re-marriages, society's position on cohabitation has changed significantly. Research shows that young people evaluate marriage and cohabitation on the same level (Pongrácz & Spéder, 2001). According to the 2001 Census, 11% of all partner relationships are cohabitations (especially for young people). Seventy-one percent of women aged 15–19 who live in relationships have chosen cohabitation instead of marriage (this ratio was only 3% in 1980). Amongst 20–24 year old women, 39% of those in steady partnerships are cohabitating, while this ratio was only 1% in 1980 (Census, 2001).

The unmarried population consists of a rather mixed group in terms of age, previous marital status and socio-economic status. Widowed persons choose cohabitation instead of marriage for financial reasons. For divorced mothers, the chance of re-marrying is very low, as finding a new partner is very difficult for this social group. The majority of women in their 30s without a steady partner are divorced mothers with children (Utasi, 2002). Young persons who choose cohabitation or life without a steady partner can also be classified into two groups. The first group includes singles, who are the most educated and well-paid group of their generation. Some do not leave the parents' home, instead living a half-adult, half-child post adolescent status. A new phenomenon in Hungarian society is that a significant number of young people remain single and a quarter of people in their 20s and one-fifth of people in their 30s have no steady partnership (Utasi, 2002).

The largest group of young people cohabitating or without a permanent partner includes those who are under-educated, permanently unemployed or living in small villages. Males who cannot find a job do not marry, since financial security is a strong expectation for establishing a family. A man who does not have a stable job and regular income often chooses cohabitation, as he is not able to support a family (Bukodi, 2002). It is also important to note that among the younger generation the education of females is higher than for males. Therefore, unemployed, less-educated young men have a disadvantageous position in the marriage market. The media and the public tend to forget this group of young people and regard the postponement of marriage as a sign of an individualistic characteristic of the younger generation.

Fertility

Together with early marriage, early motherhood is another characteristic of Hungarian society. Although families are generally having fewer children, only very few chose to remain childless. In recent decades, the two-child family model has become increasingly accepted. At the same time, compared to other European countries, there was an early reduction of the fertility rate below the reproduction level (Kamarás, 2000). Fertility has been very low in Hungary: 2.02 in 1960s, 1.92 in 1970, 1.84 in 1990, and 1.31 in 2001 (Demographic Yearbook, 1970–2001). In the 1990s, together with the postponement of marriages and the rising level of female education, women have started having children at a later age. There has been a substantial decline in the fertility of women under 24 years of age and a slight rise in that of women over 30. The average age of married women at the birth of their first child was 22.1 years in 1970, 23.3 years in 1990 and 25.4 years in 1999 (Demographic Yearbook, 1970–2001). The increase in the number of people cohabitating has brought a noticeable increase in the percentage of children born outside of marriage, from 13.1% in 1990 to 30% in 2000 (Pongrácz, 2002). The rate is especially high in the larger towns and in Budapest. In addition, the number of childless people has increased. One out of every ten women in their 20s remain childless.

GENDER ROLES

In Hungary, women first entered the job market in great numbers at the end of the 1940s and by the end of the 1980s, full employment had been realized. In 1990, 83.3% of men aged 15–64 and 68.9% of women were employed (Frey, 1997). Ninety-five percent of employees were full time workers. The state feminism of the socialist regime presented women's employment primarily as an ideological necessity (Neményi, 1996). However, in reality the economy's demand for labor had a greater role in this policy. The forced industrialization of the 1950s required a large work force. When the economy's demand for labor decreased, the Communist Party shifted the emphasis onto the family and the importance of the role of women as mothers and housewives. The introduction of *Gyes*[1] in 1969 contributed to family and social policy, and also served as a tool to withdraw women from the job market. As a result, the issue of women's employment became ambivalent. On the one hand, generations of women regarded paid work as a natural part of socialization, and an essential part of their envisaged career. On the other hand, work, especially if it was badly paid, or physically or psychologically over-demanding, meant a burden for many women and their families. The period of *Gyes* is remembered as a positive experience mainly because in this period women were exempt from the double burden of work outside and inside the home. At the same time, the number of young women who took refuge in alcohol consumption or fell into depression increased at the time of *Gyes*.

Following the regime change in 1989, 1 million jobs were lost. As a consequence, the number of employed men and women fell significantly. In 2000, 63.3% of men and 49.7% of women, aged 15–64, were employed (compared to the EU mean of 72.5% for men and 54% for women) (Frey, 2002). The transforming job market did not provide good opportunities for female employment. Although it is against the law, employers often discriminate against young women, especially young mothers. It is no wonder that most of those affected watch the shift brought about by the regime change with apprehension and worry.

Several studies have shown that Hungarian society is rather conservative in regard to gender roles and especially women's employment. Although female participation in the job market has been widespread, a large part of society views this as a forced choice. Those who thought the man's job was to support the family, while the woman's was to take care of the housework and the children, were in the majority as early as the 1970s. Research shows that the idea of a career is alien to Hungarian women, and that they give priority to the interests of the family over advancement at work (Ponrácz, 2001). Other studies suggest that the economic effects of the regime change and the spreading of conservative ideology have encouraged this opinion. For example, Frey (2001) has found that in the

1980s, 81% of women approved of female employment, while in 1999 the rate of approval was only 67%. The conservative view became especially popular with unemployed women with low levels of education who lived in declining economic regions. It would certainly be difficult for them to find jobs, and given their lack of training, any available job would be badly paid. Female employment is often accepted because of financial pressure.

Hungarian families have always needed two salaries to be able to sustain their standard of living. If either earner becomes unemployed or stops working, the family faces the danger of poverty. A significant proportion of women in this category say that they would choose to stay at home if their husbands/partners earned enough. A large proportion of even relatively highly educated women agree with this, as they find it difficult to balance the multiple roles of working person, mother and housewife. Contrary to the claims of some researchers (Pongrácz, 2002), there is also a group of relatively highly educated women in Hungarian society for whom a job means a career and self-realization. For most women who build a career, the final goal is to reconcile work and family. They expect a family policy that aids the realization of this goal in legal and institutional terms.

FAMILY PROCESSES

Families today have lived through major changes not only in the demographic sense, but also with regard to the propagation of values. The socialization of children (especially the transmission of values) is challenging. The values of the family and the values of the outside world are often in conflict. In a nationwide study of 1,000 women (Tóth, 1999), after financial problems, child rearing was the second most frequent cause of arguments in the home. The values of parents often appear to differ in today's Hungarian families with regard the children's future, their career choices, their attitudes towards cultural life, gender roles, etc. The divergence in value codes intensified as a result of the large-scale social mobility in the last decades of the regime and during the change in 1989. The direct result of social mobility (including geographic mobility) was that families became less homogeneous with regard to their cultural or religious backgrounds.

Studies of social mobility reveal that mothers have a decisive role in selecting schools and acquiring higher education (Róbert, 2000). The research suggests that the father's role in the family (and therefore his part in propagating values) has decreased. This is especially true in the case of unemployed or overworked fathers, who have little time for their families. The father is less of an authoritative figure and his emotional attachment to his children is weak. Hence, the mother's education and her attitudes towards cultural life play a greater role in the children's choice of school or their perspectives on cultural life.

The so-called dual value system is an important issue in the propagation of values within the family. Before the regime change, while many families attempted to pass on their own values, they contradicted the school's teachings and the dominant communist ideology. In this case, children's lives were clearly split between two systems, two worlds of values. The home and the outside world held different truths. This problem remains today, although in a different manner. Many families try to protect their children from commercialized culture and the lifestyle of a society oriented towards consumption and the influence of the media. Some are dissatisfied with the school system that has remained somewhat authoritarian and they seek a suitable, accessible and affordable alternative to school. If this is not a viable route, they do their best to endorse autonomy, individuality, freedom, etc. in their value codes at home. Some take their children to religious schools, even though they are not religious themselves.

Another difficulty with the propagation of values within the family is that the earlier, relatively homogeneous value systems have lost focus (Buda, 1999). The eldest members of Hungarian society have lived through at least four fundamental shifts in value systems as a result of historical changes. Today's generation of parents aged 35–45 had childhood and young adulthood experiences that directly contradict our world today. Some of their internalized values have become meaningless, while others now have a pronounced suspicion of the old regime. Furthermore, some values have become respectable even though they were barely tolerated before. At the same time, modern liberal values (such as self-realization or self-interestedness) have remained difficult to maintain. This comes as no surprise given that the confused value systems undermine people's ability to find their place in the world.

The spreading of alienation and anomie can be seen in research results of the Hungarian Household Panel (Spéder et al., 1998). At the beginning of the 1990s, an increased number of people were finding the world impalpable (Spéder et al., 1998). While in 1978 every fifth adult felt he or she could not keep up with the changes, at the beginning of the 1990s more than every second adult felt this way. In 1978, only 14% of respondents felt that it was pointless to make plans, while in the 1990s this was felt by every second participant. The experience of anomie and alienation is increased by factors such as low levels of education, poverty and old age. Although these figures were slightly better at the end of the 1990s, the high degree of anomie and alienation can still be regarded as impeding the propagation of values within the family.

In Hungarian society it is generally accepted that in order to be successful one must, to some extent, transgress norms (Spéder et al., 1998). This opinion spread

Table 3. Values in Life of Adults and Children.

	Adults M	Children M
Balanced family	3.1	3.5
Work what one likes	3.4	3.8
Clean and healthy environment	4.2	4.5
Self-guidance	4.4	3.8
Health even in old age	4.6	5.3
Friends	4.9	4.0
Orientation in the world	5.7	5.9
Success/Fame	7.1	7.4
Wealth	7.5	6.8

Source: Tóth (2001).

during the 1990s and in 1997, 43.9% of the adult population agreed entirely or to some extent (38.1%) with this view. Factors such as the sudden increase in social and financial inequalities, the spreading of corruption and the greater incidence of its revelation have caused people to feel that success, especially financial success, cannot be attained through honest means. As a consequence, the propagation of positive values within the family is strongly affected by the wide acceptance of this negative attitude.

Studies have also regularly pointed out that a large part of Hungarian society looks at the regime change with dissatisfaction and disappointment (Sági, 2000). They feel it did not bring the results that people had expected. The disappointment of Hungarian society was greatly influenced by the increase in social inequality and the fact that people had hoped that the regime change would bring greater financial security. Instead, the income of the majority of people did not increase, and for many it even decreased in real value. Furthermore since success, for the majority of people, is associated with norm violation, those who have done better than average are looked upon with jealous suspicion.

In a study carried out in 13 towns in the vicinity of Budapest, parents and children aged 12–18 were asked about the children's future and their family's value systems concerning the children (Tóth, 2001). Children were asked to rank a list of nine life goals according to their importance in their lives. Parents made the same list according to their importance in their children's lives. The ranking of the adults and the children revealed several similarities (see Table 3). The highest priority was identical, with both adults and children indicating that the most important goal in life was a balanced family life and a job that suited the child. Since girls and boys rated jobs equally high, the results suggest that holding conservative views regarding female employment is declining.

The allocation of first place to family life indicates that it is firmly established in the Hungarian value system. While this finding has been confirmed many times, it is in slight disagreement with another study that was carried out among youths of comparable ages (Sas, 2002). In that study, completed at the end of the 1970s and repeated 20 years later, 800 young people aged 14–18 were asked to write a passage describing an imaginary day in their lives in 10 years' time. Obviously, such a projective test does not show reality, but the aspirations, values and settings around which the respondents envisage their future lives. The two decades that have passed between the two data acquisitions show a dramatic change in the image that youths have about their future. Currently, family life has a very minor role in a day described by a youth, in contrast with the 1970s when large sections of the passages were devoted to the future family. Today, if starting a family is mentioned at all, it is done so in passing, in a matter-of-fact style. Alternatively, 20 years ago young people presented their future family life and their partner in a romantic way. Their plans now include cohabitation, which was unimaginable 20 years ago. Finally, almost half of today's youth make no mention of having children, while one in ten specify what kind of pet (dog, cat, etc.) they will keep. This study further confirms findings that the concept of family is acquiring new connotations in present-day Hungary and that a varied set of value systems and family styles are also appearing.

Returning to the ranking of life values shown in Table 3, differences between parents and children can be seen. A clean, healthy environment, rated fairly high by the parents, does not appear to be of such great concern to young people. Green values are not really characteristic of Hungarian youth culture. Children appear to find the ability to manage themselves more important. Since the young participants were between 12 and 18 years, it is understandable that being in control of their lives, which is of course one of the most important steps in the course of becoming an adult, is seen as having the greatest importance. It is also possible that the young respondents represent a generation, which in contrast with their parents, sees personal freedom and autonomy as not only very important, but also unrestricted by the political system. The ranks assigned by children and their parents reveal a similar difference of opinion in rating health and friendship. The adults are more likely to find a healthy lifestyle important, even during old age. In a sense, it is understandable that old age and unstable health appear distant to 12–18 year-olds, but the results of this study also show that present day adolescents are not typically health conscious. They are either not really aware of the long-term negative effects of harmful habits (alcohol, smoking, etc.) or they do not worry about them. However, preserving good health does not occupy a sufficiently prominent place in the lives of most adults either. The state of health of the Hungarian population is generally rather poor. In 1999, the life expectancy at birth of Hungarian men was

66.3 years and of women, 75.1 years (Demographic Yearbook, 2000). Combined with the prevalence of harmful habits, this fact suggests that there are few families in which this value is successfully passed on. In terms of the evaluation of friendship, the position taken by parents and children is reversed. The importance of friendship in the lives of children was rated considerably lower by the adults. The higher rating from the children is understandable, since they are at a stage where the opinions of their peers are highly important to them. Unfortunately, the replies of adults reflect the fact that a large part of the Hungarian population does not really have friends. People tend to turn towards their families mostly after their teenage years or in their early twenties.

The last items ranked by both the adults and the children were wealth, fame and success, which seem to be the least important aims in life. A possible explanation for this phenomenon could be that there may be some sort of purist ethos in the value systems of the respondents, whereby wealth, fame and success are discommendable, or something of which to be ashamed. The parents' generation was brought up at a time that viewed slow, uninterrupted material growth, rather than that which was eye-catching as setting a decent, honest man apart. Anyone who accumulated wealth at a greater pace than average was viewed with suspicion. As mentioned before, there is still a certain level of mistrust surrounding financial success. However, it is difficult to believe that parents and the majority of teenagers really do not find these ambitions important.

The children were also asked to what extent they found it plausible that they would achieve their aims. With the exceptions of wealth, success or fame, they rated the likelihood of the realization of all ambitions very similarly. That is, the mean value fell between "definitely realized" and "probably realized." The likelihood of achieving wealth or success was by far lower, with the probability of success approaching the "not realized" value. At the same time, these were the two aims where the proportion of "don't know" answers was the highest, selected in both cases by one third of the participants. The question of whether wealth and success are indeed unimportant is open-ended. Consequently, the possibility of their realization is relatively uninteresting or they are unattainable to such an extent that the majority of children do not consider them to be realistic aims. A third possibility might be that while these two ambitions are in fact exciting for many people, it is unthinkable to fantasize about them.

Young Adulthood

Before the regime change, young Hungarian people married in their early twenties and usually became parents within a year of the wedding. Due to insufficient housing and economic hardships they could not usually set up their own home. Hence, the majority of young couples started their married life by living with parents. At the beginning of the 1980s, a pattern of delayed adulthood, or post-adolescence, emerged in Hungary (Róbert & Tóth, 1984). These lingering individuals delayed their adult lifestyle because the role of adult could only be partially realized. They could not become adults in the existential or political sense and they could not take control over their lives. This frustration led to a resistance to the adult world. The only achievable part of becoming an adult left to them was to start a family. Contemporary society is more tolerant towards delayed adulthood, since there are fewer and fewer young people who can meet all of its criteria (adult age; independent household; financial independence; free decision making concerning personal affairs and the recognition of oneself as an adult) (Vaskovics, 2000).

As a consequence, relationships between young people and their parents have also changed. A study of 22–26 year olds sheds some light on the nature of the relationship between parents and their young adult children (Tóth, 2003b). Between the ages of 22 to 26, the majority of young people remain in close contact with their parents. The closest relationship occurs when the young adult shares a household with the parents. Of all the participants, 55% live with their father and 75% with their mother. These figures reveal the high incidence of divorced parents and also indicate that for young people, living with their parents is still the norm. They have their own income, and in some cases it is much higher than that of their parents. They enjoy the advantages of earning an adult income, increased freedom, as well as the status of a child being taken care of by its parents.

Close ties to parents are also suggested by the fact that a quarter of those not living with their father and a third of those not living with their mother meet their absent parent every day. The participants who have the least contact with parents are those with only an elementary education. This group also includes the highest proportion of those who do not keep in touch with their parents at all (Tóth, 2003b). The higher the level of education, the more likely the person is to meet their parents frequently. A relatively high proportion (11%) of the subjects claimed that they were without friends, 5% had only one friend, 10–15% had 1–5 friends, and 14% had more than 10 friends. Of those who had friends, 87% were satisfied with their relationships. It seems that the more friends someone has, the more satisfied he/she is with these relationships.

It is interesting that individuals at this early age are already experiencing the decline in their social life that progresses with age. Research has repeatedly shown that the concept of making friends is not characteristic of Hungarian society. There is a widespread opinion that adults are not supposed to have friends. From this point of view, these people do not appear to fit the prototype of post-adolescence, as they are very much like adults.

The previously homogeneous Hungarian society has become more diverse (Tóth, 2003a, b). Young people are not only starting their sexual lives early, but are leading varied sexual lifestyles until they marry at a later age, if at all. Others get married relatively early, in accordance with Hungarian traditions. Finally, there is a group of people who are not in a stable relationship for a long time and live with their parents in some sense, as a child. Data has revealed that the personal relationships of young people differ greatly from those of their parents (Tóth, 2003b). At this age, the parents were probably married. The proportion of those who lived in an independent single household between the ages of 22–26 was small (6%).

Hungarian society needs to acknowledge the fact that a significant proportion of the current generation of people in their 20s are choosing co-habitation instead of marriage. From the point of view of relationships, people in the 22–26 age group show a heterogeneous picture. Ties with their parents seem to be strong; the number of friends is on the decrease and a significant proportion of this generation has no friends or not as many friends as they need. In addition, the formation of stable personal relationships (not only marriage) is occurring at a later point.

Research depicts a somewhat surprising picture of the nature of young people's relationships. The main emotional support comes not from friends or partners, but from mothers. Two thirds of young people said they discussed problems with their mothers and as someone to confide in friends came in second place (58%). In other words, 42% do not have a friend with whom their relationship is deep enough to discuss problems. The attitudes of fathers towards their adolescent or grown up children is far from the idealized picture that is often painted about the family centered nature of Hungarian society (Pongrácz & Spéder, 2001). Fathers usually have little involvement in their children's lives. They know little about their children, and their relationship is relatively cold, or at least distant. A study supporting this finding indicated that only 40% of participants feel that they can turn to their father with a problem (Tóth, 2003b). Further analysis also reveals that almost all of those who can discuss their problems with their father can also talk to their mother. The reverse however, does not hold, as only half of those who can discuss their problems with their mother are able to also turn to their father.

The extent to which young people discuss their problems with their mother correlates greatly with their level of education (Tóth, 2003b). The higher the level of education, the greater the probability that they will be able to discuss their problems with their mother (51% for those with elementary education; 80% for university educated). Sex differences were negligible in this respect (i.e. men and women are equally likely to be able to turn to their mother with their problems).

Young men and women still view their mother as their primary source of emotional support. Eighteen percent of male respondents and 15% of female subjects did not have a friend or a partner with whom they could, or would want to discuss their problems. For them, the family is the only source of emotional support, which considering their age, seems to be a somewhat infantile position.

RESEARCH ON THE FAMILY

Hungarian sociologists were undertaking cross-cultural research as early as the 1980s. This was due to the relative openness of the country and the revival of Hungarian sociology. Several workshops were organized at the Institute of Sociology, Hungarian Academy of Sciences; Institute of Sociology, Eötvös University; Institute of Social Sciences; Demographic Institute of Central Statistical Office; Social Research Informatics Center. Social Research Informatics Center (TÁRKI) stepped into the International Social Survey Program (ISSP) in 1987 and the family module was conducted in Hungary in 1988, 1994 and 2003. Using ISSP data sets, some comparative analyses were done on the topic of the family.

A systematic and comparative study of the family throughout Eastern European has not been done. A significant group of family studies is dealing with the problems of fertility. Conducted by the Institute of Demography, these are mostly demographic in nature. Hungarian society reacted to the issues of decreasing fertility as family size has been decreasing for some time. The readiness of families to have more children is falling. Combined with the high mortality rate, this tendency has led to a decreasing Hungarian population. If this trend does not change in the future, Hungary, a country with 10 million people, will have a maximum of 8 million in 2050. The reasons for this phenomenon and the effect of family policy are at the center of current family studies.

Other research is focused on changing family forms. In Hungary, the decreasing number of marriages and the increasing number of cohabitations has become obvious in the past decade. Public opinion has become concerned with the situation. Another group of studies is dealing with the functioning and everyday life of families. This includes violence in the family; family economy; gender relations; generations in the family; Roma families.

CONCLUSIONS

This chapter focused on changes in family forms and family life that have emerged in the last decade in Hungary. Marriage, which used to be traditionally widespread, has lost its popularity. While re-marriage after divorce has declined, the chances of men and women remarrying after divorce are similar. The age of entry into marriage is rising. Thus, some young people continue to stay in their parents' home in a child-like status, while others choose cohabitation instead of marriage. Today, cohabitation is becoming an increasing preference among the younger generation.

Following the regime change in 1989, one million jobs were lost. The transforming job market does not provide good opportunities for female employment. Studies have shown that Hungarian society is rather conservative regarding gender roles and especially female employment. A significant proportion of women say that they would choose to stay at home if their husbands/partners earned enough. Career and self-realization in work are attractive only to a small group of well-educated women.

Families are struggling to instill their values in their children. Many Hungarians feel that the change of regime did not fulfill their expectations. Increasing inequality, along with ideological-political changes has led to increased anomie. Parents are confused as to how to socialize their children and the changing society has also had an impact on intergenerational relationships. A significant number of young people are living a post-adolescent life style. Some have no supporting friends or partners and because of this, their attachment to parents, especially mothers, has gained greater importance.

NOTE

1. Extended maternity leave allowed mothers to stay at home for 3 years after the birth of a child with a relatively low monthly salary. It also placed the employer under legal obligation to re-employ the mother after this period.

REFERENCES

Andorka, R., & Balázs-Kovács, S. (1986). The social demography of Hungarian villages in the eighteenth and nineteenth centuries (with special attention to Sarpilis, 1792–1804). *Journal of Family History, 11*, 169–192.

Buda, M. (1999). Minöség és szelekció (Quality and selection). *Educatio*, Ösz, 517–532.

Bukodi, E. (2002). A párkapcsolat-formálódás és – felbomlás néhány társadalmi meghatározója (Some social determinants of couple-formation and disintegration). In: I. Nagy, T. Pongrácz & I. Gy. Tóth (Eds), *Szerepváltozások 2001* (pp. 98–112). Budapest: TÁRKI.

Census (2001). Vol. 2. *Részletes adatok a képviseleti minta alapján (Detailed data by the microcensus sample)*. Budapest: Central Statistical Office.

Demographic Yearbook (Vols 1948–2001). Budapest: Central Statistical Office.

138   OLGA TÓTH

Frey, M. (1997). Women on the labour market. In: K. Lévai & I. Gy. Tóth (Eds), *The Changing Role of Women* (pp. 15–36). Budapest: TÁRKI.

Frey, M. (2002). Nők és férfiak a munkaerőpiacon (Females and males at the labour market). In: I. Nagy, T. Pongrácz & I. Gy. Tóth (Eds), *Szerepváltozások 2001 (The Changing role of Women 2001)* (pp. 9–29). Budapest: TÁRKI.

Hablicsek, L. (2000). Kísérlet a roma népesség előreszámítására 2050-ig (Attempt a forecounting of Roma population up till 2050). In: Á. Horváth, E. Landau & J. Szalai (Eds), *Cigánynak születni (Born to be Roma)* (pp. 243–276). Budapest: Új Mandátum.

Hajnal, J. (1965). European marriage patterns in perspective. In: D. V. Glass & D. E. C. Eversley (Eds), *Population in History* (pp. 101–143). London: Edward Arnold.

Kamarás, F. (2000). Termékenység, népesség-reprodukció. (Fertility and reproduction of population). In: T. Kolosi, I. Gy. Tóth & Gy. Vukovich (Eds), *Társadalmi riport 2000* (pp. 409–432). Social Report 2000. Budapest: TÁRKI.

Neményi, M. (1996). Social construction of women's role in Hungary. *Replika* (Special Issue), 83–91.

Pongrácz, T. (2002). A család és a munka szerepe a nők életében (The role of family and work in the life of women). In: I. Nagy, T. Pongrácz & I. Gy. Tóth (Eds), *Szerepváltozások 2001 (The Changing role of Women 2001)* (pp. 30–45). Budapest: TÁRKI.

Pongrácz, T., & Spéder, Zs. (2001). Párkapcsolatok az ezredfordulón (Couple relations at the turn of the century). In: Zs. Spéder (Ed.), *Demográfiai folyamatok és társadalmi környezet (Demographic processes and social environment)* (pp. 13–32). Budapest: Central Statistical Office.

Róbert, P. (2000). *Társadalmi mobilitás (Social mobility)*. Budapest: Századvég Kiadó.

Róbert, P., & Tóth, O. (1984). Die Institutionalisierung einer neuen Lebenspase durch verzögerten Berufseintritt. *Angewandte Sozialforschung, 12*(4), 311–322.

Romsics, I. (1999). *Magyarország története a XX. században (History of Hungary in the 20th Century)*. Budapest: Osiris.

Sági, M. (2000). Az anyagi helyzettel való elégedettség és a vonatkoztatási csoportok (Satisfaciton with the material situation and the reference groups). In: T. Kolosi, I. Gy. Tóth & Gy. Vukovich (Eds), *Társadalmi riport 2000 (Social Report 2000)* (pp. 261–297). Budapest: TÁRKI.

Sas, J. (2002). Egy napom tíz év múlva (One day in my life ten years after). *Educatio, 11*(3), 365–383.

Spéder, Zs. (2002). Szegénység: Szocio-ökonómiai jegyek és demográfiai tényezők (Poverty: Socio-economicl features and demographical factors). In: Zs. Spéder (Ed.), *Demográfiai folyamatok és társadalmi környezet (Demographic processes and social environment)* (pp. 108–121). Budapest: Central Statistical Office.

Spéder, Zs., Paksi, B., & Elekes, Zs. (1998). Anómia és elégedettség a 90-es évek elején (Anomy and satisfaction in the beginning of 1990s). In: T. Kolosi, I. Gy. Tóth & Gy. Vukovich (Eds), *Társadalmi riport 1998 (Social Report 1998)* (pp. 490–513). Budapest: TÁRKI.

Statistical Yearbook of Hungary (2001). Budapest: Central Statistical Office.

Szalai, J. (1991). Some aspects of the changing situation of women in Hungary. *Signs, 17*(1), 152–170.

Történeti Statisztikai Idosorok, 1867–1992 (Historical Statistical Data) (1992) (Vol. I). Budapest: KSH.

Tóth, O. (1999). Marriage, divorce and fertility in Hungary today: Tensions between facts and attitudes. In: A. Pető-Béla Rásky (Eds), *Construction, Reconstruction, Women, Family and Politics in Central Europe* (pp. 127–146). Budapest: OSI, CEU.

Tóth, O. (2001). Értékátadási problémák a családban (Problems of value transfer in the family). *Educatio, 10*(3), 449–460.

Tóth, O. (2003a). Hungary. In: J. J. Ponzetti (Ed.), *International encyclopedia of marriage and family* (pp. 847–851). Macmillan.

Tóth, O. (2003b). *A 22–26 éves korosztály társadalmi problémái (Social problems of the 22–26 years olds)*. Budapest: Institute of Sociology. Manuscript.

Tóth, O., & Róbert, P. (1994). Sociological and historical aspects of entry into marriage. *Journal of Family History, 19*(4), 351–368.

Utasi, Á. (2002). Fiatal, egyedülálló nők párkapcsolati esélye (Chance for couple relation of young single women). In: I. Nagy, T. Pongrácz & I. Gy. Tóth (Eds), *Szerepváltozások 2001 (The Changing role of Women 2001)*. Budapest: TÁRKI.

Vajda, Á., & Farkas. E. J. (1990). Lakáshelyzet (Flats). In: R. Andorka, T. Kolosi & Gy. Vukovich (Eds), *Társadalmi riport 1990 (Social Report)* (pp. 131–164). Budapest: TÁRKI.

Vaskovics, L. (2000). A posztadoleszcencia szociológiai elmélete (Sociological theory of postadolescency). *Szociológiai Szemle Sociological Rewiev, 4*, 3–20.

Wrigley, E.A., & Schofield, R.S. (1981). *The population history of England, 1541–1871: A reconstruction*. London: Arnold.

CHILD DEVELOPMENT AND FAMILY FUNCTIONING WITHIN THE ROMANIAN CONTEXT

Mihaela Robila

SOCIO-HISTORIC AND ECONOMIC CONTEXT

Romania is located in the southeastern part of Europe and has a population of 21.68 million, with 52% residing in urban areas. Ninety percent of the people identify themselves as Romanian, 7% Hungarian, and 3% belong to other ethnic groups (Census, 2002; Government White Book, 2001). In 100 AD., the Roman Empire conquered the local population, the Geto-Dacians, and established a province covering a large part of the current Romanian territory. Following hundreds of years of foreign influence and organization into smaller principates, present-day Romania took shape in two stages, through the union of Moldavia and Wallachia Provinces in 1859, and with the annexation of Transylvania in 1918. Following World War II, Romania fell under Soviet influence and a communist regime was established.

While Romania was primarily an agrarian society with a traditional social structure at the beginning of the 20th century, the communist development program implemented between the 1950s and the 1970s emphasized urbanization and industrial modernization (Zamfir, 2001; Zamfir et al., 2001). Communism had a negative effect on the state economic infrastructure resulting in an underdeveloped and inefficient economy. An orientation towards self-sufficiency, absolute monopoly over the internal market, rigid and technologically backward

Families in Eastern Europe
Contemporary Perspectives in Family Research, Volume 5, 141–154
Copyright © 2004 by Elsevier Ltd.
ISSN: 1530-3535/doi:10.1016/S1530-3535(04)05009-5

large enterprises, and economic sectors very dependent on massive subsidies resulted in a weak economic infrastructure (Zamfir, 2001).

The post-communist transition was influenced by the way the communist system was changed. In 1989, a popular revolution with over 1,000 deaths created an explosive situation in the country, which achieved the disintegration of the communist system in just a few days (Măarginean et al., 2001). Romanian politics and society have undergone profound change since 1989. The communist institutions and ideology that dominated the country for four decades have lost their power and legitimacy and different structures and beliefs have emerged. Nostalgia for pre-communist traditions and values immediately surfaced and combined with the assumptions and principles of communist rule that had been imposed over the preceding four decades (Fischer, 1998).

Romania's transformation into a market economy was challenging and relatively slow. Since 1989, successive governments have adopted a cautious approach to market-oriented reforms (OECD, 2000; World Bank, 1997). The relatively greater difficulties in Romania compared with other Eastern European countries lay in a particularly unfavorable set of conditions inherited from previous regimes. Although marketization and privatization have already brought significant hardships, the restructuring of the economy has barely begun. In agriculture, for example, privatization has divided the land into small plots, and the absence of machinery or the capital to purchase it has temporarily reproduced the old hardships of the traditional peasant family, with its strict gender roles and division of labor (OECD, 2000).

As in other post-communist states, Romanians have been faced with the difficulties of economic transition such as high inflation, rising unemployment, declining production, and erosion of the social safety network (pensions, health care, other benefits). Almost unknown until 1989, unemployment became a crude reality for Romanian society, with complex economic and social consequences for the population (Garai, 2001). Unemployment as a normal phenomenon of economic recession represents a difficult experience for families, especially for women, who represent the most vulnerable segment of the population. The urban unemployment rate is generally lower for those with high educational attainments, but some types of education are not very well adapted to current labor market needs (OECD, 2000). Another factor contributing to economic difficulties is the high retirement rate. For example, the percentage of the population actively working decreased from 45.9% in 1992 to 40.7% in 2002 (Census, 2002). Additionally, the income level is low, not allowing people to meet their family's minimum needs. All of these factors left 44% of the population living at or below the poverty line (CIA, 2003). Similarly, more than 35% of national survey respondents considered that their income was not enough to meet their daily minimum needs (see Table 1) (BOP, 2003).

Table 1.   Income Level and the Standard of Living.

Family Income Level	%
Not enough even for the minimum living	36.6
Enough only for the minimum living	38.6
Enough for a decent living, but we cannot afford to buy more expensive things	17
We can buy some more expensive things but we need to make restrictions	4.7
We can buy anything we want without any restrictions	0.6

Note: N = 2,100. *Source*: Barometru de Opinie Publica (Barometer for Public Opinion) (2003).

The costs of transition have affected especially poor families. Economic inequalities have increased, creating a rising gap between poor and rich people (Haibach et al., 2001). Although the discrepancies between poor and rich increased during the transition period, Romania, like other countries in the region, maintains a high level of egalitarianism. While the Gini Index, the standard measure of inequality, rose from 21 in 1989 to 31.1 in 1998 (the Gini Index has values between $0 =$ perfect equality and $100 =$ perfect inequality), it is still lower than in the U.S. (40.8 in 1997) or other Western countries (e.g. U.K. – 36.8 in 1995) (CIA, 2003; Tesliuc et al., 2001).

A series of negative phenomena such as excessive corruption, social polarization, and deepened poverty have left people unhappy and concerned for their welfare. The results of a national survey of participants 18 years and older (BOP, 2003) indicated that 72% were unsatisfied with their life (24% not at all satisfied; 48% not quite satisfied), while only 27% were satisfied (26% quite satisfied; 1% very satisfied). The perceived standard of living declined, with 48% of respondents indicating that they were doing worse than before 1989, 22% were doing the same, and 25% had a higher standard of living (BOP, 2003). Similarly, 39% of individuals reported that their current life was worse than the one they were living the year before, 44% indicated the situation was the same, and only 17% considered their life better now than in the year before (BOP, 2003). The poverty and uncertainty about the future have caused some people to regret the break with communism (Chelcea, 2000).

Research indicates that economic pressure influences the family at multiple levels (Robila & Krishnakumar, in press). A study with 239 women and their adolescent child examining the direct and indirect links between financial strain, social support, depression, and marital conflict indicated that higher levels of financial strain were associated with higher levels of social isolation and higher rates of depression and marital conflict (Robila & Krishnakumar, in press). Additionally, increased maternal depression is associated with a lower quality of parenting (lower levels of parental support and acceptance, harsh discipline) (Robila & Krishnakumar, 2002). Subsequently, lower quality of parenting is associated with higher levels of internalization (depression, anxiety) and externalization in adolescents (delinquency, violence).

The socio-political factors had significant implications at the family level. During communism, there was an intrusive involvement of political forces in family functioning. For example, in 1966, family planning and abortion became illegal, and those performing and receiving abortion or any other form of family planning were severely punished (Baban, 2000). After 1989, the State was no longer directly involved in family life, the family now regulating itself. Family planning is now widely accessible, allowing people to have more control over their lives.

Romania's political culture remains influenced by prejudices belonging to the previous political regime. During the communist era, party-controlled mass organizations including youth, women, and children's organizations, unions, and professional associations were examples of "form without the content" (Grunberg, 2000, p. 310). Most women, forced to play an active role in politics before 1989 and to be part of the corrupt communist organizations for women, were no longer interested in making policy (Grunberg, 2000); consequently, there was resistance to political forces trying to encourage women's participation in political life. Thus, women constitute only 9% of the Romanian Parliament (Evenimentul, 2001). Women need to increase their visibility in the political sphere in order to participate in developing and implementing social policies designed to support their rights.

FAMILY STRUCTURE

The Romanian Family Code indicates that only marriage at the legal office guarantees rights to spouses. Men can marry at 18 years and women at 16, and they have equal rights in the marriage (Codul Familiei, 1954, 1999). In Romania, there is a high preference for marriage and for the legalization of the relationship. Although the marriage rate is decreasing, in 2000 being 6.1 marriages per 1,000 inhabitants (the lowest level in the last 50 years), it is still relatively higher than in other Eastern European countries (e.g. Bulgaria 4.3; Hungary 4.7) (INS, 2001; UNICEF-TransMONEE, 2001; UNDP, 2000).

The average age at marriage is relatively young, although it has increased in the last decade. In 2000 it was 26.9 years for men and 23.6 years for women (Council of Europe, 2002; NIS, 2001). Eighty percent of marriages are first marriages, and, on average, the duration of marriage is 22 years, indicating a high level of family stability (UNPD, 1996). Cohabitation is still low (6% of all unions) compared with other countries, and transitory (usually until partners are 30–35 years old) (INS, 2001). The divorce rate has remained relatively steady, at around 1.3 divorces per 1,000 inhabitants (in the European context, this level is below average) (INS, 2001).

Natality is decreasing from 16/1,000 people in 1989 to 10.5/1,000 in 2000 (INS, 2001). The fertility rate is declining from 2.2 children/woman in 1989 to 1.24 in 2001 (Council of Europe, 2002; INS, 2001). The number of children per family depends on the educational background and the part of the country from which the family comes. Individuals with higher educational levels and those living in cities tend to have fewer children (UNDP, 2000). The abortion rate is decreasing from 3.15 in 1990 to 1.09 abortions for every one newborn in 2000 (INS, 2001). Women's age at the first child has increased by 1 year since 1989, from 22.5 to 23.5 in 2000. In terms of family structure, statistics show that 7% are single parent families, 85% of these being single mother families (INS, 2001).

FAMILY RELATIONS

A national survey (Barometrul de Opinie Publica, 2002) of issues related to the importance of family life indicated that the family occupied first place for 57% of people (second place for 26% of people), followed by work (for 27.4% it occupied first place, and for 25.5% it occupied second place). The majority of respondents reported having a partner as being related to happiness. Among the things that make a marriage happy, 90% of people reported love, followed by reciprocal trust, mutual support, and having a place to live. The issue of having a place to live is extremely important within the Romanian context, given the fact that housing is very expensive and frequently out of the reach of young people. This factor is even more significant since the nuclear family is considered the ideal family type and so having a personal place to live is important.

Research on marital conflict (BG, 2000) indicates that the most important factor in generating conflict between spouses is economic hardship (lack of money, impossibility of making ends met). This is more prevalent among younger couples than older ones, since the older generation have been able to acquire resources and have fewer necessities. The scarcity of housing represents one of the major problems in post-communist Romanian society, forcing many young men and women to live with their parents until they marry and often after marriage. The consequences of this include conflict between generations and lack of privacy. However, the survey indicated that the role of the family in people's lives is very important and satisfaction with the family is high, regardless of economic difficulties.

The second factor leading to marital distress was represented by difficulties related to the childrearing process (BG, 2000). This is more prevalent among women, which is to be expected, since, as in the West, the woman is the one spending most time with the children. For the younger generation, parents-in-law were considered another source of stress (BG, 2000). This result was more prevalent in situations where the new family is residing in the same apartment with the parents, not having the resources to live on their own.

Religion

Among the social institutions that represent stability, the Church has the highest level of credibility (Barometrul de Opinie Publica, 2002). The communism system tried to eliminate religion from society by removing the Church from social life and politics and by forbidding religious education and promoting atheism. This led to a secularization of public space and a decline in religious practice (Voicu, 2001). Nevertheless, religious values remained quite strong among the population, with many family practices and customs having a religious basis.

The majority of the population (87%) is Christian Orthodox (the rest is represented by Roman Catholics (5.6%), Protestants (6.8%), others and unaffiliated (0.6%) (CIA, 2003). Forty-two percent of respondents in a national survey indicated that they attended church at least twice or three times per month, while 37% reported going to church on religious holidays (BOP, 2003). Eighty-eight percent of respondents reported trusting the Church much and very much (BOP, 2003).

Gender Roles

Communist ideology reinforced the value of work outside the home for women, denigrated their unpaid household labor, and denied them the promised public facilities, convenience goods, and appliances to help with family tasks. After communism, women and men have begun to reshape some of their basic assumptions about work, family, and their own personal roles and priorities (Fischer, 1998; Harsanyi,

Table 2. Attitudes toward Relationships and Gender Roles.

Attitudes	Agree/Strongly Agree (%)	Disagree/Strongly Disagree (%)
The best thing for a women is to take care of the household	78	21
A man must have children to feel fulfilled	82.5	15.5
People need a life partner to be happy	92.9	6
What women truly want is to have a family and children	82.5	17

Notes: $N = 2,212$. The rest of the percentages is represented by the "No Answer."
Source: Barometru de Opinie (Barometer for Public Opinion) (2002).

Table 3. Gender Roles.

Attitudes	Yes (%)	No (%)
Bringing money home is more men's duty than women's		
Men	71	22
Women	69	24
Household work is more women's duty than men's		
Men	62	32
Women	66	28
Household work should be appreciated as any other work		
Men	52	28
Women	52	29
Household work is the easiest work		
Men	10	80
Women	11	82

Notes: N = 2,212. The rest of the percentages are represented by the "No Answer."
Source: Barometru de Gen (Barometer for Gender) (2000).

1993). The need to break with the immediate past produced a "confusion of values" and led men and women to turn once again to traditional institutions such as Church, ethnic group, and family in a search for personal and group identity (Fischer, 1998). Women tended to embrace pre-communist assumptions about their own status in society, most notably the value of their role in the family and the deep differences between men and women. It is still expected, both formally and informally, that women should find their satisfaction primarily in family and motherhood. While parenthood is highly desired by both men and women, household tasks are expected to be performed by women (see Table 2).

Although attitudes that are more egalitarian are emerging, gender roles are still traditional, with men being more preoccupied by providing financial security, and women as the managers of the household (see Table 3). A national survey indicated that 57% of men and 65% of women agreed that the woman is the chief of the house (28% of men and 19% of women disagreed with this statement), while 86% of men and 81% of women agreed that the man is the head of the family (7% of men and 8% of women disagreed) (BG, 2000).

CHILDREARING PRACTICES

In Romania, as in other areas of Eastern Europe, the child is considered the central value of the family (Robila, 2003; Robila & Krishnakumar, 2004). The majority of the participants in a national survey agreed that a family needed to have a child to consider itself fulfilled (BOP, 2002). Children have a duty to respect and love their parents. On the other hand, parents are expected to do whatever they can for their children, even sacrificing their own happiness. Thus, children represent the highest goal for the parent.

Women are more involved than men in childrearing activities. There are also differences between women and men's perceptions of their involvement in the family. For example, while 10–15% of men consider that they participate in childrearing or the child's education, only 5% of women agree with this (Stanciulescu, 2002). Similarly, while 17% of men indicate that they go to the doctor with the child, only 4% of women agree (Stanciulescu, 2002). Women are considered better at performing housework chores and childrearing tasks. The change in traditional attitudes towards women's double role (in the family and workplace) is only modest among the younger generation. Women's double burden is maintained, not only as a choice, but also as a necessity in order to cope with economic difficulties. During communism (and even now), the lack of economic and social resources requires parents to work in shifts to be able to take care of their children. In this situation, men's contribution to childrearing is sometimes increased (Stanciulescu, 2002).

One of the most important missions for parents is transmitting and teaching their children values, attitudes, and roles. Batar (2000) conducted a study on parental role transmission in contemporary Romanian society. The results indicate that role transmission is dependent on residential environment (rural vs. urban), parents' educational level (lower, medium, higher), and occupation (blue/white collar). In rural families, there is a continuation of the traditional role transmission from one generation to the next for both girls and boys. Batar (2000, p. 169) identified three characteristics of role transmission: (1) the normative-directional character of transmitting and learning of attributions (the child sometimes replaces the parent in performing certain tasks, becoming thus an important work source); (2) performing these roles brings recognition and prestige; (3) the manner the young adult learns the roles, determines the way he/she will be identified with the adult who will replace the parent.

Role transmission and role learning in urban areas is different, given the contextual diversity that affects family functioning (Batar, 2000). Children learn their tasks depending on their age and gender, as well as on their parent's education and occupation. Thus, mothers with higher levels of education will encourage their daughters to acquire more modern gender roles (less household work) compared with mothers with lower levels of education. The identification with the mother's gender role is more prevalent also as daughters increase their educational and occupational status. Unemployed mothers direct their daughters towards activities other than the domestic in order to compensate for their own lack of professional activity (Batar, 2000). Sons are attracted by the father's activities, especially those outside the home (occupational, relational, friends). Sons' housework activities are reduced, more prevalent being activities of maintenance and shopping. Very few differences were registered based on fathers' education or occupational status. Unemployed fathers have a lower status within the family, their economic role being reduced, while their assistance in domestic work is not significantly different from that of employed men (Batar, 2000). In urban areas, as in rural ones, youth participate in economic activities to help the family (by undertaking other members' responsibilities) while reducing their own free time. In both rural and urban areas, role transmission, as part of the socialization process, is characterized by reciprocity, meaning that there is an awareness of its necessity from both parties (parents and children) (Batar, 2000).

The Importance of Education

In Romania, as in other countries around the globe, the necessity of obtaining an education is strongly emphasized as the only way to achieve social and financial security. During the communist years, the general level of education increased, especially as a result of industrialization, which created a movement of the population from rural to urban areas (Cartana, 2000). After 1989, there was again a tendency towards increasing levels of education. During communism, education was highly politicized, with the state deciding the specializations to be promoted. In this context, social science was deemed to be less relevant and several university departments (e.g. psychology, social work) were closed. After 1989, these departments were reopened and the educational system began aligning itself to the economy's needs.

The main duty of children is to study, and parents do whatever they can to support them. Due to economic difficulties, parents' investment in their child's education is quite significant. In return, the child is expected to perform very well. Although available resources are usually modest, what is important is the parents' sacrifice in obtaining them, and this sacrifice needs to be recompensed by the child's efforts to present good, scholarly results (Stanciulescu, 2002). Education is perceived as a substitute for work and as a protective mechanism against hard work.

Education is also closely related to social mobility. Cartana (2000) conducted a study concerning the educational and socio-occupational dimensions of intergenerational social mobility in Romania (ascendant and descendent mobility) with a national representative sample (CURS Survey; 37,474 respondents). The results indicated high intergenerational mobility, particularly ascendant mobility.

The rates of social mobility show major discrepancies between urban and rural areas due to the persistence of unequal social opportunities. Cartana's study (2000) showed that educational mobility/stability is related to the father's level of education. In 1999, at the national level, only 20% of participants reproduced the educational level of the father, 78% of the population at 25 years of age having an educational status different than their father's (75% of these had a higher educational level). Women's ascendant mobility (70%) was 7% lower than that of men (in rural areas, the difference was 12.6% in men's favor). Ascendant mobility was 5% higher in urban areas (76%) than rural. Cartana (2000) suggests that these differences might be due to traditional cultural models in rural areas that provide more educational opportunities for boys. Educational immobility (the reproduction of the father's educational level) and descendent mobility are more frequent for women and in rural areas, indicating that there are more overall educational opportunities for men than for women, and more opportunities in urban areas than in rural ones (Cartana, 2000).

FAMILY POLICIES

Family policies are intended to provide benefits to support families in exercising their functions. The transition from communism to democracy brought changes in family and social policies. Policy analysis and development has been necessary with regard to family planning, which was almost non-existent during communism. As Romania attempts to shift from a reliance on abortion to a more widespread use of contraception, in 2000 the government approved policies of providing free contraceptives to target groups (e.g. unemployed, people with low income, students), their sale at affordable prices to non-targeted groups, and by distributing them through family doctors in rural areas without family planning clinics. In this context, an analysis by Sharma et al. (2001) indicates that, since government resources are limited, the effectiveness of the family planning program could be further increased by targeting the free contraceptives to the most vulnerable groups (the ones that cannot afford to pay for them). Non-Governmental Organizations (NGOs) also have an important role in supporting initiatives and campaigns on safe sex and family planning education.

A major restructuring has occurred in the policies related to parental leave. In 1999, the government introduced a 100% paid, 5-day paternal childcare leave option that can be taken up in the first 8 weeks of the child's life. The mother can take 112 days paid maternal leave with full salary. The father and the mother can also take leave for up to 2 years to care for the child, being paid 85% of salary (Ministry of Labor, Social Solidarization and Family, 2003). However, the low reimbursement, which barely meets the minimum standard of living, sometimes causes parents to reject this and to work full-time (Baban, 2000). Recently, policies to support low-income families and low-income single parent families financially were introduced. Another important initiative has focused on the prevention and eradication of domestic violence. A law to protect against family violence is in place and a National Agency for Family Protection has been created to support these endeavors. In addition, national advertising campaigns against family violence have been sponsored. In terms of child protection, the introduction of the foster care system was one of the newest interventions, which looks like a promising solution to child institutionalization.

Moving from a planned to a market economy has resulted in high costs for large sections of the Romanian population, one of them being the end of full employment. In the pre-1989 welfare system, there was no unemployment insurance and social assistance because the basic conception of welfare was that everyone had the right and the obligation to work (Haibach et al., 2001). The lack of basic welfare programs required under a capitalist market economy emerged as a social problem during the transformation, with a housing crisis, increased unemployment, deterioration of the social security system, and difficulties in coping with the increased prices for basic consumables (Haibach et al., 2001). The social protection system, introduced in 1991, is based on granting unemployment benefits and supporting allowances as a response to the sharp increase in the unemployment rate (NHDR, 2001–2002). The social insurance and pension situation in Romania remains uncertain, not only because of the lack of a more coherent policy framework, but also because there are more pensioners and fewer contributors (NHDR, 2001–2002).

RESEARCH ON FAMILY

After being closed by the communist forces since the 1970s, several social science academic departments were reopened in the early 1990s. While fields such as psychology, sociology or social work are now widely recognized in Romania, family science is still at the beginning of its development. Due to the prolonged time period without any research on the family, studies need to be conducted on a variety of issues such as marital quality, parenting, intergenerational relationships, domestic violence, etc. Some information on families can be drawn from recent surveys. For example, in 2000, the SOROS Foundation sponsored a national representative survey ("Gender Barometer") (BG, 2000) carried out by the Gallup Organization, which assessed people's attitudes on a wide range of issues related to gender socialization (e.g. gender roles in the family and society, equal rights, violence). While sets of questions regarding attitudes towards family issues have started to be included in other public opinion surveys (e.g. BOP, 2002), there is a need for moving beyond examining attitudes to focusing on family processes.

Several state research institutes have conducted periodical studies on peoples' attitudes and perceptions concerning various topics such as quality of life, social policies, inter-ethnic relations, or changes in the socio-economic and political spheres (e.g. poverty, social marginalization and exclusion). However, research needs to be conducted specifically on family issues. Family Science and Family Counseling departments need to be created within Social Studies Colleges in order to prepare family scholars and practitioners to develop and conduct systematic scholarly work with families. Institutes and/or Centers for Family Studies need to be developed in order to conduct research projects on family relationships and to attract funding. Although several works on families have been published (e.g. Mitrofan & Ciuperca, 2002; Robila & Krishnakumar, 2002), considerably more systematic research on Romanian family processes needs to be conducted.

CONCLUSIONS

This chapter has provided an overview of the impact of socio-political and economic changes on families in Romania. The transition from communism to democracy, with its appealing civil liberties and decentralized and competitive free markets, has also brought economic insecurities and challenges. Under these conditions, people in Romania have developed survival strategies to cope with the lack of resources. Families in Romania continue to remain the filters of socio-economic transformations for individuals. Family relationships and childrearing are highly valued among Romanians. As societal changes will continue to be associated with difficulties, families need to find effective ways to support both children and adults in their efforts to be successful. In this light, developing programs and policies to support families in their endeavors is of maximum importance. Therefore, systematic research on family processes in Romania needs to be conducted in order to provide basic knowledge of family matters, which would allow the development of strategies and programs to support family members during these times of significant transformations.

REFERENCES

Baban, A. (2000). Women's sexuality and reproductive behavior in post-Ceausescu Romania: A psychological approach. In: S. Gal & G. Kligman (Eds), *Reproducing Gender: Politics, Publics, and Everyday Life After Socialism* (pp. 225–257). Princeton, NJ: Princeton University Press.

Barometru de Gen. (BG) (Barometer for Gender) (2000). Bucharest: SOROS Foundation.

Barometrul de Opinie Publica (BOP) (Barometer for Public Opinion) (2002, 2003). Bucharest: SOROS Foundation.

Batar, D. (2000). Socializarea copiilor – mode de exercitare a rolurilor parentale (Child socialization – way of performing parental roles). *Calitatea Vietii (Quality of Life)*, *12*(1–4), 159–171.

Cartana, C. (2000). Mobilitatea sociala in Romania: Aspecte cantitative si calitative la nivel national si in profil teritorial (Social mobility in Romania: Quantitative and qualitative aspects at national and territorial level). *Sociologie Românească (Romanian Sociology)*, *1*, 105–124.

Census (2002). *Recensamintul populatiei*. (Census). Guvernul Romaniei.

Central Inteligence Agency (CIA) (2003). Country Reports.

Chelcea, S. (2000). Justitia sociala socialista si comunismul residual in Romania dupa un deceniu de tranzitie: O analiza secondara (Social socialist justice and residual communism in Romania after a decade of transition: A secondary analysis). *Sociologie Românească*, *1*, 125–141.

Codul Families (1954, 1999) (Family Code). Romanian Government.

Council of Europe (2002). *Recent demographic develicoemnts in Europe*. Council of Europe, Strasbourg.

Evenimentul (18 Mai 2001). Romania, codasa Europei in privinta reprezentarii politice a femeilor (Romania, among the last countries in Europe regarding women' political participation).

Fischer, M. E. (1998). From tradition and ideology to elections and competition: The changing status of women in Romanian politics. In: M. Rueschemeyer (Ed.), *Women in the Politics of Postcommunist Eastern Europe* (pp. 142–168). Armonk, New York: M. E. Sharpe.

Garai, A. (2001). Abordarea psihological a somajului in perioada de transition (Psychological approach of unemployment during the transition). *Revista de Psihologie (Psychology Journal)*, *47*(34), 261–278.

Government White Book of Romania (2001). Governance overtaking December 2000. Bucharest.

Grunberg, L. (2000). Women's NGOs in Romania. In: S. Gal & G. Kligman (Eds), *Reproducing Gender: Politics, Publics, and Everyday Life After Socialism* (pp. 307–337). Princeton, NJ: Princeton University Press.

Haibach, J., Rusu, B., Samezelus, T., Szabo, B., & Vonica, S. (2001). Globalisation and the future of welfare states – Germany, Romania and Sweden. *Calitatea Vietii*, *12*(1–4), 35–47.

Harsanyi, D.P., 1993. Women in Romania. In: N. Funk & M. Mueller (Eds), *Gender Politics and Post-Communism* (pp. 39–52). New York, NY: Routledge.

Institutul National de Statistica (INS) (2001). (National Institute for Statistics). Bucharest, Romania.

Ministery of Labour, Social Solidarization and Family (2003). Government of Romania. www.mmss.ro.

Mitrofan, I., & Ciupercă, C. (2002). *Psihologia vieţii de cuplu*. Bucuresti: SPER.

National Human Development Report (NHDR) (2001–2002). Country report: Romania.

Organization for Economic Co-operation and Development (OECD) (2000). *Review of labor market and social policies in Romania*. Paris, France. *Romanian Family Code*. Bucharest: Romanian Government.

Robila, M. (2003). Romanian families. In: J. Ponzetti (Ed.), *International Encyclopedia of Marriage and Family* (2nd ed., Vol. 3, pp. 1370–1373). New York, NY: Macmillan Reference USA.

Robila, M., & Krishnakumar, A. (2002, November). *The impact of depression and marital conflict on parenting and adolescent psychological functioning in Romania*. Poster session presented at the annual conference of the National Council on Family Relations, Houston, TX.

Robila, M., & Krishnakumar, A. (2004). The role of children in Eastern European families. *Children & Society*, *18*(1), 30–41.

Robila, M., & Krishnakumar, A. (in press). The impact of financial strain on marital conflict in Romania. *Journal of Family Psychology*.

Sharma, S., Winfrey, W., & Marin, M. (2001). *A family planning market segmentation analysis: A first step in operationalizing contraceptive security policies in Romania.* U.S. Agency for International Development: Policy Project.

Stanciulescu, E. (2002). *Sociological educatiei familiale (Sociology of Family Education).* Iasi: Polirom.

Tesliuc, E. D., Pop, L., & Tesliuc, C. M. (2001). *Poverty and the social security system.* Iasi: Polirom.

UNICEF (2001). TransMONEE Database.

United Nations Developmental Program (UNDP) (2000). Human Developmental Report 2000. Oxford University Press.

Voicu, M. (2001). Modernitate religioasa in societatea Romaneasca (Religious modernity in Romanian society). *Sociologie Românească, 1–4,* 70–96.

World Bank (1997). Romania – Poverty and Social Policy.

Zamfir, C. (2001). Introduction. In: C. Zamfir, K. Postill & R. Stan (Eds), *Poverty in Romania* (p. 5). Bucharest: Expert Publishing House.

Zamfir, C., Postill, K., & Stan, R. (Eds) (2001). *Poverty in Romania: Causes, anti-poverty policies, recommendations for action.* Bucharest: UNDP, IQL.

THE BULGARIAN FAMILY: SPECIFICS AND DEVELOPMENT FROM LIKING IN THE VILLAGE SQUARE TO LOVE IN THE "CHAT"

Raya Staykova

The opinion of the pessimist is that "The family is dead already." In retaliation, the optimists shout, "The family will continue to exist forever." These two opposing viewpoints highlight the family as the most adaptive and flexible social institution. It is also the most stable and conservative one that has survived for centuries. It is no accident that globalists such as Carter (1999), Bauman (1999), and Fukuyama (1995) focus on the model of the family as one of the main indicators for social change. They note that each historical age has modified the family institution. Regardless of varied family structures, it is the fundamental value for the majority of people. It transforms in order to help people to meet their needs and to survive. Every global change reveals the importance of the family as a social institution. Thus, it attracts the attention of researchers, politicians, etc. The current circumstances of being at the threshold of the information age in a global sense, has put personal, immediate communication in the family on a significantly new level.

Families in Eastern Europe
Contemporary Perspectives in Family Research, Volume 5, 155–171
Copyright © 2004 by Elsevier Ltd.
All rights of reproduction in any form reserved
ISSN: 1530-3535/doi:10.1016/S1530-3535(04)05010-1

ECONOMIC AND SOCIAL OUTLOOK
OF THE BULGARIAN TRANSITION

Bulgaria is a Balkan country, established in 681. It is one of the East European countries to be experiencing the transition from a centrally planned economy and a totalitarian regime, to a market economy and democracy. The current population is nearly 8 million of which 83.93% are ethnic Bulgarians, 9.41% are Turks, 4.68% are Gypsies and there are relatively small numbers of Armenians, Jews, Russians, and Greeks (Census, 2001). Historically, all ethnic groups have lived in peace, free from severe conflicts. At the community level, different religions and cultures celebrate all their holidays together. The current Bulgarian ethnic model offers a way for people striving to live together to be tolerant of difference, and a unique culture and religion.

Transitions in Bulgaria have been accompanied by severe difficulties. The economic restructuring is slow and the population is paying high social prices (see Table 1). There have been many "working poor"[1] in Bulgarian society in the past 4–5 years. In 2001, approximately 20% of employed people were extremely poor and in theory did not differ from those who lived on social benefits. In September 2003, the "working poor" represented a third of the employed population.

During the last decade and a half of transition, phenomena such as unemployment, corruption, and crime have become common. Regardless of the fact that the private sector is rising and developing, monopolies still operate. Privatization of state ownership has almost been completed. Poverty and corruption are some of the factors that cause the most alarm and create a constant feeling of distress and uncertainty for the future. Periodic surveys held since 1991 indicate that the number of people who consider their lives to be worse is constantly increasing. In 1991, at the beginning of the transition process, only 18.4% indicated

Table 1.   Basic Economic Indicators of Bulgaria.

Year	GDP Growth (%)	Inflation (%)	Unemployment (%)	Average Annual Income	Index of Income per Capita 1990 = 100
1991	−11.7	338.1	11.1	11,508	63.7
1995	2.9	62.1	11.2	91,166	40.0
1996	−10.1	121.6	12.5	158,963	28.3
1999	2.4	6.2	16.0	2,412	31.9
2000	5.8	10.4	17.9	2,856	30.3
2001	4.5	4.8	17.3	–	–

Note: In 1998 BGL has been denominated 1000 lv = 1 BG leva.
Source: Statistic Yearbook, 1995–2000, Sofia: NSI.

that their living standard had worsened. However in 1998, this rose to 68, and 87.5% assessed the changes after 1989 as absolutely negative (Staykova et al., 2000). In 2001, 74.2% of the population considered themselves poor and to be worse off than before (Dimova, 2003). The optimism of the first years of transition, including the hope and eagerness for active participation in the establishment of the new and democratic society, has ceased to exist.

The nine governments after 1989, regardless of their political ideology, have not succeeded in improving the standard of life for the average Bulgarian. This transition process is unique and is characterized by a distinctive economic phenomenon at the micro-level. There has been a continued worsening of the living standard, regardless of the stability of the national economy, for the past 3–4 years. A survey carried out by the Institute for Social and Trade-union Study with the Independent Trade-union Confederation showed that for a period of 10 years GDP (Gross Domestic Product) grew 19.8%, whereas for the same period the real salary decreased by 28.5%.[2]

Researchers are unanimous in the view that the economic hardships and social crisis which Bulgarian society is currently experiencing will have long-lasting and large-scale consequences. New values are yet to be created in place of the discarded ones.[3] This is having an especially strong impact on young people, who have grown up and formed their personalities during the years of transition.

The family has always been a stable social institution and contributed to the survival of the Bulgarian population in periods of yoke (Byzantium – IX–XII c.; Ottoman – XIV–XIX c.), wars (1913–1917; 1941–1945) and economic crisis. However, it is now confronted with hardships and troubles. Common global changes have had a fundamental influence on the family and marriage. There is a tendency in Europe for the traditional nuptial model of the family to be replaced by new types like cohabitation and incomplete families, etc. These are all processes that have found followers among the Bulgarian population. The family now has to assume complete responsibility for rearing children and the young generation. This is in contrast to the socialist period during which the state took partial responsibility for these functions. Therefore, the shaping of the new mentality, values, and norms of behavior have become concentrated within the family. How, and to what extent parents will undertake the responsibility for giving birth and raising future populations depends to a great extent on the stability of the family institution and essential values. These factors have always contributed to the successful adaptation to new situations. When the Internet and cyber space emerged, heralding the beginning of an information society, the family was the only real institution that had been bestowed with the role of guiding the growth and upbringing of the latest generation. The family creates the vital set of values and social norms. These cannot conflict with either the traditional values of the Bulgarian people, or with the new information messages of the globalized world.

The Bulgarian Family through the Centuries

The first information on the Bulgarian family was published in the middle of 19th century.[4] During that time, the population lived in rustic democratic communes and inside the communes, in families. This traditional patriarchic family was characteristic of the agrarian era. Economic interests formed the basis of spousal selection. Historically, two types of family are known in Bulgaria. The large "zadruga"[5] was the comparatively less extended family seen up until the 1980s.

The Bulgarian zadruga represented a household of several generations of monogamous families, who lived together in one house under the protection of one person (the head of the zadruga was usually the oldest man). All members of the household worked together, the ownership was collective, and they shared the profits from their labor. Monogamous marriage was for life and it excluded any infidelity on the part of either the woman or the man. Young people became attracted to each other when they met at the chain dance at the village square. However, marriage had to be negotiated by their parents. More often, young people married without knowing each other personally, but through obeying their parents' decision. Divorce and nuptial unfaithfulness were extremely rare and were viewed as a serious sin. Between the 17th and 19th centuries, the zadruga was a very common trend among the Southern Slavs, as well as on the territory of Bulgaria (Todorova, 2002).

The zadruga is a variety of the extended family in the Balkans. Its distinct characteristic is the large number of the family members who live together in one household, regardless of the kinship ties between them. It is referred to as a zadruga family when the number of its members is around 20 people or more. Historical data reveals a zadruga of 200 people. Researchers do not agree on the exact characteristics that distinguish the zadruga as a specific family type in the Balkans, from that of the Western European extended family. However, they are unanimous in their belief that the zadruga was of significant importance to the public and economic life of the country. It was the productive union that emerged out of the necessity to ensure the family's survival (Todorova, 2002).

Living together with a large number of relatives and families in one household required very strict systems of hierarchy, standards, and norms of conduct that each family member firmly obeyed. Marriages between representatives of different religions and ethnicity were not allowed and practically did not exist. If such a marriage happened, the sinners were socially sanctioned.

In the zadruga, all the members worked. Men and women had strictly defined responsibilities, and there was mutual respect between them. Tasks for men and women were different, but equally valuable to the organization of life in the household. They were equally responsible for raising the children and for preserving the family. Equality for the Bulgarian woman was based on economic power and relative freedom within the family. Traditionally, the bride brought dowry (possessions under her personal disposal) with her and according to Baldjiev (1891), some wives lent money to their husbands with interest. Additionally, others traded independently (without asking their husbands) and were responsible for their property (e.g. selling it for their own benefit). Business contracts between spouses also existed. The Bulgarian wife was even able to lend or lease her property to her husband and was able to sell it without his agreement. Such economic independence created a position of female dominance, as she took responsibility for family life. Scholars researching the Southern Slavs found that the equality between men and women, which had been established in Bulgaria for centuries, was not usual for the Slavonic tribes and had not existed in all European nations (Bogishich, 1874; Kanitz, 1876).

The organization of family life in the zadruga, and later in the Bulgarian extended family, reflected the development of the undisputed authority of the older generation. At least 3–4 families, usually from the man's line of descent, lived together. The most authoritative person was the eldest man, followed by his wife. However, there were some cases in which a woman led the zadruga.[6] With time, this authoritativeness turned into veneration and respect for the elders. This was mostly displayed in the relationship between the son and his mother and between the brother and his elder sister. The mother of the groom was, and continues to be, the strongest individual in the extended family. Today she is the first one with whom the bride has to find a common language in order to be accepted by the rest of the groom's relatives. She has traditionally occupied the roles of landlady, the person who runs the house and housekeeper (Strashimirov, 1993). Since that time, according to Bulgarian common law, while the mother is alive the son has no absolute right over his father's property. It was historically established within the Bulgarian family for the widow to take over the role of the husband and to manage the property, even if she had sons of age. She had the right to divide the inherited property, without being required to comply with the other heirs.

For centuries, the freedom of the wife has been reflected in the political life of the country. Bulgaria has a long-standing tradition of formal gender equality that is enshrined in the Turnovo Constitution of the Bulgarian Principality (1879), in the two Constitutions of 1947 and 1971, the Constitution of 1991, and in a number of additional laws that provide juridical guarantees of equality. *De jure* equality notwithstanding, *de facto* Bulgarian women in have a lower status than men. Nowadays, under the conditions of hard economic and social transitions, the position of women in society, especially with respect to authority is increasing. The reason for this is the trust that Bulgarian society has always put in the woman as a strong individual who finds balanced solutions to conflicts (Staykova, 1999).

The Family and State Policy during Socialism

Industrialization, which started developing vigorously after World War II and the establishment of the socialist order, entirely changed the way of living. The socialist state encouraged the establishment of the two and three children family model. This model involved the two parents working outside the household and having an equal obligation to contributing to the family income. However, household labor has always predominantly been the woman's responsibility.

Extensive economic development in Bulgaria required citizens to work full-time outside the home. The husband's salary was not enough to provide for a normal living standard, and thus the two spouses were required to work. Throughout the socialist era, the employment of women expanded continuously. Their rapid rise in the national labor force reached its highest levels in the mid- to late 1980s (Bobeva et al., 1992). This was accompanied by the positive growth of female participation in the non-productive sector (86% in 1986).

In time, working women increased their participation in professional occupations such as physicians, teachers, and university professors. In 1973, 39% of professionals with a higher education were women, while in 1986 this rose to 50%. The educational status of women influenced the values, needs, and spirituality of the mother, who passed these values on to her children. Bulgarian women now prefer to work outside the household and to have a professional and social status.[7] These needs are reflected the behavior of mothers in terms of how many children they decide to have and what education they provide for them. Results from studies conducted in 1985 and 1990 show that the Bulgarian woman decides how many children to have and when to have them. The opinion of her husband is important, but not decisive. This is especially true for the highly educated social strata.

The socialist state assumed part of the care for bringing up children by constructing a wide-range of nurseries and kindergartens in the cities and villages. It organized summer camps and other types of activities for children during the school holidays and during free time. From 1975, state policy was directed towards the protection and safeguarding of pregnant women and families with infants. Obviously, for the centralized state it was easier to re-distribute the income from the total state budget to young families and families with children. This policy was applicable to everyone, regardless of ethnicity, place of residence, type of work, income, etc. The legislation postulated an increase in annual paid leave and an early pension for mothers, as well as paid- and non-paid childcare leave for up to three years.[8] It also gave the family the right to choose which parent would use this leave.[9] The first three years of a child's life were considered as the pension length of service, and the absolute amounts of child allowances were constantly being increased. These allowances consisted of two types, i.e. a lump sum allowance at the birth of the child and a monthly allotment through to 16 years of age, and if s/he studies, up to 18 years. In addition, legislation provided families with lodging or with preferential loans for buying a dwelling for families with two children. There were also special social gains for the mother-students, free medicines for children under 16, etc. (Vidova, 1981).

The Bulgarian model of the nuclear family involving a marriage was maintained during the socialist period. The extended family (usually three generations in one household) also continued to exist until the 1980s, but was common mostly in the villages and small towns. In the rural areas, family ties continued to be more intensive and mutual help was expressed more strongly. Urbanization processes stimulated the separation of young families into households of their own. In the cities, these dwellings were small in most cases and did not satisfy their growing needs. A differentiation of the nuclear family began in the villages as well, regardless of the fact that several families continued living in the same house. However, these families were economically separated. Socially, connections with the extended family of up to 3 generations, found a new form of existence. Data from 1969 showed that in 58.6% of families with infants up to 3 years of age, the grandparents took over the care of children while the parents worked (for children 3–7 years of age, this arrangement occurred in 45.1% of the households) (Dinkova, 1976). In a large number of families, the grandparents took care of school-aged children, especially when the child started school and was in the early grades.

Family policy during the socialist state also had lasting negative consequences. The transfer of part of family obligations and responsibilities for childrearing to the state shaped relations between spouses and created a specific attitude towards their obligations to their children. The feeling that it was the state's obligation to provide their education and healthcare relieved parents from these responsibilities. After the changes in 1989, the claims towards the state have been large. What is more, an important part of the population opposed and refused to accept the reforms in the social sectors. Also, the crisis occurred when the existing social benefits were gradually disappearing because they were in conflict with the social policy of the market economy.

THE MODEL OF THE BULGARIAN FAMILY:
TYPES, VALUES, TRADITIONS

Children in the Family

In Bulgaria, children are greatly valued. The percentage of men and women who do not wish to have children has constantly remained below 3%. In 1900, the birthrate was 42.2 per thousand, which was the highest in Europe. However, this number has steadily declined, so that in 2002 it has fallen to 8.5 (see Table 2).

Data on birthrate and reproductive behavior indicated that in 1985 the two-child family model was firmly established, with the one-child family predominating in the country and in some social groups. The statistics revealed that 7% of the families were childless, 25% had one child, 54% had two children and 14% had three and more children. In 2001, the picture was quite different with 34.86% of families childless, 35.78% with one child, 24.08% with two children, and only 5.28% with three or more children (Census, 2001). In the past, the one-child family model was more widespread in large cities, and among women with high levels of education and a professional career. Recently it has become a common model for most people, regardless of where they live and their profession.

The strong traditional family beliefs and norms are seen in the fact that 90% of children continue to be born to married couples. This model is found among all ethnic groups with the exception of the Gypsy population. According to Gypsy culture and traditions, it is common practice for children to be born and raised by cohabitating parents. Other members of the extended Gypsy family, as well as those in the local community, also take part in rearing the children.

Table 2.   Birthrate in Bulgaria (Per Thousand).

Year	Birthrate
1900	42.2
1920	39.9
1960	17.8
1970	16.3
1980	14.5
1990	11.7
1995	8.6
2000	9.0
2001	8.6
2002	8.5

Source: Statistical Yearbooks 1991–2002, Sofia: NSI.

Regardless of the clear indicators that the extended family is disappearing and the nuclear model is prevailing, close and intensive family ties to the extended family continue to function in the present. Grandparents are still helping financially and with other means. This help is most obvious during a family crisis. Even when the children reside in different regions, the grandparents are ready to make sacrifices for the sake of their children and for their grandchildren's happiness. It is deeply rooted in the Bulgarian consciousness that it is a parent's obligation to create better living conditions for their children. This involves providing them with a good education, or with their own dwelling where they could start an independent family life. Social norms permit grandparents to participate on equal terms with the parents in the rearing of their grandchildren. Thus, the emotional relationship between the grandchildren and the grandparents is very strong and stable during the upbringing of young adults.

A change in the attitude of men over 50 years of age, regarding household duties, has also occurred. Their readiness to help in the homes of their sons and daughters is greater than that related to helping their spouses. This is not a result of retirement, as these men have continued to work. It is more a reflection of the new meaning attributed to the individual's personal and professional life and a return to family values. The increased standard of living and the differences in the intergenerational needs and views have caused conflicts, which could decrease the traditionally strong ties between generations. However, young parents are constantly seeking and expecting help from their parents. This behavior of shared responsibility was prominent during the transition period, when the need for quick and risky decisions increased. The younger generation (under 30 years of age) was not ready to make decisions and to take responsibility for its activities without the help of the older generation (over 50 years of age) (Staykova et al., 2000).

Family and Marriage

In Bulgaria, early marriages and early childbirths are the predominant model (see Table 3).

The workload of Bulgarian women outside the family is an important factor that stimulates them to have children at an early age. For highly qualified specialists, this is of great importance, because when it happens at the beginning of their professional career, early pregnancy and motherhood is not an occupational obstacle (Staykova & Gadeleva, 1989). Support from grandparents helps young parents to practice their profession and to look for opportunities, regardless of the number of children they have. The socialist state policy of stimulating birth did

Table 3. Demographic Indicators.

	1990	1995	2000	2001
Natural increase (per 1,000)	−0.4	−5	−5.1	5.6
Sex ratio (female per 1,000 male)	1030	1043	1054	1054
Birth rate (per 1,000)	12.1	8.6	9.0	8.6
Marriage rate (per 1,000)	6.9	4.4	4.3	4.0
Divorce rate (per 1,000)	1.3	1.3	1.3	1.3
Age of woman at birth (mean)	23.9	23.9	24.9	25.1
Age of woman at first birth (mean)	22.0	22.2	23.5	23.8
Age of first marriage (mean)				
Male	24.7	26.0	28.1	28.1
Female	21.7	22.6	24.7	24.8
Age at divorce (mean)				
Male	37.1	37.3	38.0	39.1
Female	33.7	34.0	34.8	35.8

Source: Women and Men in the Republic of Bulgaria, 2002, Sofia: NSI.

not have a significant impact on birth rate, but it helped to maintain the two-child family model and limited the decline in birthrate.

Until 1945, Bulgaria was characterized by relatively stable marriages and divorces were 0.40 per 1,000. By 1965, the number of divorces had increased and the country was now considered to have a high divorce coefficient (1.06 per 1,000) (Dinkova, 1976). The reasons for the rising divorce rate are complex, and not captured by such statements as "flagrant violation of the nuptial responsibilities," "physical and moral abuse," "and no cares for the family." More realistically, the cited reasons for divorce are factors such as "incompatibility of characters." Such reasons represented the differences in partners' cultural values and spiritual needs. With time, these reasons for termination of the marriage increased.

The depreciation of the legal status of marriage, the increase in cohabitation, and the emergence and spread of trial marriages in Europe all influenced the new perspective on divorce. The change of partners became acceptable in society. Numerous people (usually the educated and economically independent ones) have separated themselves from the existing life-long family model, as they can afford to overthrow this model. The most common divorces are those among well-educated, city-dwelling people.

Analysis of behavior post-divorce often reveals that the father refuses to take care of the children. Thus, the entire responsibility has to be undertaken by the mother. As a result, the mother often seeks the due allowance from the father through the courts. During the period of 1959–1973, the average number of such lawsuits was 1,400–1,600 (Dinkova, 1976). This was a period when divorce was a relatively new phenomenon in Bulgarian society and there were no norms for parents to relate to the ex-partner and his/her relatives. Children suffered not only from the lack of financial support, but also from the antagonistic behavior of other relatives. They also struggled with their parents' decision to remarry. Thus, the number of single parent families increased. During the 1970s and 1980s, these families were still not accepted by the Bulgarian society as normal. The negative attitude of society stigmatized these children and they isolated themselves from their peers.

THE CONTEMPORARY BULGARIAN FAMILY

Revolutionary transitions are typically accompanied by an overthrow of the old and an acceptance of the new. This brings insecurity and fear, and places the individual in a situation of premature choices and risk. In Bulgaria, the economic, social and political transformation took place while the nuclear family, with one or two children, was the dominant family model (Yachkova, 2002). This traditional model of marriage was the social norm in Bulgarian society in 1989. For a large sector of the population, early marriages were and still are preferred. Globalization and joining the information era, as well as the transition to a market economy, pose difficult tests for the Bulgarian family (Yachkova, 2002). Economic and social crises put the family in an extremely hard situation. The next sections focuses on two basic spheres of influence on the Bulgarian family: (1) the influence of the world changes on the model of the modern family; and (2) depreciation of traditional national values due to global changes in the cultural and spiritual spheres.

The Modern World Demographic Crisis and Process in the Family

Bulgaria is one of the countries in Europe in which the demographic problem of an aging population is especially intense. Only 19.5% of the population is 18 years of age or younger, and only 16.7% of children are under 14 years of age. Women in the fertility ages are below 40% (Census, 2001). It is estimated that in 50 years the population will be half of what is today, and in 2080 it will be around 2 million, composed mostly of old people (Balev, 2001).

Following world trends, the birthrate in Bulgaria is decreasing. Although it is the norm for women to have at least two children, in reality those who have one child are predominant (see Table 2). Since 1992, the portion of single-child families increased from 26.8 to 29.8%. Two-child families have decreased because raising one more child is seen as expensive for the family (25.5%). Parents cannot provide a normal standard of living for two children. Unemployment, poverty and economic problems, insecurity for the future and low income, have stopped parents from giving birth to a second child, even if they desire a larger family (20.9%) (Balev, 2001; Jekova, 2000). Only 8% of the one-child families indicate that this is the ideal family for them. Data shows that the basic factor for the fewer number of children is the economic crisis and the deterioration of the parents' living standard. These economic conditions impact the reproductive behavior of the families, regardless of place of residence, parents' education or religion. There are a few differences based on ethnicity. A large family with more than three children is normative only for the Gypsies. Bulgarian and Turkish customs have similar views in that in both groups the norm is two children. However, in families of Bulgarian Muslims the number of children tends to be higher.

Bulgarian women continue to give birth to children at an early age. In 2001, the average age at the birth of their first child was 23.8 years of age, while in 1990 it was 22. The same slight upward trend can be seen in the average age of the father, which in 1990 was 23.9 years. This grew to 25.1 years in 2001, which continues to be the lowest one in Europe (Balev, 2001).

Has the Bulgarian Family Model Changed?

As in other parts of the world, a slow change in the stable model of the married family has been observed in Bulgaria. New alternatives, such as cohabitation and single parent families, are more frequent. Regardless of the fact that the population already accepts the new nuptial relations as normal, the married family remains the dominating model. Approximately half of young people up to 35 years of age (46%) state that they could not possibly live without a spouse; 33% appreciate the meaning of marriage, but do not consider its absence as fatal; 12% accept marriage as a difficult relationship, which could be avoided, and for 9% marriage is an old form of life (Yachkova, 2002). The stability of marriage in Bulgarian minds is seen in the large number of couples who currently cohabit, but accept it as temporary. They view it as a trial marriage, similar to the period of the "godej" in the past, which was a traditional engagement that was followed by marriage.

Two relatively new types of family life that have been accepted by Bulgarian society are *the incomplete family* (usually single mothers) and *the cohabitation family*. The 2001 census showed that incomplete families comprise 12.39% of the population (82% are single mother families). Recently, 10–11% of all newborns belong to mothers who did not have an official marriage. Two main factors account for these out-of-wedlock births: (1) undesired pregnancy, mostly typical for the young, uneducated woman; and (2) planned pregnancy by mature women who have missed out on finding a spouse. The incidence of these women with education and professional qualifications that bring a relatively high social status is increasing. In crisis conditions these women feel immense responsibility as parenting is expected to be a first priority.

In contrast to the incomplete family, cohabitation has rapidly spread, especially recently (Spasovska, 1995). The understanding of this type of relationship is incomplete, because they have only recently been adopted by the Bulgarian people and they were not tolerated by the state. For the first time, the 1965 census registered the presence of cohabitation without a marriage contract: 1.8% of all families (71.2% of the partners were up to 16 years of age and 25.1% were 17–19 years of age).[10] These are most popular among those of Gypsy ethnicity (17.1%), and among Bulgarian Muslims (5.5%). They are also popular among the least educated people and villagers.

Cohabitation is currently on the increase as an alternative to traditional marriage. While it has different dimensions that encourage young people to select this style of family living, it is still hard to identify and is defined in different ways. According to some authors, cohabiters comprise 5% of all couples (Keremidchieva, 1998). According to others, unions without marriage amount to about 13–15% of the population (Spasovska, 1995). The profiles of these partners show they are young people less than 29 years of age. Cohabitation is favored more by men, as women tend to quickly reject this style and to register the marriage legally. Most of them live in the capital of Sofia and a few in villages (Spasovska, 1995). Some cohabiters were divorced. According to the survey, "The young for the family and marriage" (Yachkova, 2002) a major portion of those living under such arrangements believe that love is an illusion, or have experienced disenchantment in love. They are either not satisfied with the way they live, have experienced disappointments in life, or dream about living in another organized state, or another way of living. Yachkova (2002, p. 37) suggests that in psychological terms, these are individualists with place very high values on personal freedom and a sense of self-dignity and pride.

The existence of strong immigrant attitudes in young people also contributes to a rejection of legal marriage and a preference for uncommitted unions. The electronic media and especially the Internet creates a virtual world for the young, where they can ignore space and time, accept themselves as citizens of the Universe, and become bearers of a new family culture. Finding a partner through the Internet is already popular among Bulgarian youth, and also among middle-aged, single people.

Changes in family relations were evident in the early years of the transition period (1990–1991). Thus, families experienced fear of the unknown future, worries and a sense of insecurity. Potential unemployment was a new and unknown phenomenon and provoked a slow change in family relationships towards alienation and independent decision-making. The mother and the father built a strategy for their children's future. Parents voluntarily undertook the entire responsibility of providing for the future of their children. They always strove to do the best for their children.

The weakening of family kinship as a result of the transition is also indicated by analyses of developments in the private sector, especially among small and medium sized businesses. With the restitution of private ownership, conflicts between relatives who cannot agree to divide the restituted property are common. Similar antagonistic relations are even more obvious when examining the development of small private firms. They grew rapidly in the first years of the transition. Usually, these companies were organized and registered as small family businesses. It is well known that trust among shareholders is the most important factor in successful development. Such strong links based on trust are more or less family ones. Analysis of the development of small companies shows that family firms developed successfully and without conflicts, until there profits rose. This resulted in intense disagreements and usually led to the downfall of the firm. Data show that in 1991 70% of the population viewed the family as the main source of support when forming a survival strategy. Contrastingly, in 1998 only the elderly felt they could rely on support from the family. Young people up to 35 years of age seek a method of coping with situations without counting on family and relatives (Staykova et al., 2000). This indicates that internal family relations in Bulgarian society have changed. Relations between partners are based on greater free will and relative independence.

FAMILY AND MOTHERHOOD POLICY IN THE TODAY'S TRANSITION

Demographic processes that have resulted in a decreasing birthrate, the shift to a smaller family size, the increase in divorce, and the gradual establishment of partner relationships, require a corresponding policy, directed towards preservation of the family and children. Family policy is inseparable from state social policy. After the transitions, none of the governments provided a clear, precise outline of the frames of their policies and attitudes towards the family. Today, the social policy provides assistance and services that protect individuals during periods of income loss. In conditions of economic recession, families gradually lose their social benefits from the time of the socialist state. Gradually, a number of protective regulations for mothers were removed from the Labor Code. The duration of paid leave for giving birth was reduced to 135 days, and the option of using non-paid leave when the child was between the second and third year was eliminated. Additional paid annual leave for mothers with two or more children, as well as the protection of the pregnant women's work place, was also eliminated.

Significant economic changes were required for the rethinking of the aims and character of the family policy. It must be recognized that high-quality social protection for the family leads to improvements in quality of life. It also results in an improvement in the population's health, which ultimately helps families cope with economic recession. In this period, it is especially important to create an adequate family policy, which will stabilize and recognize the family as an institution, responsible for producing and socializing the next generation. These are responsibilities which until recently were shared with the socialist state. Unfortunately, the presence of a purposeful, planned, systematic policy, which would ensure the long-term protection of the family in all its varieties is currently lacking. Bulgaria is one of the few countries in Europe without a specialized state unit authorized to create national family policy. The problems of the Bulgarian family fall within the responsibility of the Ministry of Labor and Social Policy. In the Parliament there is no separate commission to countersign the changes in the Family Code. Thus, current family policy is reduced to social assistance. There are discussions about the re-introduction of a family income tax, which would have a substantial effect on the budget of families with children (such a law existed in the past recognizing the number of the family members when establishing the taxes).

CONCLUSIONS

Interdisciplinary analysis of the family in Bulgaria under conditions of globalization reveals signs of relatively rapid changes. These changes are due to two world processes, i.e. the demographic decline in fertility and the modernization of family/conjugal relations. The economic and social transitions experienced by society accelerate changes in the family. This analysis shows that the Bulgarian family is stable as a social institution and family values in Bulgaria are not endangered. Family life is still perceived as a value that occupies a high position in the hierarchy of individual belief systems and is directly related to the birth and upbringing of children. The liberalization processes require a rethinking of gender roles within couples. Nevertheless, men and women realize the necessity of matrimonial union, and of family ambience for the sake of their children. Modern communication technologies and the Internet have increased the possibility of finding a spouse throught the "chat room" and the desire is to transform the virtual communication between partners into a real family.

NOTES

1. This concept has been recently introduced in the European Union and reflects the low income of people who have jobs, but lack enough earnings to cover their expenses related to the social existential minimum.

2. Data first published in Newspaper *24 hours*, 2003, 16th October.

3. According to the operating legislation, until 1989 the primary education (8 grades) in Bulgaria was obligatory for everyone. Currently, based on data of the NSI only, in 2002 28,000 children dropped out of school, with 31% not desiring to study at all (SEGA, 2003) One of the reasons for such a sharp change in the mind set of the growing population is the widespread maxim that "in order to be rich, it is not necessary to study." Unfortunately, reality is currently supporting that maxim.

4. The first sociological survey of the Bulgarian family was conducted by Valtazar Bogishitch in 1864 and is part of the work: *Pravni obicaj u Slovena* (Dinkova, 1976).

5. Determines a large household in contrast to the small, simple or nuclear family, which includes only parents and children (Todorova, 2002).

6. The roots of the Bulgarian patriarchic family had gone through matriarchate, which meant respect for the woman: for the wife and the mother. During the five-century long Ottoman Yoke, the role of the woman was raised and she became the caretaker of the Bulgarian culture, values, spirituality, and customs.

7. In 1990 about 21–22% of the women would not work if their husbands received enough profits; 78% stated that they would continue working even if they lost the job they were currently practicing. The women indicated that they could not imagine a situation in which they would stay at home and be entirely occupied with taking care of the children, organizing the family social time, etc. For them this is a worthless life, and does not satisfy them (Bobeva et al., 1992; Staykova & Gadeleva, 1992).

8. The paid-leave is determined by its consecutiveness: for a first child – 120 calendar days, for a second child – 150, for a third – 180 days and for each next one – 120 days.

9. It was also possible for the paid leave to be used by the grandmother of the newborn.

10. According to the Family Legislation the contracting of a marriage up to the age of 16 is forbidden, and up to 18 years of age the contracting of marriage happens only with the parents' permission.

REFERENCES

Baldjiev, V. (1891). On our personal spouse law. Cited by: A. Strashimirov (1993), *Our Nation*. Sofia: YATRUS.

Balev, I. (2001). Newspaper. *Troud*, 15.11.2001.

Bauman, Z. (1999). *Globalization. The human consequences*. Sofia: LIK (in Bulgarian).

Bobeva, D., Staykova, R., Gadeleva, Z., & Dinkova, M. (1992). Special strains on women and families that impacted on children. In: *National Situation Analysis of Bulgarian Children and Families* (pp. 25–38). UN: UNICEF.

Bogishich, B. (1874). Collection of the local customs of the South Slavs, Zagreb. Cited by: A. Strashimirov (1993), *Our Nation*. Sofia: YATRUS.

Carter, B. C. (1999). *Infinite wealth. A new world of collaboration and abundance in the knowledge era.* Boston: Butterworth Heinemann.

Census (2001). Tables, electronic format retrieved September 2003 from: http://www.NSI.Census2001, www.Semeistva_files\DomSemTable.htm.

Dimova, L. (Ed.) (2003). Globalization and the quality of life. In: *Women, Labour, Globalization* (pp 69–86). Sofia: ASA (in Bulgarian).

Dinkova, M. (1976). *Modern Bulgarian family.* Sofia: Otechestven Front (in Bulgarian).

Fukuyama, F. (1995). *Trust: The social virtues and the creation of prosperity.* NY: Free Press, A Division of Simon & Schuster.

Jekova, V. (2000). Factors determining the reproductive attitudes of women in the private sector. In: J. Naselenie (Ed.), *Population, Anniversary* (pp. 120–130).

Kanitz, F. (1876). The Danube Bulgaria and Balkan Peninsula. Cited by: A. Strashimirov (1993), *Our Nation.* Sofia: YATRUS.

Keremidchieva, M. (1998). Family policy-factors influencing on its development and its specifics. *J. Naselenie, 1–2,* 104–124.

SEGA (2003, April 2). 28000 children drop out of schools for a year. Data of NSI. In: Newspaper *SEGA.*

Spasovska, L. (1995). *The celibacy.* Sofia: Acad. Press "M. Drinov".

Staykova, R. (1999) *Bulgarian women – Mentality and life strategy in transition.* Electronic format, Retrieved September, 2, 2003 from: www.phylanthropy.org/GN/KEN/gntext.

Staykova, R., Iossifov, A., & Gadelev, Z. (2000). *Risk and indemnity? Society's expectations of State responsibility in the Bulgarian transition.* Electronic format, Retrieved August, 29, 2003 from: www.univie.ac.at/iwm/SOCO.

Staykova, R., & Gadeleva, Z. (1989). Motivation structure and organization of research. In: *Bedingunen fur die Entstehung und Entwicklung neuer Forschungsrichtungen* (pp. 209–217). Berlin: Teil II.

Staykova, R., & Gadeleva, Z. (1992). Die frauen in Bulgarien – Ihre bestimmung heute und in zukunft. *Feministische, 2,* 98–103.

Strashimirov, A. (1993). *Our nation.* Sofia: YATRUS.

Todorova, M. (2002). *Balkan family structure and European pattern, demographic development in Ottoman Bulgaria* (Bulgarian edition). Sofia: AMICITIA.

Vidova, M. (1981). *Women's legal rights in Bulgaria.* Sofia: Sofia Press.

Yachkova, M. (2002). *The family in Bulgaria at the turn of the Century.* Sofia: ASSA-M.

FAMILIES IN MOLDOVA

Valentina Bodrug-Lungu

ABSTRACT

The contradictions of the transition period in Moldova promoted transformations of the structure and functions of the family. Today the term "family" is more extended, including new forms in comparison with previous generations. Under current conditions there is an increased need to understand family issues. The family is not considered as a separate cell and closed system; rather it represents a problem of national interests. Strengthening the family is important, but its realization is not easy. Problems have to be solved at the society and family level. At the society level, there is a need for systematic research on family issues, for development and implementation of family support strategy, family consultations, and family life educational programs for youth. At the family level, the focus needs to be on increasing the quality of relationships, developing a democratic style of childrearing, and restructuring the gender roles.

HISTORICAL AND POLITICAL CONTEXT

The Republic of Moldova is within the Southeast European region, situated in the basins of the rivers Nistru and Prut. Since its independence in 1991, complex issues such as the strengthening the state, the reconstruction of its economy according to market principles and democratization emerged. During the transition period, the country has encountered a wide range of social, economic and political challenges, which have been pursued by successive governments. The factors fostering social order and solidarity include the creation of a constitutional and

Families in Eastern Europe
Contemporary Perspectives in Family Research, Volume 5, 173–186
© 2004 Published by Elsevier Ltd.
ISSN: 1530-3535/doi:10.1016/S1530-3535(04)05011-3

legal foundation for the democratic state; the maintenance of historical traditions of amicable coexistence, mutual respect and cooperation among representatives of various ethnic, linguistic and religious groups; and broad involvement in European political, cultural, and economic processes.

Along with the positive changes, the situation in Moldavian society remains difficult. Political instability, socio-economic crises, and high levels of criminality and corruption undermine the transition to sustainable development. The demographic profile and health of the population is declining and the democratic educational system is rapidly weakening. Inter-ethnic relations remain tense in the country. The problems of equal rights and opportunities for men and women have been underestimated in the process of society's modernization.

SOCIO-ECONOMIC CONDITIONS

For more than ten years, the Republic of Moldova, like other Eastern European countries, has been transforming its political and economic system. During this time, the principal goal of reform efforts was to ensure the transition from an authoritarian political system and centrally planned economy to a democratic state with a market economy and civil society. While the political reforms brought the state institutions, political pluralism and individual liberties closer to democracy, the results of economic reforms are very poor.

According to the World Bank, 66% of the population lives below the poverty line, while the most affluent enjoy 50.3% of national income and the poorest 20% are left with only 3.4% (1998) (National Human Development Report, Republic of Moldova, 2000). The Committee on Economic, Social and Cultural Rights (2003) is concerned that an estimated 40% of the population lives in absolute poverty, and that extreme poverty is especially pronounced in rural areas and among children. Therefore, poverty alleviation is an urgent problem. Inhabitants from the rural areas are in the worst shape. More than 80% of the "new poor" are villagers (NHDR of Moldova, 2000). The changes promoted in the rural areas have brought more difficulties then advantages, with villagers perceiving their current situation as a threat to their welfare. During the transitional decade, the rural population's wellbeing fell, and the gap between the rural and the urban sector increased.

The socio-economic challenges of the transition period have lead some people to think and speak about the "good old days" with much regret, and others to support the radical reforms. The impact of Communism on family life was contradictory. On the one hand, a strong system of family social support was created, and on the other hand, the people became used to having the state solve their problems, thus reducing people's initiative and contributing to the development of social stagnation.

Education

The importance of education for the development and enrichment of human capital is so significant that access to education is recognized by the UN as an important human right.[1] In Moldova the access of children from villages to public education is affected by several factors. First, rural localities have a poor technical-material basis. For example, while 72.5% of urban schools have computers, only 48.7% have access in rural areas. Many village schools need major overhauls. Low salaries and delayed payments (often for several months) do not encourage young people to remain in rural localities. Pupils spend a considerable amount of time taking part in agricultural activities, and housekeeping and outside schoolwork is not encouraged. In 1999, the expenses for a child's education in an urban family were 3.9 times higher than in a rural family. These negative circumstances created serious obstacles for children in rural areas in acquiring qualified educational services. In 1999, 4,700 children abandoned school (79% were from rural areas) (NHDR of Moldova, 2000). The disproportion between the welfare of urban and rural families increases the difference between the opportunities for children from cities and villages. The UN Committee on Economic, Social and Cultural Rights (2003) reveals concern about high school non-attendance and drop-out rates in primary and secondary education, the main reason for non-attendance being acute family poverty.

Health

A population's health protection is an important characteristic of a society's level of development.[2] In Moldova the sphere of health protection is very problematic. The recent socio-economic changes placed the population (especially in rural areas) in a difficult situation (NHDR of Moldova, 2000). The eradication of the general system of public health protection transferred the responsibility to the citizens themselves. Introduction of paid services, which replaced the reduced or free ones from the previous years, created difficulties for poor families, the majority of whom could not afford expenses for medical services. The reorganization of the medical institutions led to the closing of many medical centers, forcing the rural population to ask the urban centers for assistance. Thus, the majority of rural inhabitants (constituting more than half of the population) have no possibility of claiming their social rights.

The current socio-economic situation in Moldova reveals that the social costs of the transition have been dramatic, including worsening of demographic trends, reduction in resources for education and health services, a sharp rise in income discrepancies, spread of poverty, growth of a shadow economy, corruption, and organized crime. As a result, there has been a considerable decline in the wellbeing indicators. Thus, in 2000, the GDP per capita at purchasing power parity was U.S.$2.033, life expectancy was 67.4 years, and the adult literacy rate was 96.4% (Global HDR, 2000). The Republic of Moldova, in spite of these changes in recent years, remains within the group of states with a "medium level of human development." Among 174 countries included in the United Nations Rating List (Global HDR, 2000), Moldova is 102nd, compared with 75th in 1994 (NHDR of Moldova, 2000).

FAMILY STRUCTURE

Article 48 of the Constitution of Moldova (1994) states that "the family . . . has the right to protection by the society and the State," and Articles 47, 48, 49, 50, and 51 stipulate the right of the family, mother, and child to receive special protection and assistance. In compliance with international standards, the Parliament has adopted 20 laws regulating specific situations regarding the civil, political, social, economic, and cultural rights of the child, including the Law on the Rights of the Child, the Law on Youth, and the Family Code, as well as making significant amendments to the Labor Code. According to Art. 14 of the Family Code, the minimum age for marriage for men is 18 years, whilst for women it is 16 years. This norm discriminates against women and can negatively affect their health through early marriages and childbirth.

Data indicate that 93.7% of people have families and 6.3% are single (Annual Statistic Book of the Republic of Moldova, 2000).[3] Research conducted with students (Bodrug, 1999) indicates that 75% feel the family represents an important value. The participants stated that the reasons for family creation include psycho-emotional comfort, social status, stability of sexual relations, an optimal environment for children's education, and moral and financial support. Nineteen percent viewed the family as a source of pressure because they considered it easier to solve problems when alone, and that having a career is more important. Forty-three percent of the respondents noted that in the future family will represent an important value (Bodrug, 1999).

The contradictions of the transition period promoted transformations in the structure and functions of the family. Alongside the nuclear family have appeared cohabitation, single-person households, single parent families, etc. Under these circumstances, understanding family issues is a priority. The family is not simply a refuge or "a protective umbrella," as some people think. The family is expected to ensure the physical, emotional and spiritual needs of its members, promote dialogue, and care for children. At the same time, the family is also expected to manage outside social relations, ensure flexibility in the distribution of roles, promote respect for each member, and facilitate adaptation in critical situations. Not all families are prepared to carry out these difficult functions. Today, many families struggle for survival or are consumed by internal conflicts. The decline in income and widespread unemployment has reduced the living standards of most families, especially those with children. These conditions affect families' integrity and values, increasing the number of divorces, and of children born out of wedlock. Growing legal and illegal labor migration affects children's welfare negatively, leaving them more and more on their own without a proper family environment. On the other hand, poor families cannot create favorable conditions for their children's development.

Demographics

By the end of the 1990s, Moldova was confronted with a difficult demographic situation. There was a decrease in population, a rise in the death rate, and an increase in divorces. These processes were caused by various factors including socio-economic, cultural, spiritual, geopolitical, migrational, etc. The demographic situation constitutes an integral indicator of a country's social development as a reflection of its socio-economic and moral state. The population decreased from 3,643,500 (42% urban) in 2000 to 3,617,700 (41.4% urban) in 2003 – without Transnistria region (Moldova in Figures, 2003).

The family plays an important role in the demographic development of the country. The age of spouses, the stability of the family, and the number of children affect the rhythm of population growth. The birth rate has diminished from 13 per 1,000 inhabitants in 1995 to 10.6 in 1999 (NHDR of Moldova, 2000). The number of live births decreased from 38,501 in 1999 to 35,705 in 2000 (Moldova in Figures, 2003). During this period, the average number of children a woman gave birth to diminished. As a result of the economic situation, the overall number of children in families has been dropping. However, families in rural areas tend to have more children. In general, the majority of families have 1 (54.2%) or 2 children (37%), 7% have 3 children, and 1.3% have 4 (Report – Status of Women, 1999). The number of abortions increased annually, and it is still the main form of family planning. Data indicates that abortions for the teenage group are frequent (8.9–9.7%) (Bulgaru, 2001). In 2002, the number of abortions was 15.6 per 1,000 women of fertile age (UN Economic and Social Council, 2003).

There has been a decrease in the number of marriages and an increase in divorces. For example, in 1980 there were 24.5 divorces per 100 marriages, while in 1990 and

2000 there were 32.2 and 52.4 respectively. Between 1990 and 2000 the number of marriages decreased to 53%. In 2002, 21,685 marriages and 12,698 divorces were registered (Moldova in Figures, 2003). Data revealed that 31.5% of divorces occurred in the first four years of marriage (The Annual Statistic Book, 2000). This is also the period when more than 60% of childbirths occur. In 2000, 8,209 children lived in single parent families due to divorce (Gagauz, 2001). Analysts explained the increased divorce rate as a result of women's economic independence (Bulgaru & Bulgaru, 2001; Gagauz, 2001). Other factors associated with rising divorce rates include alcoholism, weak preparation for family life, jealousy, matrimonial infidelity, conflicts, socio-economic conditions of the family, long separations from spouses due to working abroad, intervention of the parents in the life of young spouses, and infertility (Anțîbor & Rijicova, 2003; Bologan, 2001; Ovcearenco, 2003).

GENDER ROLES IN THE FAMILY

The legislation of Moldova contains no discrimination on the basis of gender. However, discriminating attitudes towards women have been noticed at different levels such as government, economic, social, and especially in families.[4] Analyzing gender role differences, responsibilities, barriers and opportunities for men and women can contribute to fighting existing gender stereotypes and establishing new perspectives on gender equality. There is a need to reconsider the roles of parents in children's education. Until recently, the traditional family represented a well-structured mechanism with precise division of roles. The husband was engaged in professional activity outside the family and had responsibility for the material support of the family, while the wife was engaged in household work and children's education and socialization. As a rule, both also had outside jobs. Maternity was transformed into a cult, while the father had a less important role (Bodrug-Lungu et al., 2001).

The current family organization is rather inconsistent. On the one hand, there are still strong patriarchal stereotypes about the traditional roles of the man (material maintenance of family, head of family) and woman (household work, children). On the other hand, especial in urban and young families, the image of the father as patriarch is changing as more young fathers wish to be present for childrearing, education, and to help with the household work. Young spouses work to build relationships on the basis of partnership and respect.

A recent study indicated that the majority (68%) of respondents from rural areas favor traditional gender roles (Bodrug-Lungu & Zmuncila, 2001). Most of the women considered household work to be similar to paid work (84% of 16–20 year old women, 76% of women 30 years and older). The majority of men perceived household tasks as simple and easy work (44% of men from rural areas and 56% from urban areas). Results show that men and older people are more traditional in their perspectives on gender roles.

The societal changes during the transition period influenced women and men's attitudes to gender roles and now they are not so strongly divided. For example, "dish washing" is performed by 40% of men, and 60% of women; "cooking" by 35% of men and 65% of women; and "education of children" by 45% of men and 55% of women. The functional roles inside the family are not so rigidly distributed anymore. Youth have a modern perspective on "masculinity" and "femininity," indicating a tendency towards gender equality in social life as well as in family relationships.

One of the problems encountered within families is domestic violence. Data from the UNIFEM Regional Survey on Domestic Violence (2001–2002) indicated that the majority of respondents (82%) mentioned the existence of domestic violence against women. Women and youth acknowledge this problem more often than men and older individuals. As in other countries, the most recognizable types of violence are physical (87.5%) and sexual (96.6%). Threats and intimidation as forms of psychological violence were reported by 69% of the respondents. Economic violence (denial of access to employment/education, refusal to give money to buy goods) was recognized by half of those questioned. Again, women much more often than men reported psychological violence. Among the most regularly noted negative consequences were woman's psychological stress (83.8%) and damage to her physical health (70.1%) (The Level of Public Awareness on Domestic Violence and Sexual Harassment at the Work Place and Its Reflection in the Media, 2003). Recommendations were made to bring the issues of domestic violence to the public's attention using various methods to inform women, especially from rural areas, about their rights, to convince them that they are equal to men, to raise their self-esteem, and to introduce the Gender Education Program into the educational system (Bodrug-Lungu, 2003). The National Center on Child Abuse Prevention (NGO) organized a special Survey with UNICEF support on "Child Abuse Evaluation in the Republic of Moldova (2000–2001)." A rise in violence against children was discovered.

FAMILY PROCESSES

A relatively new phenomenon is the increased number of cohabitations. There is a growth in the amount of non-registered marriages and young women (24–28 years old) living in "free" relationships and having children. According to a 2000 survey, only 45% of women who had children outside marriage had the option of marrying and raising children in a nuclear family (Gagauz, 2001). Research finds that 62% of respondents (students) from the urban areas and 56% from the rural areas accept cohabitation (Bodrug, 1999). Boys generally have a more positive attitude towards cohabitation compared with their female counterparts. The changes in conjugal behavior (freedom to engage in sexual relations before marriage) increase partners' satisfaction and independence. There is a more active involvement of women in public activities. These positive consequences for individual growth might be paralleled with negative consequences for society (decrease in birth rate leading to the family losing its status) (Bulgaru & Bulgaru, 2001; Cuznetov, 2000; Ovcearenco, 2003).

Another problem is the increased number of children born out of wedlock. In 2001, 22.5% of children were born out of wedlock (17.5% in 1998). The birth of children outside of marriage can be divided into two groups: (1) teenage mothers' childbirths, a consequence of early sexual activity and unplanned pregnancy; (2) births by 30–35 year old women who consciously accept responsibility for the child's rearing (Bulgaru & Bulgaru, 2001). In 1999, 1,614 children (4.2% of all children) were born to teenage mothers (42.2% of them outside marriage) (Gagauz, 2001). Teenage pregnancy is more frequent when the mother does not receive any support from a partner or relatives. This impacts their psychological and economic welfare, negatively influencing the opportunity to study, work, or have a career. In 2000 in Moldova there were 15,000 children abandoned by teenage single mothers. Many times teenage mothers have become victims of human traffic. The traffic of human beings (especially young women) is still widespread despite the various measures taken by the State to prevent and combat this phenomenon, including the adoption in 2001 of a National Plan of Action against the Trafficking in Human Beings.

Though the phenomenon is very difficult to monitor, migration of the population has been increasing since 1990 and nonofficial data estimates that 600,000 to 1 million citizens now work abroad. The migration is principally due to economic reasons and most emigrants are parents who have left their children at home with relatives or friends. In Moldova many people with high intellectual potential are compelled by economic stress to leave for Italy, Greece, and other countries to earn their living and frequently do so illegally. The consequences of such economic migration are both positive and negative. On the positive side is the reduction of unemployment, an improvement in economic welfare and the increased opportunity to provide for the education of children. However, the negative consequences include depopulation, the outflow of labor – especially by intellectuals – and the disintegration of families. With such economic migration comes a re-structuring of the spousal role; men are compelled to accept the responsibility for household work and for child rearing. As head of the family, it is often hard for them to be engaged in such traditionally female activities or to find themselves dependent financially on their wives. Some start drinking, increasing the risk of conflict and divorce. This situation indicates that gender roles need to be reconsidered and patriarchal stereotypes abolished.

TRADITIONS AND FAMILY LIFE

Traditions provide a kind of "national university" whose "graduates" have mastered the skills of a complete "course" of moral, ethical, cultural and spiritual norms, as well as having internalized civic qualities. These "schools of traditions" are very strong in Moldova in spite of the destructive pressures of socio-economic problems and the expansion of other values and ideals which have flooded the country since the collapse of the Soviet Union. Factors which encourage the preservation of traditional culture are a high percentage of the rural population (54%) and a first generation of urban inhabitants who maintain an agrarian mentality.

Role of Religion in Family Life

Religion is a significant component of Moldavians' spiritual life. During several decades of state-sponsored "militant atheism," drastic methods were used to suppress and prohibit any expression of religious life. There was a forcible destruction of religious monuments, liquidation of churches, and mass deportation to Siberia of religious people and believers of different religions. Beginning in the 1960s, after the so-called "thaw," a policy of "tolerant atheism" was promoted. It lasted until 1988–1989, when the process of democratization and the national renaissance was launched. The policy of repressing religious worship and believers was replaced by an attitude of "peaceful coexistence."

The process of democratization and the creation of conditions for the free expression of basic human rights in the Republic of Moldova was launched in the early 1990s and served as a means to accelerate the development of religious life. This tendency was observed within the traditional Christian Orthodox Church, which was the primary affiliation for the largest part of the population (93%), as well as within other churches. In comparison with the recent past, freedom of religion is indicated by the enormous increase in the officially recognized religious groups. In 2000, there were 8 religions and 12 religious associations (congregations, organizations) (NHDR of Moldova, 2000). Today, the continuity of the country's traditions is maintained alongside religious diversity. Religion plays an important role in the lives of many families. Observation of church canons (e.g. fasting), holidays (e.g. Easter, Christmas Holiday), and rituals associated with weddings, christenings, and funerals are very important. Lately, many young and elderly people (atheists before) have been going to church, especially on important religious holidays.

CHILDREN AND PARENTING STYLES

Research on parenting roles indicate that 76% of respondents considered it good to have two children, 12% preferred 3–4 children, 10% one child, and 2% wanted more than 4 children (Bodrug, 1999). Traditionally, in the majority of families, especially in villages, the authoritarian style of education of children dominated: the father had a central position and the child was expected to respect the parents' decisions, since the honor of the family was paramount. Corporal punishments were often resorted to, and there was a differentiation in education of girls (priority on household work) and boys (priority on trade). Today, the societal changes are reflected in parent-child relationships.

The results of a study carried out with 97 nuclear families indicated that 61.86% of parents practiced supervision and rigid suppression of children's actions (Morarescu et al., 2001). Parents considered they had the right to require from children obedience, submission, and acceptance of decisions. In many families, different approaches to rearing boys and girls are still observed. The boys learn to be active, to show initiative, to make their way in life, and to make a career, while the girls are taught to be diligent, careful and to administer household work.

Ninety percent of teenagers stated that parents monitored and controlled their actions and made decisions without considering the child's opinion. Only 11% of the teenagers specified that parents give them an opportunity to express their opinions. Ninety percent of them stated that their parents used sanctions and punishments as methods of compelling submission to their decisions and as infringement upon their freedom. Only 10% specified that they could discuss their problems and opinions with their parents.

Frequently, parents' behaviors carry a subconscious character, caused by the desire to help their children meet societal requirements. At the same time, parents' desire to monitor their children's actions interferes with the development of the child's independence. Another difficulty consists in reaching a consensus about educational values and standards. Many parents are not ready to educate their children, frequently reproducing their own parents' educational styles and stereotypes. This results in an aggravation of the relations with one's own children and produces conflicts in the family. Educational programs and training are needed for both youth and parents.

RESEARCH ON THE FAMILY

In Moldova, systematic research on family issues is lacking. Some studies have examined the family and its role in socializing the young, while others focus on family psychological problems (Bodrug-Lungu, 2001; Morărescu, 2000; Moraru & Borsci, 2001; Tereşciuc & Moşin, 2001). Part of these investigations has been carried out by scholars from UNICEF and UNDP in Moldova.[5] While some scholars argue that the family has mostly lost its educational function due to its focus on survival, others, on the contrary, insist on the exclusive importance of family in the child's education (Cuznetov, 2002; Ovcearenco, 2003). During the reform years within the education system in Moldova, specific steps for introducing programs of training for family life were undertaken. Thus, in some schools a new course, "Family Life Education," was introduced by the Family Planning Association in collaboration with the Ministry of Education. However, this idea has not been applied in practice due to a lack of organization and human and educational resources.

POLICIES AND PROGRAMS
SUPPORTING FAMILIES

The Government of Moldova adopted a number of strategies, concepts, and programs on social protection of the child and family, including the National Concept on the Protection of the Child and Family. The main goals of the Concept are to ensure the development and implementation of the policy on families' and children's social protection at the national and local level; to encourage the creation of new, sustainable models of social services; to create a national system for monitoring and evaluating the child and family's situation; to facilitate the participation of civil society in social protection; and to develop mechanisms for preventing social risks to children. The National Council on Children's Rights was created as part of the mechanism of children's rights protection. However, these rights are often violated due to the social and economic situation in the country.

The Government of Moldova recognized that for ensuring sustainable social assistance there was a need for reforming the system of social protection and it has started this reform. National legislation promotes the norms of social protection for most groups (but not all of them) that are covered by international laws.

The system of pensions includes the following guarantees: retirement pensions; disability pensions; and pensions in case of the loss of the breadwinner.

The Preliminary Poverty Alleviation Strategy (2002) concluded that children constituted one fifth of the poor. The poorest groups are families with many children, especially in rural areas, and single parent families, especially those with a single mother. In 2003, the Government of Moldova adopted The Strategy of Growing Economy and Poverty Reduction, directed to the improvement of people's economic situation, including families. Legislation states that maternity leave can be used by both parents and close relatives. However, data indicates that fathers do not use the leave. The image of men bringing up children is not highly promoted in the society.

In analyzing the government activity in the domain of family policies it is worth mentioning its "National Plan on Promotion of Gender Equality in Moldova 2003–2005." In accordance with this plan, the Ministry of Labor and Social Protection has coordinated a UNIFEM Project, "Promoting gender equality through legislation in Moldova," and, in collaboration with "Gender-Center" (supported by the SOROS Foundation), has elaborated the Draft Law on "Prevention of Domestic Violence."

CONCLUSIONS

Families in Moldova suffer from the changes brought about during the transition period. Urgent measures are necessary to promote policies such as stimulating investment for improving individual and family living conditions, developing social services for children and families, improving family status, and ensuring gender equality. Social policies should not only focus on quantitative aspects such as growth of fertility and population; this growth should be accompanied by an improvement in the quality of family life. The policy needs to focus on the transformation of the whole social structure to support the interests of the family and its consolidation as a social institution.

NOTES

1. For more information about the Education system in Moldova see National Human Development Report Republic of Moldova, 2000, pp. 83–87. http://www.undp.md: http://www.statistica.md.

2. For more information about the health system in Moldova see National Human Development Report Republic of Moldova, 2000, pp. 89–93. http://www.undp.md.

3. The last census was in 1989, making it very difficult to acquire statistical data for some categories.
4. See: National Human Development Report, Republic of Moldova (2000), pp. 63–69. Report Status of Women in the Republic of Moldova (1999).
5. 'Young Voices Opinion Survey of Children and Young People's Report for Moldova (2001). UNICEF. The situation of children and families in the Republic of Moldova (2002). UNICEF. National Human Development Report. Republic of Moldova (2000) UNDP.

REFERENCES

Anṭîbor, L., & Rîjicova, S. (2003). Compatibilitatea maritală – factor determinant al stabilităṭii familiale (Marital compatibility – the determinant factor of family' stability). Conferinṭa corpului didactico- ştiinṭific "Bilanṭul activităṭii ştiinṭifice a Universităṭii de Stat din Moldova în anii 2000–2002" (Paper presented at the Conference of Didactical Academia "The balance of scientific activity of The State University of Moldova from 2000–2002") (P. II, pp. 317- 318). Chişinău: USM.

Annual Statistic Book of the Republic of Moldova (2000). *Anuarul statistic al Republicii Moldova.* Chişinău: DASS.

Bodrug, V. (1999). Determinarea viziunii prospective a tinerilor asupra relaṭiilor gender în viitoarele familii (Determination of prospective visions of young peoples about gender relationships in the future's families). *Anale Ştiinṭifice ale Universităṭii de Stat din Moldova (Scientific Annals of the State University of Moldova),* P. II, 103–107. Chişinău: USM.

Bodrug-Lungu, V. (2001). Rolul familiei în educaṭia copiilor (The role of the family in child's education). *Revista Didactica Pro . . . (Journal Didactica Pro . . .), 4*(8), 44–46. Chişinău: Cartier.

Bodrug-Lungu, V. (2003). *Violenṭa din perspectiva gender (Violence from gender perspective).* Chişinău: USM.

Bodrug-Lungu, V., Saca, S., & Poustovan, I. (2001). *Gender şi Educaṭie (Gender & Education).* Chişinău: USM.

Bodrug-Lungu, V., & Zmuncila, L. (2001). Gender şi lucrul casnic (Gender and household work). *Anale Ştiinṭifice ale Universităṭii de Stat din Moldova (Scientific Annals of the State University of Moldova),* 108–110. Chişinău: USM

Bologan, L. (2001). Indicatorii calităṭii vieṭii de familie în Republica Moldova (The indicators of quality of family's life in Republic of Moldova). *Anale Ştiinṭifice ale Universităṭii de Stat din Moldova (Scientific Annals of the State University of Moldova),* P. II, 157–159. Chişinău: USM.

Bulgaru, M., & Bulgaru, O. (2001). Particularităṭile evoluṭiei proceselor demografice în Republica Moldova (The particularities of evolution of the demographics process in Republic of Moldova). *Anale Ştiinṭifice ale Universităṭii de Stat din Moldova (Scientific Annals of the State University of Moldova),* P. II, 145–151. Chişinău: USM.

Constituṭia Republicii Moldova (Constitution of Republic of Moldova) (1994). Chişinău.

Cuznetov, L. (2000). *Etica vieṭii de familie (Ethic of family life).* Chişinău: ASEM.

Cuznetov, L. (2002). *Dimensiunea psihologică şi etică a parteneriatului educaṭional (The psychological and ethic dimension of educational partners).* Chişinău: UPS "I. Creangă."

Gagauz, O. (2001). Familia tânără şi rolul ei în procesele demografice (The young family and its role in demographic process). *Buletin Informativ al Centrului Naṭional de Studii şi Informare pentru*

Problemele Femeii (Journal Informational Bulletin of National Center of Women's Studies), 4(11), 12–13. Chişinău: SA "Business Elita".

Moldova in Figures (2003). *Moldova în cifre. Short Statistical Book (Anuar statistic succint)*. Chişinău: DASS. http://www.statistica.md.

Morarescu, M., Papuc, L., & Zbirnea, A. (2001). Educaţia liberă în familie – premisă a formării personalităţii autonome (Free education in family – condition of formation of the independent personality). *Revista Studii Gender (Gender Studies Journal)*, 4, 17–21.

Moraru, I., & Borsci, l. (2001). Stabilitatea relaţiilor în cuplu (The stability of relations in couple). *Anale Ştiinţifice ale Universităţii de Stat din Moldova (Scientific Annals of the State University of Moldova)*, P. II, 97–98. Chişinău: USM.

National Human Development Report Republic of Moldova (2000). Chisinau, UNDP. http://www.undp.md.

Ovcearenco N. (2003). Suportul psihologic al relaţiei mamă-copil: Tradiţionalism şi modernism în educaţie (Psychological support of relationship mother-children: Traditionalism and modernism in education.). Materialele conferinţei ştiinţifice internaţionale (Materials of international scientific conference), pp. 327–329. Chişinău: ULIM.

Report Status of Women in the Republic of Moldova (1999). UNDP. Chisinau: Ed. Ruxanda.

Tereşciuc, R., & Moşin, T. (2001). Şcoala atitudinilor parentale – imperative al timpului (The "school" of parental attitudes – imperative of the time). *Anale Ştiinţifice ale Universităţii de Stat din Moldova (Scientific Annals of State University of Moldova)*, P. II, 133–134. Chişinău: USM.

The level of public awareness on domestic violence and sexual harassment at the work place and its reflection in the media (2003). UNIFEM. Almaty: PH "Domino Ltd." http://www.nasilie.net.

Situaţia copiilor şi familiei în Republica Moldova (2002). *Evaluare şi analiză 2000–2001. (The situation of children and family in the Republic of Moldova. Evaluation and analysis)*. Chişinău: UNICEF.

United Nations Committee on Economic, Social and Cultural Rights (2003). Consideration of Reports Submitted by States Parties under Articles 16 and 17 of The Covenant – Republic of Moldova.

Young Voices Opinion Survey of Children and Young People's Report for Moldova (2001). Berlin: UNICEF.

FAMILIES IN THE UKRAINE: BETWEEN POSTPONED MODERNIZATION, NEO-FAMILIALISM AND ECONOMIC SURVIVAL

Tatiana Zhurzhenko

THE SOCIAL AND ECONOMIC CONTEXT

The experience of the first decade of state independence changed the mood of the Ukrainian people from hope and enthusiasm to frustration and apathy. The reasons for this are manifold, including widespread corruption and the evident failure of Ukrainian democracy. For most families, the major challenge was the severe economic crisis of the 1990s. A combination of factors led to economic decline and stagnation, a dramatic decrease in the standards of living, and economic and social insecurity. Firstly, the Soviet system and its common economic space of which the Ukraine was a deeply integrated member, collapsed. Following this downfall, there was a persisting dependence on Russia in terms of oil and gas supplies. What is more, Ukrainians lacked a clear strategy for economic reforms and a political will to enforce them. Finally, a business elite, interested in suspending privatization and in blocking the implementation of a viable rule of law, was formed. Although the official unemployment rate is rather low (3.8% in 2002), the estimated rate according to the ILO (International Labour Office) methodology is over 9.8% (*Uryadovy Kuryer*, 28.02.2003). Estimations including those who are employed but on "administrative leave" raise the total unemployment rate to almost 24% (ILO, 2001). Permanent delays in the payments of salaries, pensions and social

Families in Eastern Europe
Contemporary Perspectives in Family Research, Volume 5, 187–209
© 2004 Published by Elsevier Ltd.
ISSN: 1530-3535/doi:10.1016/S1530-3535(04)05012-5

allowances became normal practice during the 1990s. Moreover, inflation and monetary reform devaluated the saving of most families. Economic insecurity forced many to look for low wage jobs and to enter informal and often illegal businesses. Between 1.5 and 2 million Ukrainians are working abroad, most of them in the low-skilled labor force.

Since the end of the 1990s, the decline of the social infrastructure was partly compensated by private initiatives. However, in some sectors, which normally fulfill the basic needs of the population, the authorities failed to prevent a collapse. For example, the lack of electricity supply, permanent difficulties with the heating in winter, serious problems with the canalization system and water purification. Since 2000 the government has been reporting economic growth, and in 2002 they even reported increase in the real income of population and slight reduction of poverty. Current surveys show that a growing proportion of the Ukrainian population evaluates the current situation as tolerable, but the majority still feels insecure (KIIS, 2001). There are, however, some signs of economic stabilization, including the normalization of electricity supplies, and the gradual liquidation of debts in salaries and social payments. Despite bureaucratic obstacles and widespread corruption, market reforms have created a legal and institutional basis for private initiative, and millions of Ukrainians are now engaged in new business activities. Due to economic liberalization, the market was filled, for the first time, with a wide variety of goods. Western standards of mass consumption affected people's expectations and life choices, even among those with low incomes. However, the social costs of market reforms were unexpectedly high, which meant that the majority of the population could not fully enjoy the achievements of the transition.

A new phenomenon can be observed in Ukrainian society. That is, a social differentiation based on the growing income gap between the richest and the poorest. According to UNDP (2003) statistics, the Gini index (which reflects the degree of income inequality) for the Ukraine was 29 in 1999. This was higher than in Hungary (24.4) and the Czech Republic (25.4), but similar to Poland and the Baltic states (UNDP, 2003). According to IMF (International Monetary Fund) analyses, during the first eight years of the transition, the Ukraine registered the highest increase in income inequality in the region, combined with a GDP falling 11% per year (compared to Poland, these are opposite dynamics) (Keane & Prasad, 2001). Due to growing inequality, there is a wider gap between Ukrainian families in terms of their economic strategies and lifestyles than was the case under the Soviet regime. Through the privatization process, financial speculations, the re-export of Russian gas and oil and privileged access to state contracts, the new class of Ukrainian capitalists has accumulated a significant share of the national wealth. The new middle class of managers and highly paid specialists are a relatively small group, which enjoys Western standards of mass consumption (e.g. holidays abroad, private schools for children).

Contrastingly, the majority of the families have been negatively impacted by the economic transition. Even having both parents employed does not guarantee a minimum standard of living. In 2000, 49% of the Ukrainian population lived on less than $1 a day, and 26.7% of the population was categorized as living in poverty. According to an ILO/UNDP survey, 46.8% of the Ukrainian population identified themselves as "poor," and an additional 36.9% identified themselves as being "not well off" (UNDP in the Ukraine, 2003). According to the Ukrainian government, the share of those employed who earn less than the official living minimum was 63.6% in 2002, indicating a high level of poverty among the working population (*Uryadovy Kuryer*, 28.02.2003). A growing number of homeless people and street children, the declining health standards, and the spread of alcoholism and drug addiction, indicate a dramatic social marginalization of many Ukrainian families. This is illustrated most strikingly by the decrease in life expectancy between 1989 and 1995 (it dropped 5 years for men and 2.6 years for women). While this indicator has improved since the second half of the 1990s (in 2001, the life expectancy was 63.4 years for men and 73.7 years for women), it still has not reached the level of the 1980s (Children, Females and Family in the Ukraine, 2002).

Certain groups (retirees, families with young children) are especially vulnerable under the present economic conditions. According to a representative household survey conducted since 1999, the risk of poverty increases with the number of children in the family (Social Indicators, 2002). Most families with children are concentrated in the low-income group, and those with three or more children have limited possibilities to enter the middle-income group. In 2001, households with one child spent on average 60.6% of their budget on nutrition, families with two children 63%, with three children 68.3%, with four or more 71.2% (Social Indicators, 2002). Consumption of more expensive food (e.g. meat, fish, eggs, vegetables) was almost twice as low in families with more than two children. Only the consumption of the cheapest products (bread and potatoes) remained the same in all categories.

The neoliberal economic reforms in the Ukraine were too incomplete and inconsistent to create a market economy. They also dismantled social guarantees and undermined social security. In the new Constitution, the Ukraine declares itself a social state guaranteeing basic social rights to its citizens. However, in reality the responsibility of the state has been reduced to limited support of the most vulnerable categories of the population. The family is expected to take full responsibility for the well being of its members, to ensure the development of children, and (given the low level of pensions in the Ukraine) to also support its senior members. Employment guarantees and social benefits for working mothers have not been officially abolished, but remain a symbolic façade of a democratic state without any legal mechanisms of enforcement. The existing recreation, sport and leisure time facilities for families, which before independence were provided by state-owned enterprises and trade unions, have been privatized or even abandoned due to the lack of money. In the absence of a modern system of medical insurance, health care has become increasingly commercialized. This means that the population has unequal access to medical services, and is highly dependent on family income. The cost of education, even in state schools, places a substantial burden on the family budget and access to higher education also depends on income. State-supported housing construction has stopped, and young families have to buy apartments for full market prices, with loans available only for people with a high guaranteed income.

During the transition, the family provided the Ukrainian people with the necessary economic, social and emotional resources (Zhurzhenko, 2001, p. 151). The costs of childbearing were to a large extent transferred to the family. Under conditions of economic crisis, the family became an important site of collective survival based on the solidarity and mutual support of its members. At the same time, families reacted to the social and economic stress through a dramatic decline in birth rates, postponed marriages and high divorce levels.

THE NEW POLITICS OF THE FAMILY

The process of nation building and the implementation of democratic institutions have brought serious changes to the politics of the family. During the Soviet era the family was interpreted as a "cell of society" and a mediator between the state and individual. However, under the new conditions it was transformed into a symbol of national revival. The neo-familialist tendency in the Ukraine contributed to the reinvention of national origins and helped to establish a distance from the communist past. Mythologized images of the "traditionally strong family," the "Ukrainian habit of having many children," and the "traditionally high status of women in Ukrainian society" became very popular in the rhetoric of state officials, academics and women's leaders. This model of the traditional family is often presented in public and academic discourse as something between the idealized Ukrainian family of the pre-Soviet past, and the American middle-class family of the 1950s. A common assumption is that stable marriage and high birth rates are fundamental to the Ukrainian ethnos, and that these were lost as a a result of anti-Ukrainian communist politics (Chyrkov & Vinnychenko, 2000, p. 120).

In this context, the family is often presented as the very basis for national revival, as it is responsible for biological reproduction and for the education of children as members of the national community. It is within the family that national identity is formed and where love for the native language and culture emerges. For example, an Ukrainain expert in children's education defines the national character in an essensialist way (hospitable, generous, hard working, searching for truth) and claims that the aim of parents is to support and develop these characteristics in their children (Shcherban, 2000, p. 39).

The discourse on strengthening the family can also be found in the election programs of political parties, in speeches of pro-presidential and oppositional leaders and in parliamentary debates. Virtually every political party in the Ukraine placed family issues among the priorities of their election programs. They admitted that the economic crisis had a very negative effect on families, and all promised more or less the same measures. That is, the support of low-income families, raising social benefits, pensions, stipends, improving the quality of medical services, and so on. In the current Ukrainian political situation, the political parties often use family politics and women's issues for populist purposes. By referring to such issues as pensions and family support, the party of power tries to gain more legitimacy, while the national-democratic opposition uses these issues to denounce the current regime.

Women's NGOs (Non-Governmental Organizations) are playing an increasing role in formulating the agenda of family politics in the Ukraine. With the exception of few feminist groups, which consider any preoccupation with the family a symptom of traditionalism, most Ukrainian women's NGOs identify with the idea of a strong family as a specific tradition of Ukrainian society. For them, this pro-familial attitude does not contradict the feminist idea of women's empowerment. The popular image of the strong Ukrainian woman is reinforced by the historical myth of the traditional matriarchal character of Ukrainian culture. According to this myth, in the past, women lived in a society in which both genders had complementary roles of roughly equal value. They enjoyed equality in difference, and their natural female roles were highly respected (Rubchak, 1996). This discourse evokes the ancient image of the Berehinia (a pagan goddess-protectress of the fireside and the home), which is widely used today as a female symbol of the Ukrainian nation. The popular view is that Ukrainian women are strong and independent, but at the same time family oriented. They are committed to their maternal duties and respectful of their husbands. Therefore, they assume leadership in their families.

Despite neo-familialist tendencies, the women's movement became an important factor in the modernization of Ukrainian society. By addressing issues of discrimination, gender inequality, access to political life and decision making, women's organizations created a space for new discourse and challenged the traditional approaches. The influence of this global feminist discourse increased especially after the World Women's Conference in Beijing in 1994. Its resolutions obliged Ukrainian state institutions to incorporate gender equality and a women's rights agenda into national politics. In cooperation with a group of women's organizations, the *National Plan of Actions for 1997–2000 on Improving the Status of Women and the Rise of Their Role in Society* was developed. In 1995, parliamentary hearings on the implementation of the UN Convention on liquidation of all forms of discrimination against women took place in Ukraine. This increased the awareness of politicians, state officials and the general public concerning the issues of gender equality and challenging traditional attitudes.

At the same time, conservative forces in Ukrainain civil soceity expressed opposing viewpoints. For example, during the International Congress on the Family, which took place in Kyiv in 2003, the head of the All-Ukrainian Charity Foundation "For Human Dignity" came out against the official legalization of abortion, sexual education of children, and the public advertisement of contraception (Caritas Spes the Ukraine, 2003).

The mixture of discourses adapted by the state rhetoric results from various factors: new social and political forces concerned with family issues, global influences, the Soviet heritage, and the search for a national tradition. Their presence helps to explain the mixture of discourses adapted by the state rhetoric. The current state ideology of family is heterogeneous and transitional, as seen for example in the *Draft for a State Family Policy* adopted by the parliament in 1999. It formulates the main principles of the state-family relationship. Firstly, it declares the sovereignty and autonomy of the family while minimizing the interference of the state and of self-administration bodies, political parties, public organizations and religion. Secondly, the state only provides social protection for disabled citizens. The third principle presumes "parity" and "partnership" between men and women in all social spheres, the provision of equal opportunities and even the "fair distribution of family duties." The fourth principle proclaims the "social partnership between the family and the state" thus replacing the compromised "state paternalism." The fifth principle guarantees the opportunities for the free development of every child. It appeals to the United Nations Convention on the Rights of the Child and ends the old Soviet approach of the "protection of childhood." Finally, the sixth principle defines the role of the family in the nation-building process, which consists of contributions to the continuity of the generations and of passing on national and cultural traditions, values and customs to the children (Draft for a State Family Policy, 1999).

FAMILY DEMOGRAPHICS IN THE UKRAINE

Traditionally, the Ukraine was a country characterized by early marriages and a high marriage rate. In terms of these indicators, at the beginning of the 20th century it was fifth among European countries, led by Serbia, Romania, Bulgaria and Hungary. Most of the population consisted of peasants, and early marriages were an economic necessity in these households. Revolutions and wars in the first half of the 20th century, as well as industrialization, forced migrations and the mass repressions under Stalin's regime destabilized the traditional institution of marriage. The Soviet legislation abolished religious marriage, legalized abortion and guaranteed full rights to illegitimate children. Divorce was allowed and it became readily available to men and women. These innovations led to a dramatic increase in the divorce rate. In 1925, almost one in five marriages was terminated by divorce and Ukrainian indicators were amongst the highest in the world. Young marriages were the most unstable, and in the countryside more so than in the cities (Pribytkova, 1995, p. 214). At the same time, the Ukraine remained a country with a high marriage rate. Despite fluctuations caused by World War II, this rate was still high during the second half of 20th century. By the beginning of the 1990s, there were 9.5 marriages per 1,000 people, and in 1991 the Ukraine had the highest rate in Europe, but then it was decreasing and finally dropped to 5.5 (the lowest level after World War II). In 2002 the marriage rate increased again to 6.6 (State Committee of Statistics of the Ukraine, 2003). Officially registered marriages have become less popular.

The divorce rate in the Ukraine was influenced by state policy. In 1944 a new law was adopted in which only officially registered marriages were recognized by the state. Also, the divorce procedure became very complicated and the divorce rate dropped. In the 1960s, legislation was liberalized again and the divorce rate increased. It seems that there is no direct correlation between economic crisis in the Ukraine and the divorce rate, which has been steadily growing since the beginning of 1970s. In 1989 there were 3.7 registered divorces per 1000 people and 3.8 in 2002 (Children, females and family in the Ukraine, 2000). The divorce rate is traditionally higher in the eastern, more urbanized regions of the Ukraine. In the western part, this rate was always low due to the absence of the experience of early Soviet modernization and a stronger church influence. From 1985, the divorce rate has also started to increase in the west (Children, females and family in the Ukraine, 2000). This tendency can be partially explained by the growing labor migration of Western Ukrainians abroad, which affects the stability of marriages.

On the one hand, the stable divorce rate may indicate that economic hardships encourage people to stay together. On the other hand, people often start a new relationship without going through a divorce process, and live for years in informal marriages. The perspectives of marriage for the middle aged and older generations are distorted due to a misbalance in the age and gender structure of the population. From the age of 29, the number of women exceeds the number of men of the same age (in developed countries this starts happening from the age of 50) (On the Situation of Families in the Ukraine, 2000).

Marriage and divorce rates during the decade of transition show that many Ukrainians postponed their marriage plans until better times, or preferred to cohabitate. The main reasons for this were the lack of separate housing and insufficient income (Lavrinenko, 1999b). Another reason, especially among the young generation in the cities, was the growing influence of alternative values (professional career, leisure time), which competed with family values. The high marriage rate in the Soviet Ukraine can be explained by persisting traditional patterns of an agricultural society. However, more importantly, high social stability and employment guarantees contributed to the high rate. Although the standard of living was low in comparison to Western countries, people accepted it as a sufficient basis for family life. Marriage was considered by young people as a means of gaining independence from their parents (although economic dependence could persist for a long time). This is why the average age at the first marriage remained low in comparison to other industrial countries.

Today, as the family is fully responsible for its well-being, and consumption standards have increased, marriage is perceived to be a more serious decision. In 1997, the average age at the first marriage was 24.7 for men and 22 for women. New opportunities in education, business and professional careers compete with traditional family values, and seem to offer a quicker way to independence. Young people have become more emancipated in their sexual behavior and less oriented to the search for a potential marriage partner (which is also due to the previously unimaginable availability of contraceptives). Meanwhile, parents have become more tolerant of "testing" marriages, or informal cohabitation of their adult children. Despite these changes, early marriages remain characteristic of the Ukraine, especially in the countryside. In 2001, in 40% of marriages the age of the bride was 20–24 and in 18% of these 18–19 years. Another 6% were women under 18. This corresponds to early motherhood, as the average age at childbirth in the Ukraine is 24, the lowest in Europe (Children, Females and Family in the Ukraine, 2002).

FAMILY STRUCTURE

At the beginning of the 20th century, the Ukraine experienced a disintegration of the traditional multigenerational peasant family. Instead, the nuclear family emerged as the dominant form. This process started in the Ukraine earlier than in Russia due to some peculiarities of agrarian relations. In 1926, the average size of a blue collar worker's family was 3.91 persons, among white collar workers it was 3.61, and among various categories of peasants it was between 4.04 and 4.79 (Prybytkova, 1995). The number of families with children was more than 75%.

Today, the average size of the family is 3.2 persons. Elderly people (retirees) represent 80% of the one-person households. More than 2 million (around 14%) families consist exclusively of retirees, a fact which illustrates the aging of the family in the Ukraine. This has created new challenges for the state's social policy. According to the same study, 55% of families have children (up to 18 years), most of them (60%) have only one child, 34% have two children, and 4% have three. The average number of children per family is 1.5 (1.3 in the cities, 1.7 in rural areas) (On the Situation of Families in the Ukraine, 2000).

The decline of the birth rate occurred during the last century as a result of the increasing modernization and urbanization of Ukrainian society. Progress in women's education and rising employment also contributed. Additionally, the economic crisis of the 1990s affected reproductive behavior. The birth rate decreased from 12 (in 1990) to 7.7 per 1000 people (in 2000) and only in 2002 it increased to 8.2 (State Committee of Statistics of the Ukraine, 2003). The total fertility rate dropped to 1.1 in 1999 (half of what is required for population replacement at the same level) (Children, Females and Family in the Ukraine, 2000). Other indicators (for example, the growing share of first births among the total number of births) show that families are not having a second or third child. According to a survey conducted in 1996, around 60% of young couples intended to have two children and around 10% more than two (Chuyko, 1999, p. 257). Economic and social insecurity affect the decisions of young families concerning the number of children.

Women often assume maternity and family obligations before they finish their studies or find a job. To some extent, this is a remnant of Soviet reproductive culture under conditions of full employment. During this time, many women were oriented not to a professional career, but to a job which could be easily combined with motherhood. Furthermore, the lack of modern contraception and the popularity of abortion created a specific pattern. That is, couples tried to regulate their reproductive activity only after having their first child. In the countryside the level of early maternity is twice as high, and not only because of traditional attitudes. The problem of housing is not as dramatic as in the cities, expectations concerning the level of income are lower, and the young couple can rely on the support of parents.

According to national data, 10.6% of families in the Ukraine consist of single mothers with children and single fathers represent 1%. While most single parent households have one child (71.1%), many single mothers still live with their relatives and rely on their support (On the Situation of Families in the Ukraine, 2000). These families have a low income and the level of poverty among them is higher (42.9%) than in the rest of population (32.5%). Women earn 70% of the average male salary, and for most single mothers this is the main source of income. Social transfers to these families are very low. The contribution of the ex-husband to the family depends on personal agreement, rather than on official regulations. One of the rarely discussed problems in Ukrainian society is the lack of communication and contact between the father and his children following divorce. Ukrainian legislation does not discriminate against either parent, but in practice it is the mother who makes all the decisions concerning the child. Communication with the father is often discouraged. In many cases, fathers themselves do not insist on having an opportunity to communicate with their children and do not take on the financial obligations of supporting their former family.

As well as divorce, births to unmarried women are a source of single parenthood. In the Ukraine, the rate of births to unmarried women has risen from 11.2% in 1990 to 19% in 2002 (Children, females and family in the Ukraine, 2002; State Committee of Statistics, 2003). Again, regional differences are important as this indicator reaches 20–26% in the east and south, and only 6–9% in the west (Children, females and family in the Ukraine, 2002). There are no estimates of how many children are born to single mothers and how many to women cohabitating with partners. Unlike some western European countries, the low level of social benefits for single mothers does not make this status economically attractive.

During the 20th century, the tendency towards the nuclear family has a long history in Ukrainian society, and this model has remained dominant until today. However, under conditions of economic crisis, and more importantly, with the deficit in housing it is more difficult for young families to start an independent life. According to a 1996 survey on young families, 36.2% lived with their parents, 30.5% in a separate house, part of the house or apartment, 10.6% in youth residences, 9.4% rented a room or an apartment, and 3.3% shared apartments (Chuyko, 1999, p. 262). Even if the young family lives separately, the support of the parents is often considerable and family ties are important. More than 60% of young families receive regular financial support from the parents, 2/3 receive food and consumption goods, more than 1/3 get help in solving housing problem, and 60–70% of the young families get regular help in the household. In addition, elderly people are usually economically supported by their children (because pensions are very low), and in the absence of special state institutions for seniors, it is the family who has to provide care for them. Therefore, it is not only low living standards, but also the lack of social support for young families with children and for seniors, which impedes the movement towards the nuclear family.

GENDER ROLES

In the Ukraine, gender roles and gender inequality in the family have not been studied systematically. This section is based on data from the 2002 survey, "For equal rights and opportunities" (UISR; Gender Mainstreaming, 2002). According to this survey, almost the same proportion of men and women considered their profession to be "important" or "rather important" (women 53/25%; men 63/22%). The same consensus applied to the importance of the family (women 85/10%; men 80/14%). Seventy-four percent of women and 78% of men agreed that "for a child of preschool age it is not good if the mother works," 63% of women and 75% of men agreed that "women's duties are connected first of all with the family, and men's duties with the profession." At the same time, 62% of women and 50% of men did not feel that "higher education is more important for men." Almost all of the participants (96% of women and 93% of men) were convinced that both parents are equally responsible for the education of children and family decisions. Interestingly, 55% of men thought that they should be privileged over women in cases where there is a deficit in jobs (among women, 37% agreed and 56% disagreed with this idea). The different responses of men and women represent a certain mixture of Soviet egalitarianism (for example in education issues) with a strong conviction regarding "natural" gender roles (the responsibility of women for the family and the natural priority of men in the professional sphere).

The survey shows that the status and authority of both parents is relatively high in Ukrainian families, although that of the mother seems to be granted more respect. Women showed higher awareness of children's problems and interests than men. They also help their children with homework more often, read books with them, visit museums, cinemas and exhibitions, discuss their problems and involve them in housework. Men seem to be responsible for sports, hobbies and excursions into nature. Among the duties to be fulfilled almost exclusively by women, are taking care of the child when sick and visiting doctor with them. About 70% of the respondents state that it is the mother who takes the child to the kindergarten or school and back, as well as puts the child to bed at night. Thus, it can be concluded that women do the majority of family duties connected to education and childcare. As a result, the relationship between children and their fathers is more distanced.

Apart from the children, the woman is also in charge of most other family responsibilities. According to the UISR survey, women do most of the cooking, washing, ironing, cleaning and dishwashing. The male contribution is mainly in the area of shopping. However, in the countryside men perform many household activities, in addition to their farm work. On average, a wife performs 63% of the housework, a husband 16%, a mother/mother in law 13%, a father/father in law 1%, children 4%, other relatives 2% and paid services 1%. Traditionally, the grandmother provides a significant level of support to the family, while the grandfather's contribution is reduced. The contribution of men to the household depends on their age and education, with those younger than 24 and older than 49 helping their wives most often. Middle-aged men invest more time and efforts in their professional career and in earning money. Men with a higher education are more active in the household. However for women, age and level of education have no influence on their share of housework.

In general, the division of gender roles in Ukrainian families remains rather traditional, despite the high level of female employment. Only a small number of men manage to be breadwinners under the current economic conditions, and women still carry most of the responsibility for the family. This leads to physical and psychological stress for many women, and challenges their professional development (Gender Mainstreaming, 2002). However, gender inequality in the family has not become an issue in Ukrainian society and it is only recognized as a problem by some feminist groups. Paradoxically, most respondents said they were "satisfied" or "rather satisfied" with the distribution of duties in their families (27/41% among women, and 31/43% among men). Still, the percentage of women who are not satisfied with the distribution of family duties is 19% against 11% of men.

FAMILY TRADITIONS

The Ukraine is a multinational state and numerous nationalities have lived on its territory for centuries. These include Russians, Jews, Crimean Tatars, Karaims, Gagaus and many others. The focus of this section will be the family rituals of Ukrainians. Most of them have an archaic, pre-Christian basis, which was later influenced by the church (Catholic or Christian Orthodox, depending on the region). Due to the turbulent history (foreign invasions, revolts, and massive migrations), family relations in Ukrainian local communities were initially regulated by common law. The church came to impose its authority relatively late, around the 17th century. In certain periods, "civic" marriages without a church ceremony were widespread. For the community, a wedding celebrated according to Ukrainian customs was important for legitimizing the new couple. Without such a celebration, a church wedding was not valid. In some regions, civic marriage formed a part of the resistance of Orthodox peasants to the forcefully imposed Catholicism and to Polish dominance. Divorce was relatively easy, although common law discouraged people from terminating their marriage (Polishchuk & Ponomariov, 2000). The situation changed in the 18–19th centuries, when the growing authority of the church introduced the idea of divorce as a sin and a source of shame for the family. The role of the Church in regulating family life was (and still is) especially important in the western part of the Ukraine. In the Eastern and Central regions some attitudes were less rigid (for example, attitudes towards pre-marriage sexual relations and illegitimate children). They became even more liberalized due to the more intensive capitalist development and industrialization in the second part of 19th century (Polishchuk & Ponomariov, 2000).

In the Soviet Ukraine, the role of the church in family life was reduced to a minimum. Through educational and medical institutions, youth and women's organizations, the state fought against what it considered to be "superstitions." To some extent, the Party replaced the church in its function of controlling the family and sexual behavior. New Soviet marriage and family rituals were introduced and gradually accepted, especially in the cities. Apart from the regular registry offices, special wedding palaces were offered to make the ceremony more attractive to young people. Official registration was usually followed by a visit to one of the Soviet memorial places. Elements of Ukrainian folklore were integrated in the official ceremony of marriage registration (e.g. the use of *rushnyki*, i.e. embroidered towels). In fact, this secularized wedding ceremony persists in the post-Soviet Ukraine, with Soviet symbols being replaced by national ones (portraits of the Ukrainian poet Taras Shevchenko, national flag). The non-official part of the wedding is usually celebrated at home in the villages, and in cafés or restaurants in the cities. Despite the economic difficulties faced by many families, a lot of money is usually invested in the wedding. It integrates important elements of the traditional Ukrainian wedding, which is performed as a play according to certain rules. For example, the groom and his guests go to the bride's home to pick her up before registration, he negotiates her "price" with her siblings or neighbors, and the special bread (*korovay*) presented to the couple by the groom's mother plays a symbolic role. The party itself is often organized with the help of a professional, who arranges speeches, dancing and entertainment according to a scenario. The married couple has a passive role in this scenario, and often it is not until the second day that the young people are able to have their own party and are not disturbed by their parents. In less traditional environments (among intellectuals) these customs are often ignored.

Among family rituals the most significant is probably the child's baptism, which is celebrated as an important event together with relatives and friends. This ceremony was even practiced during the Soviet era, although it had to be hidden by parents who were active in public life. According to tradition, the godparents are responsible for the child's education and become close relatives of the family. Godchildren are supposed to visit their godparents on Christmas Eve in order to offer ritual food.

There are also traditions related to death in the family. The last fifteen years have seen a shift from a secularized funeral ceremony in the cities, often in a crematorium, to the traditional funeral with the priest presiding. As in other cultures, the priest is supposed to help the dead in his/her transition to the other world, and to protect the rest of the family from the dangerous contacts with death.

The role of religion in Ukrainian society has increased considerably over the last fifteen years. There influence of non-traditional religions and sects has also grown.

At the same time, reanimation of national traditions and customs are encouraged in schools and by the media as a way to establish Ukrainian identity, which was lost under Soviet rule. There are still persisting cultural and religious differences between the urban and rural areas, as well as between the eastern and the western regions of the country.

CHILDREN AND PARENTING

There have been several changes that have made parenting in contemporary Ukrainian society more problematic. These include the economic and social instability of the transition period, the conditions of the market economy, informal employment, and some of the effects of postponed modernization in the private sphere (liberalization of sexual relations and differentiation of family patterns). According to data a significant portion of Ukrainian society is quite skeptical about the ability of the family to provide an appropriate education under the current conditions (Education in the Family, 2002). Mentioned among the obstacles to fully-fledged education in the family were a lack of time (49% of the women, 46% of the men) and overwhelming economic problems (83% of the women, 81% of the men).

The economic crisis in the Ukraine has not only curtailed the material basis for the education of children, but it has also affected family relations with the outside world and posed new challenges for parenting. There are four factors involved:

(1) A lack of time for communication with children. This concerns those parents with a low income who have to combine two or more jobs, as well as those who are run a relatively successful private business. Further difficulties arise for those parents who regularly work abroad and are absent from home for a long time.
(2) The growing income gap combined with the growing influence of Western mass consumption standards. Many families cannot afford to satisfy their children's expectations concerning clothes and entertainment. Family income often becomes a basis of inclusion/exclusion in peer groups, creating a social hierarchy.
(3) The debasement of the social environment (e.g. the rise of criminality). Parents with a higher economic and social status try to isolate children from the street, to prevent them from trying drugs and alcohol. At the same time, today's parents have less control over the social contacts of their children.
(4) Cultural factors have created an existential gap between generations. These include rapid changes in the official ideology, the growing role of religion, and

the re-evaluation of the country's history and of social experience during the last fifteen years.

In the Ukraine, there is almost no reliable systematic research on issues of education in the contemporary family. However, the results of surveys, conducted by the UISR and the Institute for Problems of Education at the Academy of Pedagogical Sciences, and "Education in the family in contemporary situation" can be drawn on. The data shows that parents prioritize the qualities they try to develop in their children in the following way: independence and self-confidence, perseverance, the ability to act in any situation, respect for the parents, diligence, religious values, the ability to save money, healthy way of life, respect for the traditions, awareness of the national culture, patriotism, honesty and openness, tolerance and respect towards others (Education in the Family, 2002, pp. 45–46). These reveal the educational priorities of Ukrainian parents, as well as the changes to their own system of values. Obviously, those qualities that are necessary in a liberalized market society take the leading positions. Traditional values are only second, and old-fashioned qualities (honesty and tolerance) are even less popular.

As previously mentioned, while in most families the authority of the parents is respected, it is the mother who was recognized by a higher percentage of the respondents. Sixty percent of the mothers, compared with only 46% of the fathers confirmed that children share all their problems and secrets with them. According to the children's survey, the older their age, the more difficult communication with their parents becomes, especially with the father. Seven percent of 11–12 year olds admitted they have difficulties in communication with their mothers, and 20% with their fathers. Among the 13–14 year olds it was 10 and 31%, among the 15–16 year olds 17 and 40% (Education in the Family, 2002, p. 55). Two thirds of children agreed they have as much support from their mothers as they need. In terms of their father, only 51% of the 11–12 year olds and 42% of the 15–16 year olds gave this answer (Education in the Family, 2002). The report indicates that in the Ukrainian family the father is often alienated from education, and it is the mother who mainly provides support, control and a point of communication for children.

The data also reveals that parents prefer authoritarian childrearing methods to liberal ones. Traditional differences between urban and rural families are most evident in common family labor activities. In the countryside, in 96% of families the children work together with their parents in the household and in the garden. In addition, they help with taking care of cattle and selling products at the market. In the cities, children regularly help in the household in only 47% of families, and in only 11% of the families are children involved in other labor activities (e.g. help in private business) (Education in the Family, 2002).

To conclude, the conditions for parenting have changed significantly since the end of the Soviet system. Under the previous regime, parents had more support from the state, but at the same time they were expected to share the official communist ideology and values. Moreover, the state and its institutions competed with the family. Soviet schools claimed control over educating children and leading and enlightening parents on these issues. The whole system of Soviet institutions was designed to provide paternalist support. Today, parents have a more flexible range of choices, and they possess the right to follow their own system of religious, cultural and political values. They can also choose between various schools, pedagogical approaches and methods of teaching. However at the same time, the family is fully responsible for performing its educational role, and in addition it has to resist the growing social anomie. If the family fails in its educational efforts, the consequences for children are considerable. The programs for homeless children or drug addicts are designed not to support or replace the family, but to deal with the consequences of what is referred to as family failure.

RESEARCH ON FAMILY

Initial attempts to collect knowledge on families in the Ukraine were made by historians, geographers and ethnographers in the 18th and 19th centuries. Systematic research was organized for the first time in the Soviet Ukraine, when the Institute of Demography at the Academy of Sciences was established in 1919. Among the works of the Ukrainian school of demography, which played a leading role in the development of this field in the USSR, was the first significant research on Soviet families by Khomenko (*Family and the Reproduction of Population*) published in the 1930s. However, the institute and its staff eventually fell victim to Stalin's repressions. New demographic research was organized in the 1960s and was concentrated mainly at the Institute of Economics at the Ukrainian Academy of Sciences. One of the most important works on the Ukrainian family in the Soviet period is, *Marriages and Divorces* (1975) by Chuyko. Research on families also took place at the Academy of Pedagogical Sciences, and occasionally some departments of sociology, psychology and pedagogy at the other universities.

After 1991, when the Ukraine was proclaimed an independent democratic state, a national strategy and political agenda emerged on such issues as family, youth, women's rights, and child protection. The negative economic and social tendencies of the transitional period, the worsening of the situation of most families, and the decline in birth rates made the development of a family policy even more urgent. Some new institutions were established (and old ones invested with new functions) to organize research, monitor and support family issues. In the framework of the *National Plan of Actions for 1997–2000 on Improving the Status of Women and the Rise of Their Role in Society* adopted by the government in 1997, the State Committee on Statistics started to regularly publish a special collection of data on "Children, females and family in the Ukraine." Three of these collections containing information on demography, employment, household incomes and expenditures, health care, education and other subjects were published in 1998, 2000 and 2002. Since 1999 a representative household survey has been conducted annually using international methodology, which reveals living standards, household expenditure and income.

The State Institute for Family and Youth Affairs was founded by the Cabinet of Ministers of the Ukraine in 1991. It aimed towards providing the government and general public with research, and educational and consultative services on the issues of family and family politics. At the same time, a group of members of the institute also registered a non-governmental organization (NGO) called the Ukrainian Institute for Social Research (UISR). Both are in fact two faces (state and public) of the same organization. This is a popular strategy in the Ukraine and usually helps to diversify the sources of funding. Throughout this text, the name UISR will be used for this organization. Among the aims of the Institute are the theoretical and applied studies of the family, women, youth and children. In addition it will explore the processes related to young people's integration into society in the context of social and economic transitions, and the development of economic, social, administrative and legal mechanisms of family policy (Ukrainian Institute for Social Research, 2003). Among its research priorities are social support of young families, children with special needs, prevention of alcohol and drug abuse by children, and reform of the childcare system. The Institute conducts several large-scale opinion polls and is involved in international projects. Together with the State Committee on Youth Policy, Sport and Tourism (which is also in charge of family policy) the UISR prepares the official annual reports on the Situation of Families in the Ukraine. Five reports have been issued thus far. Among them are reports on education in Ukrainian families and on problematic families. UISR is the only research institution in the Ukraine that focuses primarily on the family. It is also involved in comparative international projects on youth and family.

The Institute of Pedagogy and the Institute for Problems of Education at the Academy of Pedagogical Science conduct research on education and on the relationship between family and school. The Institute of Sociology at the Ukrainian Academy of Science lacks a special department or a research project on family. Lavrinenko, a member of the Institute, published a book on the social status of Ukrainian women, which also contains a chapter on family (Lavrinenko, 1999a). The Kiev International Institute of Sociology (KIIS) conducted some research projects on issues related to the family. This is a private institution founded in 1991 and is heavily involved in international projects. The research work of the Institute is focused on poverty, employment, political orientations, and socio-cultural parameters of the Ukrainian population (Kiev International Institute of Sociology, 2003). Although the KIIS does not conduct research on family, its projects are sometimes relevant to this subject (e.g. women's reproductive health).

The development of gender studies in the Ukraine after 1991 was one of the factors that stimulated a new interest in the family as a site of gender inequality and power relations. Research institutions of a new type, i.e. women's non-governmental organizations (NGO), initiated a number of projects such as "Gender Analysis of Ukrainian Society" (Gender Bureau, in cooperation with UNDP, 1998) and "Gender Mainstreaming in the Context of Social and Economic Transformation" (UISR, in cooperation with the Canadian-Ukrainian Gender Foundation, 2002). Apart from problems of gender inequality in economic and political life, these publications focus on gender roles, distribution of duties, and decision-making in the family. The all-Ukrainian organization "League of Women Voters 50/50" with the support of UNDP initiated a project entitled "Gender Expertise of Ukrainian Legislation." In the framework of this project, family legislation was also analyzed from the point of view of providing gender equality (Romovska, 2001). The author of this chapter studied the new relationship of the family with the state and with market institutions as a gender issue under conditions of economic transformations in the Ukraine (Zhurzhenko, 2001, 2004).

Although since 1991 a few projects and opinion polls have acquired information about the family under post-Soviet conditions, there has been no systematic research on family processes. This is due to the incipient state of social sciences, limited financial support, sociological studies completed for political purposes, the underestimation of the family as a secondary subject, and insufficient contact with the international academic community.

FAMILY POLICY

Family policy in the Soviet Ukraine was not a separate sphere of state interest, but was primarily a part of labor market regulations. Its object was the working mother, rather than the family itself. Traces of this approach can still be found in the new family policy. For example, despite several amendments, the Labor Code has in fact been in force since 1972 and still reflects the Soviet model of the relationship between the working women and the state-employer. It contains a significant amount of social guarantees for working women, which exceed International Labor

Organization (ILO) recommendations. That is, prenatal and postnatal leave (56 and 70 days respectively) and three years childcare leave with the right to keep one's position during this period. The Labor Code provides health protection for pregnant women in the work place, employment guarantees and protection against dismissal. It also enforces restrictions on the use of female labor for heavy or harmful work. The Law *On the Employment of Population* provides guarantees of resettlement for women with children and for single mothers by reserving 5% of all enterprise vacancies (quota) for this category. One of the first documents representing state family policy in the independent Ukraine, the *Long-term Program for the Improvement of the Position of Women, Family, the Protection of Motherhood and Childhood* (1992), was based on the same approach. However, under conditions of redundancy and hidden unemployment, unofficial labor arrangements and the difficult financial situation of many enterprises, the enforcement of these rights and privileges is rather problematic.

The *National Program on Family Planning* adopted in 1995 reflects a growing concern about worsening demographic indicators. It attracted public attention to the high level of maternal and child mortality, to the deterioration of public health, and to the high rate of abortions due to lack of knowledge about modern contraception. To encourage some positive achievements, another program *Reproductive Health 2001–2005* has been implemented. The *"Children of the Ukraine" Program* (1996) defined the new concept of state policy towards children and undertook urgent measures of support for certain groups (e.g. those who lack parental care or who live in unfavorable conditions).

Faced with the worsening demographic situation, the state paid special attention to the problems of young families. The Law *On the Promotion of Self-fulfillment and Social Development of Youth in the Ukraine* (1993) established the principles of state youth politics under the new conditions. This followed the abolition of the Komsomol (Soviet youth organization, controlled by the Communist Party). The Law included some guarantees for employment, as well as special measures to solve the problem of housing for young families. Among other programs to be mentioned is the *National Plan of Actions for 1997–2000 on Improving the Status of Women and the Rise of Their Role in Society*. This was designed to introduce the issue of gender equality to the discussions on family policy.

In 1999, the Ukrainian parliament adopted the *Declaration on General Fundamentals of the State Policy in the Ukraine Concerning Family and Women*, and the *Draft for a State Family Policy*. These documents defined the main principles of family policy in the context of national consolidation, democratic transformation and the market economy. In 2001, the Cabinet of Ministers adopted a new program, *Ukrainian family*, which is based on these earlier documents. In 2002, the new Family Code was adopted by the parliament.

According to the Law "*On the State Assistance to Families with Children*" the following allowances and payments for families with children are offered (as of January 1, 2002): onetime assistance for pregnant women (78.2 hryvnia; 1 U.S. Dollars = 5.5 hryvnia), onetime assistance connected with the birth of a child (121 hryvnia), childcare allowances (until the age of 3) (29.1 hryvnia per month), allowances for parents with three or more children (until the age of 16) (35 hryvnia per month), assistance for single mothers (12.8 hryvnia per month), for parents with disabled children (45.5 hryvnia per month) etc. In comparison, in 2002 the average wage was 391 hryvnia per month, whereas the living minimum was officially fixed at 329 hryvnia. At the end of the 1990s there was a rising debt in social payments to families with children. In 1996 it was 20.1 million hryvnia, and by 2000 it had grown to 61.5 million. This debt started to decrease in 2001, and the situation now seems to be under control. In general, this assistance list corresponds with the legislative standards of most welfare states. However, the problems are: (1) the small amount of payments; (2) the frequent disregard of the declared social guarantees; and (3) the constant delays in the distribution of payments.

Until 2001, most payments for families with children were calculated as a percentage of the officially established minimum wage (50–100%). However, the minimum wage was far lower than the actual living minimum, which demonstrated the inability of the government to provide essential guarantees. In 2001, the minimum wage rose and state social assistance to families was officially reduced to 25–35% of the minimum wage. In 2000, the *Law on State Social Standards and State Social Guarantees* established the living minimum as an official social standard and as a basis for calculating salaries, pensions and social allowances. However, due to economic instability the new standards based on the living minimum have not been implemented. In 2003, the minimum wage was reported to have grown in 2002 from 38.4 to 45.2% of the living minimum. The government viewed this increase as a big success. The growing problem of poverty forced a transformation in the system of social support to make it more effective. In 1999, the government created a system of targeted social help for low-income families. These families were eligible for assistance if their average income did not exceed an officially established norm. Application for social support could only be satisfied after an evaluation of the living conditions of the family. Since 1999, some attempts have been made to improve this program to make it more available to eligible families.

One of the relatively efficient programs of social support has been that which involves subsidies for housing and compensation for utilities. From the middle of the 1990s the accelerating rise in housing rents and the cost of utilities (electricity, heating and hot water) became a real burden for family budgets. This led to an accumulation of huge debts to service providers. To solve this problem, the program of subsidies was initiated to cover a part of these payments. Families who apply for subsidies have to meet certain requirements concerning living space and average family income. Recently, the program has become more selective and targets only the poorest families.

In order to provide social support for the most vulnerable groups of families, the *Measures on the Improvement of the Situation of Families with Many Children* was adopted in 1999. The implementation of these measures depends on the financial resources of the local administration. This is an attempt to provide non-monetary privileges and state services for children from these families (e.g. free school uniforms and breakfasts). Compared to Soviet times, the reason for assisting families with many children is not the encouragement of birth rates, but the recognition that these families are the most impoverished and in need of support.

Among other programs are those targeted to special categories of children, such as those who are homeless or without parents (there is encouragement to set up "family type" establishments). In this field there is active cooperation between the state social protection offices and NGOs. The victims of the Chernobyl nuclear plant disaster formed a special category of families. In 2002, 1,048,928 children were classified as being affected by the disaster and half of them still live on the territory affected by the nuclear pollution. There are also families whose members are officially recognized as having "participated in the liquidation of the consequences of the Chernobyl disaster." These families have special privileges concerning the use of public transport, health care and recreation. They are also given free housing in cases of insufficient living conditions.

CONCLUSION

The situation of the family in the post-Soviet Ukraine reflects the complicated dynamics of the transition to democracy, economic liberalization and nation building. This chapter analyses three main factors involved in this process.

Firstly, conditions for most families today are affected by the economic crisis, social and economic insecurity, growing income differentiation and the rise in poverty. While some have benefited from economic liberalization and had new opportunities for private entrepreneurship, the majority of families have to cope with economic survival. This effort affects the reproductive behavior of young couples, who often postpone childbirth. In everyday life, cultural activities have become a luxury. In addition, communication among family members and the time available for children's education have been dramatically reduced. Rather than strengthening solidarity, the need for economic survival perpetuates gender inequality in the family.

The new political agenda of nation building, which helped consolidate the post-Soviet Ukrainian elite of both communist and national-democratic origins. Additionally, it propagated neo-familialism as the new state ideology. The former communists, now known as "the party of power," gave up official Soviet egalitarianism and embraced traditional values. Alternatively, the democrats criticized Soviet paternalism and considered the family as an important institution of civil society. However, both agree that the traditional Ukrainian family is an important symbolic resource of nation building. The conservative part of the emerging civil society (even in the women's movement), as well as various churches in the Ukraine, also support (and benefit from) neo-familialist ideas.

Finally, but most importantly, there are the effects of postponed modernization in the private sphere. These were encouraged by political and market liberalization, the flows of uncensored information and the impact of Western mass culture. There are several factors that have made the young generation of Ukrainians very similar to their western counterparts. These include the availability of modern contraception and literature about sexual issues, which was unimaginable under the puritan Soviet regime, the growing plurality of family models, the emergence of alternative lifestyles, the acceptance of sexual minorities and their presence in the public discourse, western feminist ideas. This postponed modernization might fill some gaps left from Soviet modernization. For example, the previous system was concerned with women's emancipation in the interest of the state, rather than for the benefit of women themselves. However at the same time, this process poses new challenges for families in the Ukraine.

REFERENCES

Cabinet of Ministers of Ukraine, http://www.kmu.gov.ua/.

Caritas Spes Ukraine (2003). International Congress of Family, May 16–18 2003. http://www.caritas-spes.org.ua/2003/18_05_e.html.

Children, females and family in Ukraine (2000). Collection of statistics. Kyiv: State Committee of Statistics of Ukraine (in Russian).

Children, females and family in Ukraine (2002, 2003). Collection of statistics. Kyiv: State Committee of Statistics of Ukraine (in Russian).

Chuyko, L. (1975). *Marriages and divorces.* Moscow: Nauka (in Russian).

Chuyko, L. (1999). Ukrainian families and their children. In: *Gender Analysis of Ukrainian Society* (pp. 247–269). Kyiv: UNDP (in Russian).

Chyrkov, O., & Vinnychenko, I. (2000). Ethno-demographic development in Ukraine: History, contemporary state, perspectives. *Suchasnist*, 7–8, 118–122 (in Russian).

Draft for a State Family Policy. Decree of the Ukrainian Parliament from September 17, 1999 (in Russian). http://zakon.rada.gov.ua/cgi-bin/laws/main.cgi.

Education in the family in contemporary situation (2002). Thematic state report on the situation of families in Ukraine for 2001. Kyiv: State institute of family and youth affairs (in Russian).

Gender analysis of Ukrainian society (1999). Kyiv: UNDP (in Russian).

Gender Mainstreaming in the Period of Formation of Ukrainian Society (2002). Kyiv: Canadian agency for International Development; Embassy of Canada in Ukraine; Canadian-Ukrainian Gender Foundation; Ukrainian Institute for Social Research (in Russian).

ILO (International Labour Organisation) (2001). Ukraine: A land of economic insecurity (ILO Socio-Economic Security Programme Home Page, country profiles. http://www.ilo.org/public/english/protection/ses/info/database/ukraine.htm.

Keane, M. P., & Prasad, E. S. (2001). Poland: Inequality, transfers, and growth in transition. *Finance and Development (A quarterly magazine of the IMF)*, *38*(1), March 2001. www.imf.org/external/pubs/ft/fandd/2001/03/keane.htm.

Kiev International Institute of Sociology (KIIS) (2001). Public opinion in Ukraine: January 2001. http://www.kiis.com.ua/index.shtm.

Lavrinenko, N. (1999a). *Woman: self-realization in family and in society (gender aspect)*. Kyiv (in Russian).

On the situation of families in Ukraine (2000). Report for 1999. Kyiv: State Committee for youth policy, sport and tourism in Ukraine, Ukrainian Institute for Social Research (in Russian).

Polishchuk, N., & Ponomariov, A. (Eds) (2000). *The Ukrainians*. Moscow: Nauka (in Russian).

Pribytkova, I. (1995). *Foundations of demography*. Kyiv: Artek (in Russian).

Romovska, Z. (2001). Family legislation in Ukraine. Gender expertise. Kyiv: Logos (in Russian).

Rubchak, M. (1996). Christian virgin or pagan goddess: Feminism vs. the eternally feminine in Ukraine. In: R. Marsh (Ed.), *Women in Russia and Ukraine* (pp. 315–330). Cambridge: Cambridge University Press.

Shcherban, P. (2000). *National education in the family*. Kyiv: Boryviter (in Russian).

Social indicators of the standard of living of the population (2002). Collection of statistics. Kyiv: State Committee of Statistics of Ukraine (in Russian).

State Committee of Statistics of Ukraine (2003). http://www.ukrstat.gov.ua.

Ukrainian Institute for Social Research http://www.uisr.org.ua.

Ukrainian Parliament (Verchovna Rada) (1999). http://www.rada.ua.

UNDP in Ukraine (2003). http://www.un.kiev.ua/en/mdg1/.

UNDP (United Nations Development Program) (2003). *Human development reports*. http://www.undp.org/hdr2003/indicator/indic_126_1_1.html.

Uryadovy Kuryer (Governmental Courier, the daily newspaper of the Ukrainian Government), cf. http://www.kmu.gov.ua/control/uk/publish/; see also http://uamedia.visti.net/uk/indexe.shtml.

Zhurzhenko, T. (2001). *Social reproduction and gender politics in Ukraine*. Kharkiv: Folio (in Russian).

Zhurzhenko, T. (2004, forthcoming). Strong women, weak state: Nationalism, state-building and family politics in post-Soviet Ukraine. In: K. Kuehnast & C. Nechemias (Eds), *Post-Soviet Women Encountering Transition*. Baltimore: Johns Hopkins University Press.

FAMILIES IN LITHUANIA

Irena Juozeliūnienė and Loreta Kuzmickaitė

SOCIO-HISTORIC AND ECONOMIC
CONTEXT OF THE COUNTRY

Lithuania has had a long and tumultuous history. Balts, an Indo-European ethnic group, was the first civilization to live in this territory, dating back to the 10th-3rd centuries BC. The first written mention of Lithuania appeared in the German historical documents "Annals Quedlinburgenses" in 1009. In 1236, Mindaugas became the first Grand Duke of a region encompassing Lithuania, Kaliningrad and part of Poland. Mindaugas converted to Christianity and was crowned king of Lithuania in 1252. In 1323, the capital city of Vilnius was mentioned for the first time. For the first 200 years of its existence, Lithuania was under attack from both the Teutonic and the Livonian Orders. Despite this, by the end of 14th century, it managed to become one of the most powerful states in Eastern Europe. Grand Duke Vytautas the Great, who ruled from 1392 to 1430, extended the great empire from the Baltic Sea to the Black Sea. At the Union of Lublin in 1569, the Polish-Lithuanian kingdom was merged into a Commonwealth headed by a monarch. It was weakened by the wars against Russia, the Ukraine, and Sweden during the 16th–18th centuries. The end of the 18th century was marked by three partitions of the Commonwealth. In 1795, after the Third Partition, Lithuania lost not only tangible traits of statehood, but also its name. As a result, it became part of the Russian Empire.

The collapse of Tsarist Russia restored Lithuania's freedom. On 16th February 1918, it proclaimed itself The Independent Republic of Lithuania. However, by the end of the war in 1945, Lithuania was firmly under Soviet control and widespread mass deportations to Siberia of leading politicians and intellectuals started. The

Families in Eastern Europe
Contemporary Perspectives in Family Research, Volume 5, 211–224
Copyright © 2004 by Elsevier Ltd.
All rights of reproduction in any form reserved
ISSN: 1530-3535/doi:10.1016/S1530-3535(04)05013-7

period of 1944–1953 was marked by the most violent armed resistance against the Soviet occupation. The defiant forces consisted of an organized and well-structured army of about 40,000 partisans. In the late 1980s, the Soviet Union underwent several political and economic crises. In 1988, the Lithuanian Reform Movement "Sajūdis" emerged, involving millions of people of different nationalities.

Restoration of an Independent Lithuanian state was proclaimed in 1990, but was soon marked by an economic blockade. Soviet intervention in 1991 resulted in 14 unarmed civilians being killed at the TV tower in Vilnius. After the Moscow putsch collapsed, Lithuania won international recognition and was admitted to the United Nations Organization in September 1991. In 1993, Lithuania became a member of the Council of Europe and in 1994 became the first Baltic state to apply for NATO membership. Lithuania has been a member of NATO since March 29, 2004. In 1998, Lithuania became an Associate Member of the EU and in 2000 it began negotiations for EU accession. During the referendum in 2003, the majority of the population expressed a desire to enter the EU, and is now a member of the EU since May 1, 2004. Today the Republic of Lithuania is an independent democratic state. The foundations of the social system are enforced by its Constitution, which was adopted in 1992.

Social Forces

The population of Lithuania grew until the early 1990s, when it started declining. It went from 3,747,000 to 3,469,000 people in 2002 (Demographic Situation, 2002; Lietuvos Gyventojai, 2003). Before the 1990s the Total Fertility Rate (TRF) was 2 and later decreased from 1.97 in 1992 to 1.24 in 2002 (Demographic Yearbook, 2002).

Lithuania has always been home to different nationalities, and the ethnic composition of the population has varied over time. According to the 2001 Population Census, it contained 115 nationalities. This census recorded the highest share of Lithuanians in the present territory (83.45% of the population), with Poles representing 6.7%, Russians 6.3%, Belarusians 1.2%, Ukrainians 0.7%, and Jews, Germans, Tartars, Latvians and Romanians making up around 0.1% each. People of other nationalities made up 0.2% of the population, and the remaining 0.95% refused to identify their nationality (Results, 2002).

Economic Conditions

Since the 1990s, the economic situation in Lithuania has been affected by crises. These are due to the transition from a centralized planned to a market economy and privatization. The transitional period was marked by significant changes in the economic structure, increased unemployment and inflation. In 1990, a new law on the Employment of Population was passed. The definition of unemployment was introduced and an official registration system of the jobless was implemented. According to a labor force survey, unemployment dropped from 17.4% in 1994 to 13.3% in 1998, followed by an increase to 17% in 2001 as a consequence of the Russian economic crisis. Employment among men is higher than that of women (52.6 and 45.8% in 2001) (Demographic Situation, 2002; Results, 2003; Statistical Yearbook, 2003). Two distinct trends have appeared in unemployment. Firstly, there are an increasing number of unemployed professionals whose services in low demand on the labor market. This leads to a mismatch between supply and demand on the labor market. Secondly, the rate of unemployment among young people under 25 years of age is particularly high (31% in 2000).

Despite the rapid economic growth, the increase in wages has been very low (3 times lower than in Latvia and Estonia), with as much as two-thirds of the population not earning the average wage. In 2003, food prices were 2.1% lower than in 2002, whereas housing, water, electricity and gas prices were 3.8% higher (Ambrazas, 2003). In 2000, 16% of the population lived below the poverty line. Lithuania's current economy is characterized by economic growth and low inflation.

Impact of the Socio-Political and Economic Context on Family Life

The Soviet period was characterized by rapidly growing industrialization, urbanization and collectivization of the country after World War II. A range of factors influenced families. These included violent armed resistance against the Soviet occupation, mass deportations to Siberia and labor camps, the changing ethnic structure of the population due to Soviet national policy and migration. Additionally, a full employment policy and a considerable increase in the number of women working also had a direct impact on family life.

Family ideology during this period was based on the constructed Soviet family. This model contained various dogmatic values regarding gender roles, interrelations between spouses, as well as child-parent and family-state relations. The Soviet family was viewed as the only normal form of family life, and all others were considered to be deviant and unworkable (Juozeliūnienė, 1999). According to the full employment policy, female participation in the labor force was not an option but a duty that excluded the possibility of choosing a different lifestyle. Politically based slogans affected the role of women in family life and in work outside the home. Family and children were automatically assumed to be a woman's primary concern and their participation in the labor force did not change this attitude (Juozeliūnienė & Kanopienė, 1995).

Soviet national policy was designed to abolish obstacles (secular, religious) to the formation of multiethnic families. New industrial centers were established to protect and employ large groups of new immigrants (especially Russians). In addition, privileges were implemented for members of multi-ethnic families to allow them to advance in social and professional careers (Kalnius, 1989; Kuzmickaitė, 1992). Thus, the late European marriage pattern, which prevailed in Lithuania until the mid-20th century, was replaced by early marriage. During the Soviet period, family formation through marriage remained universal. Therefore, cohabitation and births outside marriage were stigmatized, as they corresponded to neither the Soviet family ideology nor the Catholic tradition. Single parent families were rare and a decline in traditional large families resulted in an increase in small families.

After restoration of an independent Lithuanian state, the country faced important changes in family life and patterns. These included a decrease in the number of marriages, postponement of first marriages and parenthood, and an increase in both divorce and cohabitation. The economic crises of the early 1990s determined these changes. The transition from a centrally planned to market economy and privatization, new migration features, new trends in family ideology were all contributory factors (Stankūnienė et al., 2003). The transitional period was marked by economic instability, a significant decline in living standards, a rise in unemployment, changes to economic activity (employment in private and public sectors, financial mediation and commercial activities), the formation of a dwelling market, and a steep rise in housing prices. The new migration features were seen as a direct response to declining living conditions (Sipavičienė et al., 1997).

In addition to the structural and economic changes, the liberalization of society also had a significant impact on family life. It determined changes in values such as increased individualization, freedom and independence, reduced acceptance of normative constraints and institutional regulations of the state and the church. New demands such as faithfulness, mutual understanding, and respect regulated the quality of interpersonal relations (Jonkarytė, 2001). Fluctuations in demographic indicators and changes in matrimonial behavior are seen as a specific adaptive reaction to rapidly and controversially changing conditions.

FAMILY DEMOGRAPHICS IN LITHUANIA

Recent changes in matrimonial and fertility behavior have raised the question of whether the family still maintains a stable position among other Lithuanian values.

Data obtained from the European Value Study (EVS) carried out in 1990 and 1999 indicate that the family has not lost its priority compared to friends, jobs, politics, religion, or leisure time. It was rated the highest value in both 1990 and 1999. Respondents who reported that family was important in their lives constituted 94% in 1990 and 96% in 1999. In both years it was women who assessed the family as being more important (Mitrikas, 2000a, b).

Marriage

Since 1987, a decrease in the number of marriages has been evident in Lithuania. The number of marriages dropped from 36,300 in 1990 to 15,800 in 2001, with a slight increase to 16,200 in 2002 (Demographic Yearbook, 2003). A shift in marriage timing has also taken place. The mean age of women at their first marriage increased from 22.4 in 1990 to 24.3 in 2002. What is more, men are getting married 1–2 years later in age than women (Demographic Situation, 2002; Demographic Yearbook, 2003; Statistical Yearbook, 2003).

The Fertility and Family Survey (FFS) conducted in Lithuania in 1994–1995 showed that changes such as postponing marriage and the spread of cohabitation occurred in the cohort born in the early 1970s, especially among men (Stankūnienė, 2001). In the late 1980s and early 1990s there was a sharp increase in marriages for men aged 19–21. Before the declaration of independence, young Lithuanian men started families earlier in order to escape military service in the Soviet army. Marriage and childbearing were legal ways to be granted exemption from service in the army. Young women born between 1970 and 1976 demonstrated unusual strategies in marital behavior. Unemployed women with a lower education married early, raised children and defined themselves as housewives. Women seeking a higher education (university degree) postponed marriage and were more interested in their professional career (Stankūnienė et al., 2000).

Family Structure

The average size of the family has decreased from 3.57 family members in 1959 to 3.18 in 2001 (Demographic Situation, 2002; Results, 2003). In 1989, there were 1,000,000 families comprising 3,220,400 people. By 2001 there were around 962,600 families comprising 3,059,000 people. The number of families consisting of three or more persons has been falling from 722 (per 1,000 families) in 1959 to 643 in 2001. The number of families consisting of 2 persons increased from 278 (per 1,000 families) in 1959 to 357 in 2001 (Demographic Situation, 2002; Results,

2003). In 2001, nearly one third of all families consisted of two people, 28.2% of three and 24.5% of four people. Almost one in nine families are comprised of five or more persons (Results, 2003). The Household Budget Survey from 2001 indicated that 5.4% of families were headed by a single mother and 0.2% by a single father. Childless couples made up 18.4% (*Women and Men*, 2002).

Until recent years, due to the cultural and Catholic traditions, cohabitation was considered as a deviant partnership and was an infrequent occurrence in Lithuania. However, since the 1990s cohabitation has rapidly increased, either as a precursor or an alternative to marriage. According to the FFS findings, each younger cohort has a greater number of experiences of living in a consensual union. Eight percent of men and 12.1% of women in the 1971–1975 birth cohorts had experienced living in a consensual union, whereas in the 1946–1949 birth cohorts these rates stood correspondingly at 0.4 and 3.1%. Younger cohorts perceive consensual unions as socially tolerated. However, more women than men view that living together as socially unacceptable (Stankūnienė, 1997). In support of the growing popularity of consensual unions is the increasing number of children born outside marriage since the beginning of the 1990s. In Lithuania, the proportion of such children has increased from 7% in 1991 to 27.9% in 2002 (Children, 2002; Demographic Situation, 2002; Demographic Yearbook, 2003).

Postponement of births to a later age can be observed among younger people. The abortion rates have gradually decreased in recent years, from 44.2 per 1,000 women in 1990 to 14.1 in 2002 (Demographic Situation, 2002; Demographic Yearbook, 2003). FFS findings indicate that generally both women and men want to have two children. However, the proportion of voluntary childlessness seems likely to rise, especially in younger cohorts (born in 1975–1977), as 10% of men and women indicated that they would not like to have any children. The number of women who wanted to have one child varied from 21% in the older cohort (1945–1950) to 6% in the youngest cohort (1975–1977). Among the dominant reasons given for the unwillingness to have more children or to have them at all, were materialistic concerns, namely the fact that "it is expensive to raise children." Difficulties in combining maternal and professional careers were also cited reasons (Stankūnienė et al., 2000). Data obtained by the European Value Study (EVS) also indicated that while children are still considered important for marital happiness, they are no longer the highest priority. Faithfulness, mutual respect and understanding within a couple are now given greater value (Mitrikas, 2000a, b). Women consider having children a priority among other family issues such as psychological support, marital quality, feelings of security, sexual relations, etc. Men consider having children as being less important compared to the issue of supplying a family with the means to survive (Purvaneckas & Purvaneckienė, 2001).

GENDER ROLES IN THE FAMILY

Although gender equality was proclaimed in the Soviet period, the domestic domain was treated as a private sphere, and the behavior of women and men was not widely discussed. The upbringing of children was considered a mother's natural duty, while the issues of the father's obligations and role remained a private matter. According to the 1988 Lithuanian Population Survey, the approval of traditional gender roles persisted, especially among men. The primary role of women was viewed as taking care of the family, and the devotion of the majority of their time to household duties. Regular participation in the performance of domestic duties by the husband only took place in one-third of the families. Male participation in housework was more commonly represented in the younger generation and the more highly educated (Juozeliūnienė & Kanopienė, 1995).

Research shows that household chores occupy 2.5 times more of a woman's life than a man's (Karalienė, 1991). Following the restoration of the independent Lithuanian state, the socialist slogan: "a woman worker in production" was changed to "woman mother in the family." Her homemaker role was viewed as the most desirable from the perspective of women, family, and society. FFS findings (1995) reveal that the main role allocated to the man in the family was that of breadwinner. The greatest responsibility for the care of the family, such as taking care of disabled or sick family members, and the raising of children, lay with women. They undertook the greatest amount of routine housework, cooking, cleaning, and laundry. In contrast, men were more engaged in activities outside the home. Few women received assistance from their husbands (Kanopienė, 1999).

The data on attitudes towards gender roles indicate changes in the preferred family models. In 1991, 62% of respondents preferred the traditional model of the family, where the husband is the breadwinner and the wife is the housekeeper. In 2000, 67% preferred the symmetric model, where both husband and wife are engaged in professional activities and share the responsibilities of family life (Purvaneckienė, 1995). At that time, the proportion of women who preferred to stay at home decreased from 51 to 20% in 1994. The proportion of women who preferred to be involved in professional activities with a high salary increased from 45 to 79% (Purvaneckas & Purvaneckienė, 2001).

FAMILY PROCESSES

In Lithuania, there were many rituals and customs related to birth. The birth of an infant was considered an important event not only in the life of the family, but for the whole community. These customs can be divided in two periods: (1) before childbearing; and (2) after child bearing. The first one included customs related to pregnancy, i.e. following inherited traditions concerning the fate and happiness of the child. The second period started after the delivery, when the infant was introduced to the family and community.

Over fifty years of Soviet rule resulted in many changes to family customs and traditions. During this period new social rituals were also introduced such as those related to retirement, transition to adulthood, and Women's Day (Vyšniauskaitė et al., 1995). In the Soviet period, a number of marriage ceremonies disappeared (e.g. matchmaking, and the return visit of the newly weds to the bride's home), while others such as parties where everybody brought their own treats, most often held in the bride's home, survived. Other family festivities included christenings, Christmas Eve, name days and birthdays, Mother's Day and Father's Day.

Religion had an important impact on family life in Lithuania. In 1251, the Grand Duke of Lithuania Mindaugas adopted Catholicism. From 1799 to 1915, the Russian Orthodox faith was the official religion, while during the period of the Lithuanian Republic (1918–1940) the Catholic Church regained its rights. Lithuania's occupation by the Soviet Union caused major losses to all churches. In 1990, the Act of Restitution of the Catholic Church was promulgated. By 2001, there were 12 religions registered (Results, 2002).

Lithuanian family life from the 19th century until the beginning of the 20th century was closely related to the Catholic Church. The greatest influence from the clergy came through the preachment of the Christian family model in encyclicals and sermons, and through administration and supervision of the matrimony sacrament. Also, the Sacrament of Penance had a particular impact on the family life. The religious community was focused on the spiritual development of children, and taught them to follow the postulated requirements of moral education. In the second half of the 20th century, the influence of the Church on family life greatly declined, and now remains only in the form of various rituals.

CHILDREN IN LITHUANIA

In 2002, there were 828,000 children under 18 years of age (23.8% of the population) (Children of Lithuania, 2002). In 2001, there were 13,500 orphaned and homeless children, 57% of whom lived in families, 3% in foster families, and 40% in different child care institutions. A hundred and eighty children were adopted during 2001, with approximately every fourth child adopted by a foreign family. Before 2001, foreigners adopted about one-third of all adopted children.

In the 19th century, the Lithuanian family was playing the main educational role, with the father at the top of the hierarchy of family relations. The wife's duties included caring for the physical and emotional well-being of her husband and children (Vasiliauskas, 2002). The degree of child socialization was dependent not only on the conditions in the family, but also on how actively the child was involved in the life of the neighborhood or religious community.

In the Soviet period, rural children were traditionally disciplined for farm work, and importance was attributed to fostering their diligence, care for the environment, orderliness, and love for the motherland (Rupšienė, 2001). However, both in the countryside and in the cities, the Soviet ideology caused complications for parent-child relations. The value of children also changed significantly. As the birthrate declined, their importance increased, and more attention was paid to their full-scale education, and more leisure time was spent with them. Opinion polls revealed that families with underage children were more likely to use moral rather than physical means of persuasion (Vyšniauskaitė et al., 1995).

A poll conducted in 1990–1993 showed that parents generally assessed communication with their children positively. Forty-four percent stated that their relations were cordial, while 52% wished that their relations were closer and more open. Only 4% were dissatisfied with their relations, saying that over time it was increasingly difficult to communicate with their children (Grincevičienė, 1997).

Among other issues, international studies on the health and behavior of school children conducted in Lithuania in 1994 and 1998 looked at their relationships with parents, siblings and peers (Zaborskis & Makari, 2001). The results indicated that older boys and girls found their relations with parents more difficult than the younger ones. Both boys and girls found it easier to come to an understanding with their mothers than with their fathers. Additionally, more girls than boys indicated that was difficult to share their worries with their fathers. As a girl grows, her relations with her father become much more complicated (in the 1998 study, only one-third of the girls indicated that they could talk openly with their fathers) (Zaborskis & Makari, 2001). Comparison of the results of the 1994–1998 studies revealed a noticeable downward trend in open communication with parents. They showed that most of the teenagers had two or more close friends, with younger teenagers, especially boys, claiming to have more friends. This could indicate that the social integration of boys was better than that of girls.

RESEARCH ON THE FAMILY

Different aspects of family life are studied at Lithuanian Universities as well as Research centers. The Fertility and Family Survey (FFS) was undertaken by the Population Activities Unit (PAU) of the United Nations Economic Commission for Europe (UN/ECE). The main topics of this study were population size and age structure, fertility, mortality, household composition, partnership formation and dissolution, children, values and beliefs, women's education and employment. The 1994–1995 study by the Demographic Research Center under the Lithuanian Institute of Philosophy and Sociology involved a sample of 5,000 respondents (3,000 females and 2,000 males) aged 18–49 (Stankūnienė et al., 2000).

The Second European Comparative Survey on the Acceptance of Population-related Policies (PPA2), was carried out in 2001 by the Demographic Research Center under the Lithuanian Institute of Philosophy and Sociology. This study analyzed the following topics: attitudes towards marriage, divorce, and cohabitation, the number of children in a family, out-of-wedlock births, single parent families, opinions on the role of the government in solving problems such as youth employment, combining professional activity with childcare, housing, health protection, and care for the elderly. The sample included 1,400 respondents (787 females and 613 males) aged 18–75 (Stankūnienė et al., 2003).

Values related to family issues as well as to work, friends, leisure, politics, and religion were examined through the European Value Study (EVS) conducted in 1990 and in 1999. This study was requested by the center for "Baltic Research" at the Institute of Culture and Art. The sample included 1,020 respondents (in 1990) and 1,018 respondents (in 1999) aged 18–75 (Mitrikas, 2000a, b). In 1993–1994 the international comparative six-country sociological study "Social Change in Baltic and Nordic Countries" (including a sample of 1,483 respondents) was conducted. Also, in 1995 the "Lithuanian Household Panel Study" was carried out as a part of the international project "Family and Living Conditions in the Baltic States." Both studies were completed by the Lithuanian Institute of Philosophy and Sociology and included a study of household tendencies such as family income management and survival strategies (Everyday Life in the Baltic States, 1997).

Attitudes towards marriage, divorce, the ideal family model, children, abortion, abuse in the family, equal opportunities for men and women, and views concerning the government's implementation of social policy in Lithuania were analyzed in the "Gender Roles in the Family" study. This was carried out in 1994 and 2000 with a sample of 1,522 respondents (Purvaneckas & Purvaneckienė, 2001).

In Lithuania, sociological research on the family was dominated for a long time by the structural functionalism perspective. The family was defined with the help of structural elements and socially normative functions. New trends in family research and the diversity of the conceptualization of the family in Western sociological theories have introduced new family research methodologies in Lithuania (Juozeliūnienė, 2003).

POLICIES AND PROGRAMS
SUPPORTING FAMILIES

During the Soviet period, assistance for families was on a theoretical level. Only a few specific measures were implemented. These included paid maternity leave (16 weeks), benefits for children from large families up to five years of age, and benefits for children up until the age of eight in poor families. An institutionalized childcare system was developed as a part of social policy. These measures were closely connected with both the full employment policy the model of the family budget based on two wages (the husband's and the wife's). In the early 1980s, other significant family assistance measures were adopted. However, these were only important in terms of the care of very small children. The main goals of the new family policy were formulated in the Population Program, prepared in 1989–1990. Family policy in Lithuania in 1989–1992 focused mainly on increasing the financial support for families with young children. Many people were paid benefits, but only in very small amounts (Stankūnienė, 1995).

In 1994, a working group composed of scientists and representatives of governmental and non-governmental institutions worked out the development strategy of a national family policy. It was entitled, Conception of Lithuanian Family Policy and Program of Actions. The document contained the objectives and principles of family policy, and actions of family policy. That is, the economic basis of family viability (participation in the labor market, housing arrangements, financial support of families by the government), family stability, maternal and child health, family planning, child care, and child protection, integration of elderly and disabled people in society, gender equality and equity (Stankūnienė et al., 1996).

While family policy in Lithuania is still being developed, it is already systematic and complex in character. Assistance offered to families raising children includes family benefits, family and labor market policy, preferential health care services, preferential terms to buy or rent housing, discounts to use public transport, and discounts to rent and purchase land (Mikalauskaitė et al., 1999). The Social Support Conception adopted in 1994 stipulates that support will be offered to eligible persons so that they can become fully or partially independent.

There is also a Law on State Allowances to Families with Children, which has been applicable in Lithuania since 1994. In the period of command economy, the key objective of family policy was higher birth rates in order to provide the country with a workforce. Therefore, the policy of family allowances was also targeted towards an increase in births. The present family policy is different, not only in terms of the objective to increase births, but also with regard to balancing family life and career, compensating the costs of raising children, and providing aid to poor families. Efforts are being made to strengthen the protection of specific groups (multi-child families, children in risk groups, students, etc.). The de-institutionalization policy is underway in which preference is given to family-like homes as an alternative to public childcare institutions. What is more, efforts are being made to reduce the institutionalization of risk groups through the development of new models of social services (Lazutka et al., 1999). In 1996, the Concept of Youth Policy was approved to develop and implement measures for professional orientation and integration of youth into the labor market. Policies that are targeted at different risk groups offer assistance to alcohol and drug addicts and their families, as well as individuals following imprisonment.

REFERENCES

Ambrazas, G. (2003). Ekonominis fenomenas prieštarauja logikai. *Respublika, liepos, 31* (Economic Interest Contradicts the Logic. *Republic, 31*).
Children of Lithuania (2002). Vilnius: Lithuanian Statistics.
Demographic situation in Lithuania 1990–2001 (2002).Vilnius: Lithuanian Statistics.
Demographic Yearbook 2002 (2003).Vilnius: Lithuanian Statistics.
Everyday Life in the Baltic States (1997). M. Taljūnaitė (Ed.). Vilnius: Institute of Philosophy and Sociology, Centre for Russian and East European Studies, University of Goteborg.
Grincevičienė, V. (1997). Tėvų ir vaikų santykių sistema Lietuvai atgavus nepriklausomybę (1990–1993). *Pedagogika, 34,* 42–52 (The System of the Parents-Children Relations in Lithuania after the Restoration of Independence (1990–1993). *Pedagogics,* 34, 42–52).
Jonkarytė, A. (2001). Family and fertility in Lithuania: Between traditional and post-modern values and norms. Unpublished paper presented at the Euro-Conference on Family and Fertility Change in Modern European Societies: Explorations and Explanations of Recent Developments, Bad Herrenalb, Germany.
Juozeliūnienė, I. (2003). Janas Trostas ir šeimos sociologija: naujos tyrinėjimo galimybės. Vilnius: Garnelis. (Jan Trost and family sociology: New trends in research studies. Vilnius: Garnelis.)
Juozeliūnienė, I. (1999). Political systems and responsibility for family issues: The case of change in Lithuania. *Marriage & Family Review, 28*(3/4), 67–79.
Juozeliūnienė, I., & Kanopienė, V. (1995). Women and family in Lithuania. In: B. Lobodzinska (Ed.), *Family, Women, and Employment in Central-Eastern Europe* (pp. 155–165). Westport, Connecticut, London: Greenwood Press.
Kalnius, P. (1989). *Šeima tautinių santykių kolizijoje. Komjaunimo tiesa, gegužės, 12.* (*Family and the collision of ethnic relations. The truth of the Young Communist League, 12.*)
Kanopienė, V. (1999). Women and labor market in Lithuania. In: G. Purvaneckienė & J. Šeduikienė (Ed.), *Women in Lithuania* (pp. 62–78). Vilnius: Women's Issues Information Center.
Karalienė, M. (1991). Women status in the family and society. *The Economist of Lithuania, 3,* 3–4.
Kuzmickaitė, L. (1992). Etniškai mišrios šeimos Lietuvoje. In: I. Juozeliūnienė (Ed.), *Pasaulis ir Šeima* (pp. 45–50). Vilnius: Institute of Philosophy, Sociology and Law. (Inter-ethnic families in Lithuania. In: I.Juozeliūnienė (Ed.), *World and Family* (pp. 45–50). Vilnius: Institute of Philosophy, Sociology and Law.)

Lazutka R., Bernotas, D., Deveikytė, R., Jočytė, R., Karčiauskienė, A., Karpuškienė, V., & Žalimienė, L. (1999). *Socialinės paramos šeimoms, auginančioms vaikus, ekonominio efektyvumo įvertinimas: Pranešimas*. Vilnius: Socialinės apsaugos ir darbo ministerija, Socialinės politikos grupė. (*The evaluation of economic efficiency of the support to the families with children: Report*. Vilnius: The Ministry of Social Security and Labour, The Group for Social Policy).

Lietuvos Gyventojai Pagal Amžių 2001–2003 (2003). Vilnius: Statistikos departamentas. (Population of Lithuania in age groups 2001–2003. (2003). Vilnius: The Department of Statistics.)

Mikalauskaitė, A., Mitrikas, A., & Stankūnienė, V. (1999). Family policy in Lithuania: Principles, experience, and expectations. *Revue Baltique*, *13*, 198–213.

Mitrikas, A. (2000a). Šeimos vertybių pokyčiai. *Kultūrologija*, *6*, 215–223 (The changes in family values. *Culturology*, *6*, 215–223).

Mitrikas, A. (2000b). Šeimos vertybių pokyčiai pastaruoju dešimtmečiu. *Filosofija, Sociologija,*, *4*, 66–73 (The changes in family values during the last decade. *Philosophy, Sociology*, *4*, 66–73).

Purvaneckas, A., & Purvaneckienė, G. (2001). *Moteris Lietuvos visuomenėje: palyginamoji tyrimų analizė*. Vilnius: Danielius. (*Women in the Lithuanian society: Comparative analysis of research data*. Vilnius: Danielius.)

Purvaneckienė, G. (1995). *Moteris Lietuvoe visuomenėje. Tyrimo ataskaita*. Vilnius: Jungtinių tautų vystymo programa. (*Women in the Lithuanian society. Report on the survey*. Vilnius: UNDP.)

Results of the 2001 Population and Housing Census in Lithuania: Employment (2003). Vilnius: Lithuanian Statistics.

Results of the 2001 Population and Housing Census in Lithuania: Households (2003). Vilnius: Lithuanian Statistics.

Results of the 2001 Population and Housing Census in Lithuania: Population by Sex, Age, Ethnicity and Religion (2002). Vilnius: Lithuanian Statistics.

Rupšienė, L. (2001). *Šeimotyros įvadas. Studijų knyga*. Klaipėda: Klaipėdos universiteto leidykla. (*Introduction to family studies. Textbook*. Klaipėda: Klaipėda University Press.)

Sipavičienė, A., Kanopienė, V., Stankūnienė, V., Česnuitytė, V., & Čiurlionytė, R. (1997). *International migration in Lithuania: Causes, consequences, strategy*. Vilnius: United Nations Economic Commision for Europe.

Stankūnienė, V. (1997). New phenomena in family formation: Case of Lithuania. *Revue Baltique*, *8*, 55–65.

Stankūnienė, V. (1995). Family policy in Lithuania: Experience and attitudes. In: M. Taljūnaitė (Ed.), *Lithuanian Society in Social Transition* (pp. 60–69). Vilnius: Institute of Philosophy, Sociology and Law.

Stankūnienė, V. (2001). A changing Lithuanian family throughout the 20th century. Unpublished paper presented at the XXIV General Population Conference, Salvador – Brazil.

Stankūnienė, V., Baublytė, M., Kanopienė, V., & Mikulionienė, S. (2000). Fertility and family surveys in countries of the ECE region: Standard country report; Lithuania. *Economic Studies, 10q*. United Nations Economic Commision for Europe, United Nations, New York and Geneva.

Stankūnienė, V., Jonkarytė, A., & Mitrikas, A. (2003). Šeimos transformacija Lietuvoje: požymiai ir veiksniai. *Filosofija, Sociologija*, *2*, 51–58 (Family transformation in Lithuania: Features and factors. *Philosophy, Sociology*, *2*, 51–58).

Stankūnienė, V., Mitrikas, A., Svirskaitė, I., Gruževskis, B., Klimas, V., Lazutka, R., Purvaneckienė, G., Vainauskienė, V., & Žibaitis, R. (1996). *Family policy in Lithuania: Principles and actions*. Vilnius: Institute of Philosophy and Sociology.

Statistical Yearbook of Lithuania 2002 (2003). Vilnius: Lithuanian Statistics.

Vasiliauskas, R. J. (2002). *Lietuvių liaudies pedagogika – jaunosios kartos socializacijos fenomenas (XIX a. antroji pusė – XX a. pradžia)*. Vilnius: Vilniaus pedagoginis universitetas. (*Lithuanian folk pedagogy – The phenomenon of the socialization of young generation (XIXth second half – The beginning of XXth century)*. Vilnius: Vilnius Pedagogical University.)

Vyšniauskaitė, A., Kalnius, P., & Paukštytė, R. (1995). *Lietuvių šeima ir papročiai*. Vilnius: Mintis. (*Lithuanian family and customs*. Vilnius: Mintis.)

Women and Men in Lithuania 2001 (2002). Vilnius: Lithuanian Statistics.

Zaborskis, A., & Makari, J. (2001). *Lietuvos moksleivių gyvensena: Raida 1994–1998 metais ir vertinimas tarptautiniu požiūriu*. Panevėžys: E.Vaičekausko leidykla. (*Everyday life of Lithuanian school children: Development in the period 1994–1998 and international Estimation*. Panevėžys: E.Vaičekauskas Press.)

MARRIAGE AND FAMILIES
IN LATVIA

Parsla Eglite

SOCIO-HISTORIC AND ECONOMIC
CONTEXT OF THE COUNTRY

Latvia is situated on the Eastern Coast of the Baltic Sea – on the shipping route between North-West Europe and Russia. Because of its location, this territory has been conquered and re-divided by crusaders from Germany, Poland, Sweden, and Russia. As a result of repeated wars, Latvians were enslaved for seven centuries and partly mixed with warrior populations. Only after World War I in 1918 was the independent state of Latvia established. Its peaceful development was interrupted by the beginning of World War II. On the basis of the Molotov-Ribbentrop pact between Stalin and Hitler, Latvia was forcibly annexed by the Soviet Union. The country suffered enormous population losses. During the first year of Soviet rule, the subsequent years of Nazi occupation, military pursuits, people seeking refuge in the West (around 200,000), and the Stalinist repressions and deportations to Siberia, Latvia's net loss in population amounted to 30% of the prewar population. It is doubtful whether any other nation, except for the Jews, ever suffered such enormous population losses as a consequence of World War II. Only a third of them returned to Latvia after 10–15 years' exile in Siberia.

In the meantime, thousands upon thousands of migrants from other Soviet republics, especially from Russia, flooded into Latvia. It was among the most developed areas of the Soviet Union, and massive migration did not stop until the late 1980s. During the last two decades of the occupation, net migration in Latvia

Families in Eastern Europe
Contemporary Perspectives in Family Research, Volume 5, 225–236
Copyright © 2004 by Elsevier Ltd.
All rights of reproduction in any form reserved
ISSN: 1530-3535/doi:10.1016/S1530-3535(04)05014-9

exceeded natural population growth (Demographic, 2002). The total number of migrants and their descendants reached nearly 36% of the country's population before the Soviet period ended in 1989 (Results, 2002). It made ethnic Latvians, like other small nations, very sensitive as regards the survival of their language and culture.

The independent state of Latvia was restored in 1990 when the former USSR and the totalitarian Soviet regime collapsed. On a global scale it is a small country, with only 2,331,000 people in 2003 (Demographic, 2002). Population numbers have been declining because of both emigration of former colonists and a decrease in the natural growth of the population.

Social Forces

Latvia is a parliamentary republic with a president having mainly representative functions. Deputies to the Saeima – the Latvian legislative body – are elected in universal, direct, competitive elections according to parties' lists. During 50 years of the occupation there were no democratic elections and only one ruling party. New parties' leaders do not have political skills and experience (e.g. in organizing parties, running elections). The Constitution states that the sovereign power in the Latvian Republic is the people. In reality, election campaigns and other activities of the more visible parties are funded by the wealthy – banks, owners of property secured in the process of recent privatization, and probably also international companies interested in securing advantageous conditions for their businesses. After the collapse of the former USSR, only prewar citizens and their descendants were granted citizenship and electoral rights. People from other territories of the Soviet Union are allowed to become naturalized, provided they know the state's language – Latvian. Up until the end of the 20th century, this was done by almost 40% of Russian-speaking residents, while 21% of the population remains non-citizens (Demographic, 2002).

Economic Conditions

A centrally planned economy, which existed in the former USSR, including annexed Latvia, proved to be inefficient. The standard of living and the competitiveness of Soviet enterprises on the global market were correspondingly low. The latter led to a high unemployment rate during the transition. The lack of savings and private capital prevents people from starting their own businesses or restoring and using denationalized houses or farms.

During the 13 years of transition to a free market economy, Latvia has not yet managed to achieve the levels of developed countries. In 2001, the Gross Domestic Product (GDP) was 4.4 times less than in the USA or 3.1 times less than the average in the European Union (Population, 2003). Average income per family member in 2000 was only US$115 per month and almost 40% of expenditures were spent on food (Household, 2001). Household ownership of appliances and long-term use items corresponds to the level of income. In 1999, only 30% of households had a car, 69.3% had a laundry washing machine, 86% had a refrigerator, and 4% had a PC at home (Eglite, 2001). Income and ownership of different appliances differ by type of household. For example, single persons have 1.25 times more income than average; couples without children have 1.13 times more; but couples with children under 16 have only 93% of the average; and one adult with a child or children under age 16 has 77% (Household, 2001). Nevertheless, couples with children are better equipped than all others with respect to modern appliances: cars are owned by 55% of them, laundry washing machines by 84%, refrigerators by 93% and PCs by 10%.

Impact of Socio-Political and Economic Context on Family Life

The loss of many of the men and the separation of couples during both World Wars I and II, as well as the massive deportation of the population to the Eastern part of the USSR in 1949, poverty, and fears of repressions resulted in a decrease in the number of births and in the proportion of happy families. The number of children in families has been also impacted by changes in the state's social policy. At the beginning of the 1980s, partly paid childcare leave was introduced in the USSR, creating a 10% increase in the fertility rate.

At the beginning of the transition period, the state's support to families changed. Under the Soviets, the goal was to achieve full employment of mothers and to provide childcare in childcare state centers. Since the transition to a free market economy, mother's care for children up to 2–3 years was given priority. A large number of nurseries were closed, and the women' employment rate decreased to 88% that of males. As the childcare allowance in Latvia is only half the minimum wage, single parent families are among the poorest strata of the population. The percentage of families under the poverty line is proportional to the number of children in the family (Latvia, 1997). This situation has led to a further decrease in fertility below the replacement level and the number of children desired. In families with low income, expenditures for the child's nutrition and additional education are limited, and therefore satisfaction with family life and the stability of marriage has declined.

FAMILY DEMOGRAPHIC PATTERNS IN LATVIA

According to the Latvian Civil Code, only unmarried or divorced heterosexual people 18 years of age or older are allowed to marry. Spouses and parents have equal rights and responsibilities. A wife is allowed to keep her previous surname and nationality, her place of residence, and to manage her own property. A marriage may be officially registered either at a church or at the civil registration office. Out of wedlock children have the same rights to state support as those born to married couples. However, the allowance in case of a parent's death, or in the case of alimonies or heritage, are available only to children born to married parents or if the paternity is recognized by the father or by the court. Divorce is allowed only in court and alimonies are proportional to parents' income.

The equal rights for married and unmarried couples and their children give no advantages to marriage. This may be one of the reasons for the considerable decrease in the marriage rate from 9.2 per 1,000 inhabitants at the end of the Soviet period to 3.9 in 2000. Cohabiting increased (especially premarital) up to the birth of the first child (Eglite, 2002). Nevertheless, 60% of Latvian women consider that the traditional concept of family is not out-dated (Markausa, 2002). The main reasons for the low marriage rate are the state's insufficient support for new families (67% of respondents), increased independence of women (47%), and lack of appropriate men for marriage (41%) (Markausa, 2002).

For six centuries, marital behavior in Latvia has followed Christian customs, but during the last century it experienced several changes according to the social situation. Since an independent Latvian Republic was declared, the civic registration of marriages and divorces has been allowed but has happened rarely. In 2000, the mean age at marriage was 26 years for men and 24 for women, after they had gained a safe job or acquired some property (Demographic Yearbook, 2001). Under the Soviets, marriages were used as a means to obtain a right to live in a certain city or to obtain an apartment. It was one of the reasons, between 1940 and 1989, people used to marry at rather a young age (but marriages were often dissolved).

Couples now tend to marry only after they have achieved some economic stability, graduated, and obtained a safe job. As a result, the mean age at marriage has increased. Also, premarital cohabitation is rather popular among the younger generations. In spite of the mixed composition of population by ethnicity, most people tend to marry a spouse of the same ethnic group.

Family Structure

The proportion of people living in families decreased in Latvia, from 85.6% in 1989 to 83.1% in 2000 (Results, 2002). Young couples tend to leave the parents' house as soon as possible. Only in 20% of families are three generations living together (Eglite, 2001). Separate living adds to the difficulties of childcare and contributes to the limited number of children. Almost 25% of families are childless and 45% have only one child; 24% have two children; and 7.3% have three or more (Results, 2000). Nowadays, only 60% of children are born within marriage; almost 30% among cohabiting couple with recognized paternity; and 10–12% to single mothers (Eglite, 2002).

A pension system has existed in Latvia since the 1930s – at first for civil servants, and later for all the employed. Consequently, children no longer feel responsible for providing for elderly parents. Nevertheless, according to public opinion and the Civil Code, children are expected to take care of old or sick parents. A recent survey shows that 1.7% of the fertile age population having no desire to have a child at all, and up to 6% have not thought about it (Fertility and Family Survey, 1998; Reproductive, 1998). The most popular family size remains the one with 2 or 3 children. An important reason for having a small family is represented by the large economic resources necessary for raising each child (Pavlina & Eglite, 2002). Nevertheless, not only children can ensure happiness in family life, and having them is not enough to keep the couple together forever. Among the divorced, 66.2% had common children; 45.8% had one child; and 20.7% had two or more children (Demographic, 2002).

ROLE OF WOMEN AND MEN IN THE FAMILY

In Latvia, the husband is expected to be the main earner and the wife is expected to take care of the house, children and disabled family members. However, enormous losses in the number of men during World Wars I and II, as well as in the Nazi and Stalinist repressions in the 1940s, caused a high level of women's employment. Due to the equal opportunities granted at all stages of education, women's full-time employment during the second Soviet occupation (1944–1990) equaled that of men. It led to women's economic independence and an equal role in the family's decision-making but also to a "double burden" of being both earner and homemaker. Surveys from 1972, 1987 and 1996 show that employed women spend only 4 hours a week less than men at the job but provide up to 28.8 hours housework per week (almost twice as much as men) (Time use, 1998). This resulted in rather limited leisure time for women (21.7 hours a week) – especially for wives and mothers. This situation was used as a ground for the revival of patriarchal gender roles during the transition period.

Latvians are not unanimous in their attitude toward gender roles in the family. Women with a higher level of education, and therefore with better opportunities in the labor market, tend to have full-time employment and fair division of labor within the household. Men – especially those of younger generations – increasingly share this attitude and devote an equal part of their time to family duties. Older generations support the non-equal family roles. Survey data show that 3/4 of active women and 2/3 of men support the equality of roles in a family (Rungule, 1997).

FAMILY RITUALS AND CUSTOMS

The German crusaders Christianized Latvians during the 13th century. Since then, rituals of Christian ceremonies such as confirmation, marriage and burial by a clergyman dominated up to the middle of the 20th century. During this time, many ancient customs were cultivated in addition to or mixed with Christian or other official rituals. The most popular feast for ethnic Latvians is Mid-Summer. All activities during this shortest night are devoted to raising the productivity of crops, cattle and also having children. Young girls predict their eventual wedding by putting crowns made from flowers into a stream; if two crowns meet, a wedding will take place in autumn. After the official ceremony in a church or civil registration office people continue the celebration at home, using rituals such as changing the girl's crown with the wife's cap, or stealing of the bride by the bridegroom's friends.

Easter in Latvia continues to be called the Great Day, as its length exceeds that of the night. Young boys would push girls in large wooden swings and girls offered them painted eggs. Afterwards, the eggs are put on a slope: if they meet on their way down, a wedding is expected. At Christmas, young people used to gather, dress in the costumes of different animals, and walk from home to home and at each of them play games involving catching and escaping. Again, during these games, some couples may well form. Thus, most customs are connected with family formation.

Role of Religion on Family Life

There is a wide religious diversity in Latvia. In 2000, 14% of people were Lutherans, 13% Roman Catholics, 15% Orthodox (Russian), 13.5% of different Christian denominations and 42% without any religious background (Eglite, 2002). Being used to such differences, people are tolerant of others' feelings. According to the Constitution, civil registration of marriages and divorces are allowed as well as voluntary attendance at religious lessons in schools.

Under the Soviets, marriages performed in church were not recognized as official. Although some people registered both in the church and at the civil office, the proportion of secular marriages increased significantly. The same thing happened with the divorce rate per 1000 of population, reaching a maximum of 5.5 at the end of the 1970s (Demographic, 2002). After Latvia's regained its independence, couples could choose a church or civil ceremony. Up to the end of the 20th century, the proportion of marriages in church had risen to 23.4% (Demographic, 2002). However, the proportion of religious families is smaller due to the growing percentage of cohabiting couples. Some people prefer to marry in church in the hope that it could help to prevent a divorce. Research indicates that religion alone does not add to the stability of marriage (Eglite, 2002). Ethnic Latvians choose for their children specific Latvian first names rather than Christian ones, regardless of their religiosity.

CHILDREARING PRACTICES

From birth up to 18 months, childcare is usually done at home by the mother. The parent assuming this role receives childcare allowance. This option is taken up by 80% of employed mothers, but very few fathers. The problem is that the allowance is only 50% of the minimum wage and job interruptions may well cause loss of the job or other career handicaps. Grandparents often participate in childcare. From the age of two, the state or private childcare centers can be used, although help from grandmothers, nurses or neighbors with children of the same age is more often the case. There is a certain distribution of childrearing tasks between the parents, with fathers being mainly engaged in playing (sports) and mothers in physical care (see more details in Table 1). These data show that the frequency of certain activities aimed at the child's development increases in families with highly educated parents.

The once dominating patriarchal relations in families from the 1930s have been replaced by children-centered patterns. Parents are striving to develop the child's talents in different musical, art or sports schools or in additional foreign language classes. Unfortunately, during the transition period, such possibilities are limited by the level of the family's income.

Peer Relations

During the 19th century, differences in parents' attitude toward children based on birth order and gender were evident. The oldest son of farmers and other owners of property were entitled to an inheritance, the second son used to be educated as his part of the inheritance, while daughters received a dowry. Today, the majority of families have two children and there is no difference in the parents' childrearing

Table 1. Participation of Parents in Activities With Children (1998).

Activities	Mainly Mother Education		Mainly Father Education		Both Equally Education	
	Secondary	Higher	Secondary	Higher	Secondary	Higher
Guiding in washing, cleaning	51.6	46.2	2.9	3.8	42.6	47.7
Instructing in work	40.8	25.7	11.8	12.1	40.1	53.1
Accompanying to school or nursery	62.1	47.5	8.6	12.1	22.0	26.8
Assistance in school tasks	69.5	72.2	2.9	2.5	24.2	23.0
Tales or reading before sleep	71.0	49.0	5.4	4.2	15.2	21.8
Answer on questions	33.6	26.1	3.0	2.5	58.7	62.3
Mutual singing, music	65.6	42.5	4.5	6.3	9.3	12.6
Mutual culture and entertainment	28.9	17.9	1.8	2.5	50.4	56.9
Ball games, gambling	28.1	4.9	23.4	31.4	34.2	36.4
Earns living	21.8	5.0	33.8	31.0	39.4	48.1
N	559	239	–	–	–	–

Source: Eglite, P., Pavlina I., & Markausa I. M. (1999). *Situation of Family in Latvia* (p. 82). Riga: Institute of Economics.

attitude. Regardless of gender and birth order, they can aspire to an equal degree of education and at least part of an eventual inheritance. According to the Civil Code, even in a case where a late parent's will leaves all the property to one of the children, 50% is to be divided equally among the others.

Education

Since 1919, boys and girls have been entitled to a mandatory sixth-grade education. Further education was not free of charge and parents of moderate income preferred to promote boys' education. During the Soviet occupation, all levels of education were free of charge. Among the younger generations, girls received more education than boys. This process has continued following the transition to a free market economy. Although only nine grades are mandatory, 88.3% of boys and 92.7% of girls aged 16–18 are enrolled in secondary education and 54.2 and 90.6% respectively of those 19–23 years of age are in tertiary education (Educational, 2003).

Parents support their daughters' schooling because it offers the possibility to obtain a safe workplace such as that of a teacher, physician, civil officer, clerk in financial institutions, artists, etc. Education is especially important in a situation of unemployment and heavy competition in the labor market. In addition, most parents do their best to support their children's education in music, arts and sports. Educational activity is higher in families where the parents have college degrees. Some less educated parents prefer to encourage their children to work on their farm instead of sending them to school.

RESEARCH ON THE FAMILY

Research on the family conducted in Latvia during the last 20–30 years has been inspired mainly by the problems connected with family life: low birth rate and high divorce rate. Studies have focused mainly on demographic and sociological topics including: actual and desired number of children according to parents' generation, educational level, employment, income, ethnicity, etc. (Fertility, 1998; Pavlina & Eglite, 2002; Zarina, 1995, 1999); use of time on unpaid house care by each of the spouses according to age and type of family (Eglite et al., 1999; Time, 1998); men and women's attitudes towards gender roles, distribution of tasks, women's employment and independence (Koroleva, 1999; Rungule, 1997).

During the transition period, Latvian methodologies have converted from the Soviet to international standards; thus, the data can be used in international comparisons. Yearly data on demographic events and household budgets are available. The Central Statistical Bureau has also conducted some regional cross-cultural surveys, e.g. on the population's living conditions in 1994 and 1999 as well as a time use survey in 1996 according to Eurostat methodology. Several specialized cross-cultural studies were maintained by different scientific institutions and health protection agencies. Among them were the Family Fertility Survey, conducted by the Demographic Centre of Latvian University in 1995, using common internationally accepted methodology, and surveys on reproductive health supported by the World Health Organization (1997). In addition, Latvian researchers have been active in presenting the results of inter-country studies at international conferences of demographers and sociologists, both abroad and in Latvia (e.g. on men's role in the family, organized in Riga in 1998).

POLICIES AND PROGRAMS SUPPORTING FAMILIES

Policies

Having regained independence from the former USSR, Latvia developed its own family policy in 1991. It is aimed mainly at reversing the decrease in birth rates characteristic of the transition period, a trend viewed as dangerous to the survival of small nations such as Latvia.

Maternity benefit. Women are entitled to maternity benefits for 56 or 70 calendar days preceding the expected day of delivery and 56 or 70 calendar days (in case of complications) after delivery. These benefits are at a rate of 100% of the wage during the last 6 months.

Birth grants are paid from the state budget to the mother in the amount of 100% of the "childcare set" (a definite value of necessary goods). The amount is around US$330–340.

A *childcare allowance* is paid from the state's budget to a mother or father not employed full-time or taking childcare leave for a child up to two years of age. Since 1998, the allowance is around US$50 per month. By comparison, the minimum wage is almost US$135 and the official subsistence minimum is US$140–150.

Childcare leave since 1996 is available to an employed mother or father.

The State's *family allowance* is paid to a mother residing in Latvia for no less than six months for every child until 15 years of age (or longer if the child attends secondary school). Since 2003, the allowance has been US$10 per month for the first child, 1.2 times more for the second, 1.8 times more for the third and further children.

A *sickness benefit* for the care of sick children under 14 years of age for up to 14 days is paid as social insurance to employed parents.

In addition, a few minor programs for children are operated through other social programs, such as a disabled children allowance (pension program), a foster children allowance, and a lump-sum payment (social assistance programs). Since the amounts of the family and childcare allowances were kept constant for several years while the consumer price index continued to rise, the current social guarantees for families with children are of little help in their overall expenditures.

Family Support Programs

Attempts to improve families' economic conditions have been made through several laws and programs accepted by the Government. A part of the program for improvement of the country's demographic situation (1998) was devoted to the strengthening of the family and increasing of the birth rate up to replacement level. Other measures were aimed to help families in some crisis situations and to care for orphans.

Since 1995, there has been a Law on Social Protection, which requires that, in the case of a parent's death, the children receive a monthly allowance. Households living under the poverty line are entitled to municipality grants (e.g. free lunches at school, transport to the school and textbooks, partial payments for housing and heating).

In 1998, a Concept on Family Education was accepted by the Ministry of Education and Science, but no eligible activities were commenced due to lack of financing. In autumn of 2001, a Concept for Promotion of Gender Equality was accepted by the Government. One of its priorities is the elimination of domestic violence. Again, no full program of activities has been elaborated by the end of 2003. One more Concept on the state's support for families rearing children was prepared in 2002 but was not accepted during the following year. In 2002, a Minister for Family Issues and Protection of Children was introduced, and in 2003 the Consultative Commission on Demographic and Family Issues was created.

CONCLUSION

Since the proclamation of the independent Latvian Republic in 1918 up to the beginning of the 21st century, marriage and family have changed significantly, especially during the 13 years of transition to democracy and the free market economy. The model of Christian life (e.g. long marriage) has given way to freely chosen cohabitation and secular marriages. Patriarchal norms of family life have been replaced by mainly egalitarian relations between spouses (both being employed outside the home), by democratic attitudes toward children as equal family members and friends, and by a child-centered distribution of expenditures. In spite of the prevalence of the modern family model, remnants of patriarchal gender roles persisting in public opinion cause certain difficulties. As almost everywhere, wives and mothers are responsible for home and children, bearing the double burden of paid and unpaid work. The latter could hardly be replaced by services because most Latvians, and especially families with children, are living under the subsistence minimum. In this situation, the state's financial support to the families rearing children should be expanded.

REFERENCES

Demographic Yearbook of Latvia (2002). Riga: Central Statistical Bureau of Latvia.

Education Institutions in Latvia at the beginning of the school year 2002/2003 (2003). Riga: Central Statistical Bureau of Latvia.

Eglite, P., Pavlina, I., & Markausa, I. M. (1999). *Situation of family in Latvia.* Riga: Institute of Economics L.A.Sc.

Eglite, P. (2001). Household composition. In: E. Vaskis (Ed.), *Living Conditions in Latvia* (pp. 30–43). Norbalt – 2. Riga: Central Statistical Bureau of Latvia.

Eglite, P. (2002). Statistics about changes in family formation in Latvia during the XX century. In: P. Eglite (Ed.), *Family Formation and Relevant Policy in Latvia After Regaining Independence* (pp. 6–30). Riga: Institute of Economics L.A.Sc.

Fertility and Family Survey in Countries of the ECE Regions, Standard country report, Latvia (1998). New York and Geneva: United Nations.

Household Budget in 2000 (2001). Riga: Central Statistical Bureau.

Koroleva, I. (1999). The views of young people on the role of the man and the woman in the family. In: I. B. Zarina (Ed.), *Man's Role in the Family* (pp. 47–55). Riga: Latvian Women's Studies and Information Center.

Latvia. Human Development Report 1997 (1997). Riga: UNDP.

Markausa, I. (2002). Women's attitude to family and marriage in Latvia. In: P. Eglite (Ed.), *Family Formation and Relevant Policy in Latvia After Regaining Independence* (pp. 72–88). Riga: Institute of Economics L.A.Sc.

Pavlina, I., & Eglite, P. (2002). Parents' views about extension of the family, happened in 1999 and 2000. In: P. Eglite (Ed.), *Family Formation and Relevant Policy in Latvia After Regaining Independence* (pp. 48–64). Riga: Institute of Economics L.A.Sc.

Population et Societes no 392 (2003). Paris: INED.

Reproductive Health of the Population of Latvia. Evaluation and Recommendations (1998). Riga: UNDP.

Results of the 2000 Population and Housing Census in Latvia (2002). Riga: Central Statistical Bureau.

Rungule, R. (1997). The role of parents – fathers and mothers – in the family and in society. In: I. Koroleva (Ed.), *Invitation to Dialogue: Beyond Gender (In)equality* (pp. 311–322). Riga: Institute of philosophy and sociology, Latvian Academy of Sciences.

Time Use by the Population of Latvia. Statistical Bulletin (1998). Riga: Central Statistical Bureau of Latvia, Institute of Economics, Latvian Academy of Sciences.

Zarina, I. B. (1995). Actual and desired family models in Latvia. *Latvian Journal of Humanities and Social Sciences*, 2(7), 48–61.

Zarina, I. B. (Ed.) (1999). *Role of men in the family*. Riga: Latvian Women's Studies and Information Center.

FAMILY RELATIONS IN 20TH CENTURY RUSSIA AS A PROJECTION OF POPULAR BELIEFS, SCHOLARLY DISCOURSE AND STATE POLICIES

Valentina I. Uspenskaya and Dmitry Y. Borodin

The renowned Russian actress Faina Ranevskaya, who had an established reputation for her sharp tongue, is reported to have once remarked in response to the question why she had no family: "The family supersedes all other aspects of human life, so before acquiring the family, one really has to make a choice: whether to have a family or to enjoy all other aspects of life." Ranevskaya might have hit the mark, for her witticism reflects the general belief that the family is the single most important event in the life of a Russian woman. Moreover, she belongs to the generation that experienced the most radical change in the social order, i.e. the Stalinist revolutionary years and socialist transformation, which left a lasting imprint on the public consciousness. It also served as a "formative experience" for the ruling elite (Fitzpatrick, 1989) and resulted in a dramatic reshuffling of the staff and agendas within academia.

This chapter will examine the influence of popular beliefs during the 1920s–1930s on ideas of family relations held by the Communist party leadership. It will also look at how the ruling elite managed to develop an ideological frame for coping with family issues, partly ousting rival visions and partly incorporating them into the mainstream ideology. Furthermore, there will an analysis of how the elite initiated the emergence of a new scholarly discourse on the family. Finally, this chapter will look at how several decades later it managed to disseminate

Families in Eastern Europe
Contemporary Perspectives in Family Research, Volume 5, 237–248
© 2004 Published by Elsevier Ltd.
ISSN: 1530-3535/doi:10.1016/S1530-3535(04)05015-0

those ideological postulates, now presented as "scientific findings," among the population. Chronologically, this survey covers the historical period from 1903 to 2003. Methodologically, the analysis was built on the provisions of social constructivism. Therefore, the main argument is that the notion of the Russian family was being socially constructed and the Soviet state was the primary, although not the only, agent of this construction. In post-Soviet Russia, the state monopoly in shaping academic discourse has come to an end. Emerging institutions within civil society (especially by women's organizations and other Non Governmental Organizations) have challenged the leading role of the state in determining family relations (and defining the family).

HISTORICAL PERSPECTIVES ON RUSSIAN FAMILIES

During the first two decades of the 20th century, the Russian family went through some institutional transformations. Peasant migrations (from European Russia to more distant destinations, and more importantly, from the countryside to the cities), World War I, the upheavals of the revolutionary period and the Civil War years all changed the country's demographic situation. This led to more women (at least in the cities) being employed outside their households. Their sub-standard living conditions and legal vulnerability attracted the attention of intellectuals (Engel, 1991) and helped reformulate the women's question, which had by then become one of the central issues of the political and intellectual life of the country. Alongside the quest for equality from upper and middle-class women, which was manifested in the burgeoning public and literary life of the *Fin-de-Siécle* Russia (Engelstein, 1992), emerged "Marxist feminism." This movement assumed the task of promoting the rights of working women and the destruction of (bourgeois) gender inequality. It also played a decisive role in shaping scholarly discourse on the family and state policies towards it. Despite the dramatic social changes, they did not readily bring about alterations in popular mentality, particularly in popular attitudes towards the roles played by men and women within the family. Barbara Engel (1991, p. 147) has observed that:

> Revolutionary transformation did not end most women's loyalty to the family and especially to their children. However, food shortages, poor housing, lack of job opportunities, and especially family instability made women's traditional responsibilities considerably harder to fulfill. The deserting husbands and short-term unions that led some women to seek abortion prompted others to demand more conservative family policy to ensure their ability to provide for their children. Instead of unions easily contracted and dissolved they wanted strong and stable marriages.

Meanwhile, during the first post-revolutionary decade, some representatives of the new elite regarded the family as holding the most strength within the *ancien régime*, which was doomed to collapse as new relations between the sexes and among generations were getting stronger.[1] A great deal of writing produced in the 1920s by Communist theoreticians discussed questions related to the pace, social context and forms in which the withering away of the family might manifest itself (Preobrazhenskii, 1923; Trotsky, 1923). It also examined the problems of sexual ethics and the upbringing of genuinely collectivist-minded people (Kollontai, 2003a–c; Lunacharsky, 1927; Zalkind, 1923 (reprinted in 2001)). "There are reasons to believe," argued Bukharin (1921, p. 170) "that in the Communist society, as the private property vanishes for good, the family and prostitution will follow suit." He also stated his opposition to the family's rearing of the younger generation: "The future lies with the communal upbringing. The communal upbringing will enable the Communist society to bring up the young in the way it deems appropriate, minimizing efforts and expenses" (Bukharin, 1920, p. 197).

Alongside the radical criticism of the family and marriage as institutions, the 1920s witnessed a revival of a more conservative approach to the problem. The proponents of this approach shared patriarchal views of the family, denounced divorce and were inclined to persecute those violating the traditional norms of family life. These were norms that the Soviet regime had inherited from its tsarist predecessors (Preobrazhenskii, 1923; Yaroslavskii, 1925).[2] The 1920s was a period when prospects of the new family were still widely discussed. These prospects involved a form of association within which women and men could communicate as equal members of the Communist society. They were tied to each other only through bonds of mutual love and a feeling of solidarity, which constituted a "longstanding alliance for the sake of the shared living and rearing of the children" (Kollontai, 2003a–c, p. 242; Lunacharsky, 1927). "The whole hostel must be re-organized, so that it resembled a club, and every resident forgot that there was any other family apart from the collective family – the hostel" (Shchekin, 1924, p. 56).

The prominent Bolshevik and champion of the cause of women's emancipation Alexandra Kollontai made a significant contribution to the theory of family relations. In the early 1920s she wrote a number of striking articles and essays, exempt from capitalism, that were devoted to the family, motherhood, relations between the two sexes (Uspenskaya, 2003). Nowadays her writings would be considered as quite moderate, but in the 1920s, they were regarded as radically feminist. Her ideas were not a mere integration of women's demands into the new state political agenda (which she actually never endorsed), but a radical emancipation of women as a result of the victorious world revolution. More specifically, Kollontai sought to emancipate Russia's women from several facets of the bourgeois legacy. These included the sphere of family and everyday life, dependence on men and the bourgeois morality, which confined women to the performance of maternal duties.

Kollontai (2003a–c/1921) believed that complete equality for women could be brought about by a radical disruption of family relations. This would promote their economic independence and involvement in material production. The primary task of the Soviet state, according to Kollontai (2003a–c/1921), was to ensure that instead of women spending their time on domestic chores and childcare, they were focused on the production of material wealth and on serving the interests of the state and collective labor unit. "It is necessary to save women's efforts and to avoid unproductive labor expenditures related to the family in order to use (women's labor) in a more rational way in the best interests of the labor unit" (p. 219); "The established labor unit (*kollektiv*) will triumphantly overcome the contemporary isolation of the family unit" (p. 219). The Revolution was one of the basic prerequisites for the emancipation of women. In Kollontai's view, household chores were to be substituted by a ramified network of public consumer services, while the state was to assume all responsibilities related to childcare: "Kitchens, which really have turned the woman into a slave, cease to constitute a prerequisite for the family existence" (Uspenskaya, 2003, p. 231). Childbirth and breast-feeding were the only responsibilities a woman still had to bear until her children were mature enough to go to the nursery house. As the upbringing of the younger generation was regarded as the principal vehicle for the making of "new Soviet citizens," it could no longer remain just a private matter. It was assumed that children could only be successfully infused with socialist values if the indoctrination was put into the hands of professional pedagogues. Parents were deemed unfit for that task due to their alleged "backwardness" and questionable reliability.

However, as mentioned above, the transformation that the family underwent in the 1920s proved to be substantially different from what Kollontai had envisioned. Both the material conditions, on which the new (liberal), hypothetical marital relations could be built, and the popular *mentalité* lagged behind the advanced family legislation. Nevertheless, the vast majority of Russia's women were unable to take advantage of all the rights granted to them, due to their illiteracy. They lacked readiness, let alone enthusiasm, to dissolve their marriages or to pass their children to the state's guardianship. In her essay, "Some Theses on Communist Morals in the Society" Kollontai had to admit that there still existed "a married couple as a distinct social unit," i.e. the family (p. 247).

Kollontai's (1972) concept of motherhood attracted attention among other approaches to the family in Russia. It "used to constitute an integral part of the state policy during the Soviet period of Russian history and underlies present day public views on the status of mothering in society" (Kozlova, 2002, p. 118). Her assumption about childbirth as the sole responsibility of women was adopted as a principle around which the Soviet state built its demographic policy. In particular, it served as a theoretical substantiation of the ill-reputed Abortion Ban Act of 1936. Kollontai's theory of sexual relations and her vision of social institutions such as marriage were not implemented under Communism. Instead, a set of compulsory social roles, embodied in the slogan, "a working woman and a housewife – two in one" was imposed on all Soviet women. The strictly confined niche of normative motherhood proved to be a heavy load for women, for they alone were expected to take care of their families. This is a symptom that can hardly be interpreted as a sign of further emancipation of women.

THE STATE AND THE FAMILY

Throughout the Soviet period, the state's attitude towards the family as a social institution remained somewhat ambiguous. On the one hand, the Marriage Act of 1926 signified a retreat to pre-revolutionary family values and reinforcement of the nuclear family. "Free love" was to be abolished as a bourgeois phenomenon, and homosexuality was outlawed. The divorce procedure was gradually made more complicated and state officials came to regard the family as an institution designed to stabilize society during the periods of transition. On the other hand, the state was still suspicious of the family, and was aware that as an institution of the private sphere, the family could not altogether come under the sway of its political manipulations and ideological indoctrination (Tartakovskaya, 1997). In this respect, the family remained the locus of property accumulation, even though this accumulation was limited and insignificant in the Soviet era (Tartakovskaya, 1997).

Changes in state policy towards the family, and the re-introduction of patriarchal legislation immediately affected the literary and scholarly discourse. Social Sciences after 1938 could only repeat the new canonical text, which contained just one phrase on the women's question and family issues. From the 1936 USSR Constitution: "The woman has been granted rights, equal to those of the man in every sphere of human activity" (*The Brief Course*, 1946, p. 330). All works published from the mid-1930s till the mid-1950s that were devoted to family issues merely reproduced that conclusion, adding some quotations from the works of Marxist authorities (primarily Stalin himself). Additionally, they severely criticized the bourgeois family on the basis of Friederich Engels' (1884) compilation "The Origins of the Family, Private Property and the State."

The change in the literary discourse was also striking. On the one hand the literary works glorifying women revolutionaries were still widely read (they were included in the school list of compulsory reading). On the other hand, in the late 1920s the first signs of the forthcoming changes appeared. Female characters now became more maternal, feminine, family-oriented and concentrated on the housekeeping and everyday problems. Reading was the most popular leisure activity among the younger generation and the writers were state-controlled in unprecedented proportions. Thus, it seems legitimate to claim that the state found a very efficient way of strengthening traditional family values (Borodina & Borodin, 2000).

Generally speaking, during the Soviet era the state made an unparalleled intrusion into family relations. It sanctioned marriages and divorces, registered births and deaths, regulated relationships between spouses. The state's occasional appearance in the role of guardian of women's rights limited the traditional powers of the patriarch. However, since the late 1920s it has never challenged the existing gender contract (that of the "working mother"). Moreover, the state often reinforced traditional gender roles through ideological manipulations.

After Stalin's death, the ideological grasp of the state loosened to a degree that allowed academia to turn to real social issues. The 1960s witnessed a temporary return of historical debates (although these debates could only be held within the Marxist-Leninist framework) and a revival and institutionalization of sociology. The family and marriage-related problems were on the list of subjects studied by Soviet sociology. Initially these problems were treated as marginal. Sociologists examining the family employed a functionalist approach, focusing on social functions of the family (reproduction, socialization, property acquisition etc.). The first more or less consistent theory in the Soviet sociology of the family was developed by Alexander Kharchev (1964). According to his perspective the family operated in the everyday sphere of the social life and its function was mainly reproductive. This theory disregarded the micro-level of analysis, as it failed to pose any questions about the relations of the two sexes within the family unit. Instead, it took the existing gender order for granted and focused on the functions rendered by the institution of the family for society at large (Kletsin, 1998). Representatives of other disciplines (economists or demographers) were even less sensitive in this respect.

CONTEMPORARY RUSSIAN FAMILIES AND THE CHALLENGES OF THE TRANSITION ERA

Since the Perestroika era of the mid-1980s there has been a revival of public and scholarly interest in developments taking place within the institution of the family. Economists and demographers were the first to influence Gorbachev's reformers. The belief that widely circulated among the Soviet elite during the first Perestroika years was that women should return to their homes and families and take care of their children, while men should provide for their families and attend to politics. The mass media made major contributions to spreading and strengthening patriarchal attitudes.

These traditional views were matched by the "alarmist" approach to the family within Arts and Social Sciences that was typical of the late Soviet and post-Soviet periods (Malysheva, 2001). According to this approach, shared mostly by demographers and some sociologists, the contemporary Russian family is experiencing a deep crisis, which manifests itself in the increasing number of divorces, decreasing birth rates (the prospect of depopulation of the country), and the growing number of single-parent families (Antonov & Medkov, 1996; Borisov & Sinel'nikov, 1996). These authors focus on the reproductive function of the family, observing with regret that in the mid-1990s, small families made up about 90% of all Russian families (Antonov, 1999, p. 96), with an average birth rate approaching 1.6 per woman of fertile age (Matskovskii, 1993, p. 15).[3]

Alternatively there are some scholars, mainly historians, economists and sociologists who analyze a broader set of variables (e.g. employment, economic status, inter-family gender relations, etc.). These individuals view the changes taking place within Russian families as a normal part of modernization. Admitting the significance of the "alarmist" issues, these scholars tend to avoid emotional estimations of social reality, focusing instead on the variety within family forms. Most students who are studying the family and working within this "modernization paradigm" eagerly use the feminist scholarly tradition and recent achievements of Gender Studies. Recently, an egalitarianist approach to family relations has emerged, which seeks to promote equality between spouses and to encourage partnership within the family (Malysheva, 2001; Rimashevskaya et al., 1999). What the alarmist and modernization currents seem to share is the acknowledgement of the crucial role played by the state and its legislation in the shaping of public opinion and family relations. Alarmists tend to favor a broad range of state-sponsored propaganda campaigns that seek to promote changes in reproductive behavior and stimulate higher birth rates (Antonov, 1999, p. 96). Alternatively, proponents of the modernization paradigm seem to believe that a new social doctrine adopted by the state should leave more options for people to choose the most suitable family forms (Zdravomyslova, 2003, p. 30).

Currently, the family debate which transcends academic boundaries and often involves politicians, state officials, journalists, public activists and (thanks to mass media)[4] a large proportion of Russia's population, is at the foreground of the Russian political agenda. During parliamentary (and forthcoming presidential) elections the ruling elite seeks to find some common ground with the society at large, and the family provides quite a promising issue. Family issues are addressed in the political programs of most candidates who promise to alleviate the situation (proposed solutions range from the unlikely introduction of polygamy to the all too likely prohibition of abortion. These are coupled with standard promises of improvement to the welfare system). The vast majority of these political programs seek to revive "our family traditions," thus elevating the position of the family. However, they fail to acknowledge the existing ethnic, cultural, social, and economic diversity (as well as the differences caused by age/generation, sexual orientation, gender) of family forms in present day Russia.

There is a trend that runs counter to this convention. Social scientists working within the modernization paradigm, regardless of their disciplinary identification, raise questions that help disclose the mechanisms through which society constructs both the institution and the notion of the family. The first question raised is "Which family?" To ask this question means to admit that there exists, ". . . a great variety of the family forms" (Rimashevskaya, 2003, p. 159) and that for a social scientist there is no such a thing as just the "Russian family." They recognize that it is necessary to account for the existing ethnic, demographic, cultural, economic heterogeneity of this institution. Furthermore, scholars often introduce their own taxonomies, which make the analysis of the family increasingly sophisticated. Thus, Matskovskii (1995) identifies marginal families, families in crisis, successful families and prosperous families (pp. 32–34).

According to Golod's (1999) taxonomy, three forms of monogamy (patriarchal, in which a man is the main breadwinner; pedocentric, which focuses on child-raising; and the spouse family, based on partnership between the spouses) are predominant in Russia (p. 92). Rimashevskaya (2003) observes that chronologically, the patriarchal family dominated Russia until World War II. This was succeeded by the pedocentric family, a model that most people followed until the mid-1980s. The 1990s witnessed the rise of the spouse model of the family. "It should be made clear, that all the three forms of monogamy co-exist, but the proportion of the families taking each of those patterns changes from period to period" (Rimashevskaya, 2003, p. 160). Zdravomyslova et al. (2002) support the idea of the existence of two different "family contracts."[5] That is, the traditional (breadwinner/housewife roles) and the egalitarian (partnership between the spouses) (Zdravomyslova et al., 2002, pp. 482–483).

The family is currently regarded as the most stable social institution, able to make the transition period less painful for the Russian population. This potential stems from the socio-historical context of contemporary Russia. The destruction of old social ties and roles has made the family the locus of social integration. Due to the emergence of the small businesses, the economic role once played by the family seems to have returned. The family serves as a psychological shelter for the individual and it provides the material basis for physical survival of the people. It provides support for the most disadvantaged sections of the population and is a catalyst for social development. As such, it will pave the way for the emergence of a middle class (Rimashevskaya, 1997, pp. 116–117). Both alarmists and proponents of the modernization paradigm emphasize the economic causes of the contemporary crises. A recent survey has demonstrated 69% of Russian citizens believe that the main problem faced by their families is low income (while only 3% mentioned tensions within the family) (Levada, 2003, p. 6). Thus, the lack of economic stability, low income and virtually non-existent state support of the family are generally believed to be responsible for the current crises of the family.

As it is an urbanized area, European Russia is mostly populated by nuclear families, although emotional ties with a broader range of relatives are often preserved. Marriage is still considered to hold great significance among the young, although traditional adherence to the idea of pre-marital chastity is now considered to be outdated. About one third of all families consist of single parent households and the level of fertility has decreased by 35%. The rate of divorce is high, with one of two marriages ending in divorce (Rimashevskaya et al., 1999). The number of officially registered marriages in Russia has dropped within the last decade. In the early 1990s, there were 7.1 marriages per 1,000 people while in 2000 there were only 6.2 (Rimashevskaya, 2003). A substantial proportion of young people prefer cohabitation to official marriage (6–8%) (Rimashevskaya, 2003). As a result, more than 50% of children under 18 will experience life in some form of deviant family (single parent family, divorced, cohabitation) (Matskovskii, 1993, p. 17).

An ongoing study of the attitudes of university students towards family life, conducted by Tver State University Center of Women's History and Gender Studies (preliminary results), partially supports these conclusions, although there are some disparities. Most students do not rate the family as a top priority in their lives. For them, the prospect of family life does not seem to be something that should be taken for granted. Those married often regard their marriage as an opportunity to enjoy life with their partner, and many postpone childbirth (some of them do not plan to have children at all). Quite a substantial number of respondents (of both sexes, though female students take the lead in this respect) are favorably inclined towards the idea of gender equality and partnership. When asked about life priorities, a significant proportion of female students at Tver State University (40%), demonstrated strong adherence to pursuing a professional career. Half believed that the most important thing was success in their family life, while 10% were eager to achieve success in both spheres.

These results are consistent with the study entitled "The Woman of New Russia," conducted in 2002 in 12 regions of the Russian Federation and the two capitals (i.e. in Moscow and St. Petersburg) (Gorshkova & Tikhonova, 2002). According to this research, most Russian women attribute the highest value to the family and aspire to have a "happy family" (96.3% of the respondents). In contrast, among the younger generation (17–18 years old) every 13th respondent did not have such aspirations and every 10th did not plan to have children (Gorshkova & Tikhonova, 2002). In terms of these women defined a happy family, 87.3% believed that a family should be founded on mutual love, and 86.9% affirmed that a happy marriage should have at least one child. In addition, 69% assumed that a happy marriage was one officially registered by the state (50.4% of the interviewed were not officially married). According to 60% of the respondents, a happy family should possess its own separate living space. A considerable percentage of the women (56.5%) characterized a happy family as one where the husband was the primary breadwinner. At the same time, however, 70.2% made it clear that they were strongly inclined in favor of equality between the two sexes (Gorshkova & Tikhonova, 2002, pp. 62–64).

With the end to the state monopoly on ideology and state support of the family on the decline, the efficiency of state efforts to maintain traditional family relations was considerably reduced. Furthermore, a number of new players joined the game, with NGO and foreign non-profit organizations being the most noticeable. Ideas of gender equality have already made their way into scholarly discourse and to a lesser degree into politics. Despite the dramatic changes that have occurred in the social environment since the late 1980s, there has been a lack of major transformation of popular stereotypes. While many families have been facing the challenges of the market economy, and experiencing the actual disappearance of traditional gender roles, stereotypes are being constantly revived. This socio-psychological inertia is reinforced by state efforts to mobilize popular support through the appeal to "traditional values" and "natural roles." At the same time, a single scholarly discourse, which could be used to uphold the state's agenda, has ceased to exist. Currently, scholars studying the family in Russia often criticize state policies from different ideological positions.

NOTES

1. It is worth noticing that within the Communist social engineering project, the two intertwined problems – those of abolishing the "old" (bourgeois) family relations and shaping the "new" (communist) family – were approached in terms of women's emancipation (which in turn was deemed a by-product of the socialist revolution).

2. Among those conservative thinkers was Emel'yan Yaroslavskii, one of the key spokesmen for the cause of Stalin's "revolution from above." Those members of the emerging party bureaucracy who saw, despite all their revolutionary rhetoric, "the socialist construction" merely as building of a more modern (and hence more powerful in terms of international politics) state, which could mobilize its population at will. Therefore, the state, which was keen on organizing the population into some standardized collective units,

or cells (*yacheiki*), that were easier to deal with and exercise control over, could hardly be enthusiastic about daring experiments in family life, typical of the early 1920s. For a discussion of those experiments and changes in state policy towards the family see: R. Stites, *Revolutionary Dreams. Utopian Vision and Experimental Life in the Russian Revolution*, Oxford University Press,1989; see also B. E. Clements "The Birth of the New Soviet Woman" in *Bolshevik Culture: Experiment and Order in the Russian Revolution* (Ed.), A. Gleason, P. Kenez, R. Stites, Bloomington, Ind., 1989.

3. By 2001 this index had become even lower – 1.25 births per woman of fertile age (Rimashevskaya, 2003, p. 47).

4. The "All-Russian Public Movement *My Family* (*Moya Sem'ya*)" headed by the deputy of the State Duma Valery Komissarov is of special interest here, as it illustrates how relevant the family problem is for the Russian political agenda. Having started as a talk show on one of the two major state-sponsored TV channels, aimed at dissemination of traditional (i.e. patriarchal) values and pro-family attitudes, this project soon turned into a large commercial enterprise, with the publishing house as one of its spheres of profit-making.

5. The most important proponents of the concept of different "gender contracts" operating within the society are, however, two sociologists from Saint-Petersburg (Anna Temkina, Elena Zdravomyslova) and their co-author from Finland Anna Rotkirch, whose theoretical framework cannot be reduced to the modernization paradigm. Being feminists, these scholars quite successfully employ post-modernist research techniques in their analyses (Rotkirch & Temkina, 1997; Zdravomyslova & Temkina, 2002).

REFERENCES

Antonov, A. (1999). Sem'ya, rynochnaya ekonomika, gosudarstvo: Krizis sotsial'noi politiki. *Vestnik Moskovskogo Universiteta*, Series 18, #3, 87–103.

Antonov, A., & Medkov, V. (1996). *Sotsiologiya sem'i*. Moscow: Gardariki.

Borisov, V., & Sinel'nikov, A. (1996). *Brachnost' i rozhdaemost' v Rossii: demografscheskii analiz.* Moscow: Rosspen.

Borodina, A., & Borodin, D. (2000). Baba ili tovarishch? Ideal novoi sovetskoi zhenshchiny v 20-kh–30-kh godakh. In: V. Uspenskaya (Ed.), *Zhenskie i gendernye issledovaniya v tverskom gosudarstvennom universitete* (pp. 45–52). Tver: "Kompaniya Folium".

Bukharin, N. (1920). *Azbuka kommunizma*. Moscow: Pravda.

Bukharin, N. (1921). *Teoriya istoricheskogo materializma*. Moscow and Petrograd: Pravda.

Engel, B. (1991). Transformation versus tradition. In: B. Clements, B. Engel & C. Worobec (Eds), *Russia's Women: Accommodation, Resistance, Transformation* (pp. 135–148). Berkeley: University of California Press.

Engelstein, L. (1992). Keys to happiness: Sex and the search for modernity in the *fin-de-siécle*. Russia: Ithaca and London: Cornell University Press.

Fitzpatrick, S. (1989). Civil war as a formative experience. In: A. Gleason, P. Kenez & R. Stites (Eds), *Bolshevik Culture: Experiment and Order in the Russian Revolution* (pp. 57–75). Bloomington: Indiana University Press.

Golod, S. (1999). *Sem'ya i brak. Istoriko-sotsiologicheskii analiz*. Saint-Petersburg: Aleteya.

Gorshkova, M., & Tikhonova, N. (Eds) (2002). Zhenschina novoi Rossii: Kakaya ona? Kak zhivet?K tchemu stremitsia? Rossisskaya politicheskaya encyclopedia (Rosspen).

Kletsin, A. (1998). Sotsiologiya sem'i. In: V. Yadov (Ed.), *Sotsiologiya v Rossii*. Moscow: Izdatel'stvo Instituta Sotsiologii RAN.

Kollontai, A. (1972). *Obshchestvo i materinstvo. Izbrannye stat'i i rechi*. Moscow: Prosveshchenie.

Kollontai, A. (2003a). Sem'ya i kommunizm (originally published in 1920). In: V. Uspenskaya (Ed.), *Marksistskii feminism: kollektsiya tekstov A. M. Kollontai*. Tver: Feminist Press, Russia.

Kollontai, A. (2003b). Liubov' i novaya moral' (originally published in 1918). In: V. Uspenskaya (Ed.), *Marksistskii feminism: kollektsiya tekstov A. M. Kollontai*. Tver: Feminist Press, Russia.

Kollontai, A. (2003c). Tezisy o kommunisticheskoi morali v oblasti brachnykh otnoshenii (originally published in 1921). In: V. Uspenskaya (Ed.), *Marksistskii feminism: kollektsiya tekstov A. M. Kollontai*. Tver: Feminist Press, Russia.

Kozlova, N. (2002). Obshchestvo i materinstvo v kontseptsii A. Kollontai. In: V. Uspenskaya (Ed.), *Aleksandra Kollontai: Teoriya zhenskoi emansipatsii v kontekste rossiiskoi gendernoi politiki*. Conference Papers. Tver: Zolotaya bukva.

Levada, Y. (2003). Some results of the public opinion poll conducted by WCIOM (10.10.–14.10.2003). *Moskovskii Komsomolets, 6.*

Lunacharsky, A. (1927) V. *O byte*. Moscow and Leningrad: OGIZ

Malysheva, M. (2001). *Sovremennyi patriarkhat. Sotsial'no-politicheskoe esse*. Moscow: Academia.

Matskovskii, M. (1993) *Sem'ya v krizisnom obshchestve*. Moscow: URSS.

Matskovskii, M. (1995). Rossiiskaya sem'ya v menyayushchimsya mire. *Sem'ya v Rossii*, 3–4.

Preobrazhenskii, A. (1923). *O morali i klassovykh normakh*. Moscow and Leningrad: OGIZ

Rimashevskaya, N. (1997). Rol' sem'i v usloviyakh sotsial'nykh transformatsii. In: V. Tishkov (Ed.), *Sem'ya, gender, kul'tura*. Moscow: Institut Etnologii i Antropologii.

Rimashevskaya, N., Vannoi, D., Cubbins, L., Malysheva, M., Meshterkina, E., & Pisklakova, M. (1999). *Okno v russkuyu chastnuyu zhizn': supruzheskie pary v 1996 godu*. Moscow: Academia.

Rimashevskaya, N. (2003). *Chelovek i reformy: sekrety vyzhivaniya*, Moscow: RITs ISEPN.

Rotkirch, A., & Temkina, A. (1997). Soviet gender contracts and their shifts in contemporary Russia. *Idantutkimus*, *4*, 6–24.

Shchekin, M. (1924). *Novyi byt, novaya sem'ya*. Kostroma: Krasnyi Volzhanin.

Tartakovskaya, I. (1997). *Sotsiologiya pola i sem'i*. Samara: Parus.

Trotsky, L. (1923). *Voprosy byta: epokha "kul'turnichestva" i ee zadachi*. Moscow.

Uspenskaya, V. (Ed.) (2003). *Marksistskii feminism: kollektsiya tekstov A. M. Kollontai*. Tver: Feminist Press, Russia.

Yaroslavskii, E. (1925). *Polovoi vopros*. Moscow: Pravda.

Zdravomyslova, E., & Temkina, A. (2002). Sovetskii etakraticheskii gendernyi poryadok. In: N. Pushakreva (Ed.), *Sotsial'naya istoriya-2002*. Moscow: ROSSPEN.

Zdravomyslova, O. (2003). *Sem'ya i obshchestvo: gendernoe izmerenie rossiiskoi transformatsii*. Moscow: URSS.

Zdravomyslova, O., Arutyunyan, M., & Mezentseva, E. (2002). Rossiiskaya sem'ya v 90-e gody: zhiznennye strategii muzhchin i zhenshchin. In: *Gendernyi kaleidoskop*. Moscow: URSS.

ABOUT THE AUTHORS

Marina Adler, Ph.D., is Associate Professor of Sociology at the University of Maryland Baltimore County. Her research specializations focus on comparative race, class, and gender inequality with a special interest in European social policy dealing with gender, work and family issues. For the last 13 years she has been studying the effects of German unification on women's lives in East Germany.

Valentina Bodrug-Lungu, Ph.D., is Associate Professor of Pedagogy and Psychology at Moldova State University and Director of Gender Center. She is the author of numerous studies on gender issues, pedagogy, family issues, and educational management. She is contributing directly to the development of Gender Mainstreaming in Moldova, including Gender Education Strategy. She oversees activities and advises the implementation of numerous projects on Gender Issues and Social Sector.

Suzana Bornarova, M.A., is Teaching Assistant at the Institute for Social Work and Social Policy, Faculty of Philosophy, St. Cyril and Methodius University in Skopje, Republic of Macedonia. Her Master Thesis examined social policy and social services for the elderly. Her fields of interest are: Social Work with Families, Gerontology, and Social Policy. She also serves as Project Coordinator for projects realized within the National Center for Training in Social Development, at the Institute for Social Work and Social Policy.

Dmitry Y. Borodin, M.A., is Assistant Professor in the Department of Sociology and Political Science at Tver State University, Tver, Russia and a Junior Research Fellow at the University Center of Women's History and Gender Studies. He holds an M.A. in Comparative History of East-Central Europe from the Central-European University (CEU), Budapest, Hungary, and is currently a Ph.D. Candidate at the CEU History Department. He has written a number of articles on gender relations in Russia (together with Anna V. Borodina).

Danuta Duch, Ph.D., is Assistant Professor in Research Unit on Women and Family in the Institute of Philosophy and Sociology, Polish Academy of Sciences.

Her particular fields of interest are women's reproductive health, women's status in a family, unpaid women's work, glass ceiling – barriers and limitations of women career in Poland. She is the author of the book: *Marriage, Sex, Procreation, Sociological Analysis* (1998). Currently she is working on a book devoted to power relationships in a family.

Parsla Eglite, Ph.D., Hab., is corresponding member of Latvian Academy of Sciences; working as Head of a Research Team of Population Studies in Institute of Economics, Latvian Academy of Sciences. Her scholarly interests are social and family policy; dynamics, composition and projections of population in Latvia; vital and reproductive behaviors; time use, leisure and family education. In addition she is a member of EAPS (European Association of Population Studies) and International Sociological Association (ISA).

Jarmila Filadelfiová, M.A, is Sociologist at the Centre for Work and Family Studies in Bratislava (former the Bratislava International Centre for Family Studies). She has conducted research on demographic development, family and gender issues, and violence against women. She is the author of numerous articles and has contributed to several books on these topics.

Irena Juozeliūnienė, Ph.D., is Associate Professor of Sociology in the Department of Sociology, Faculty of Philosophy at Vilnius University, Vilnius, Lithuania. Her scholarly interests include family sociology, contemporary sociological theory, and the problem of identity in sociology. She is the author of numerous articles as well as several books, namely, *Society and Agency: contemporary sociological interpretation* (1999) (in Lithuanian), *Jan Trost and Family Sociology: new trends in research studies* (2003) (in Lithuanian). She is a member of International Sociological Association (ISA) and Nordic Family Research Network (NFRN).

Loreta Kuzmickaitė, M.A., is Researcher at the Institute for Social Research Vilnius University. Her scholarly interests include sociology of culture, ethnicity, family sociology, and interethnic families issues.

Divna Lakinska, Ph.D., is Professor at the Institute of Social Work and Social Policy, Faculty of Philosophy, SS. Cyril & Methodius University, Skopje, Republic of Macedonia. She teaches courses on General and Social Pedagogy and Andragogy, Gerontology, Social Work with Families and Social Work in Schools. Her particular fields of interest and expertise are adult education, social research, social work with families, and Roma population. She is an active participant in domestic and foreign events (conferences/seminars/forums) related to social policy and social work and author of more than 60 publications in the same domain. Since

1998, she is a Chief of the National Centre for Training in Social Development which operates within the Institute for Social Work and Social Policy.

Hana Maříková, Ph.D., is Researcher at the Institute of Sociology, Czech Academy of Sciences. Her main areas of interest are the position of women and men in the Czech society – on the labor market and in the family, gender questions and women in leadership. She has published works in various journals and collections. In 1999, she edited the publication *Society of Women and Men from the Gender View* (in Czech) and in 2000 she edited the book *Changing Czech Family: Family, Gender, Stratification* (in Czech).

Mihaela Robila, Ph.D., is Assistant Professor in Family Science in the Department of Family, Nutrition and Exercise Sciences at Queens College, City University of New York. Her scholarly interests are family functioning in diverse cultural contexts (especially in Eastern Europe), impact of poverty on families, resilience, and immigration. Dr. Robila published a number of articles on these topics.

Raya Staykova, Ph.D., is Senior Researcher at the Center for Science Studies and History of Science, Bulgarian Academy of Sciences. Her scholarly interests are the development of human resources, organizational behavior, including cultural and gender based differences, social capital, networks and partnership in knowledge-based society.

Anna Titkow, Ph.D., is Associate Professor of Sociology. Since 1994, she is Chairwomen of Research Unit on Women and Family, Institute of Philosophy and Sociology, Polish Academy of Sciences. Her main fields of interest and research activities are: gender identity of Polish women, gender contract, unpaid women work and relations between medicine and society. Since 1995, she is conducting, with Malgorzata Fuszara, the Seminar: Women – New Tendencies in Theory and Social Legal Practice in Graduate School for Social Research, Institute of Philosophy and Sociology, Polish Academy of Sciences. She is a co-founder of Sisterhood is Global Institute and member of International Sociology Association.

Olga Tóth, Ph.D., is Sociologist at the Institute of Sociology, Hungarian Academy of Sciences. She has conducted empirical research on family structure, gender relations, attitudes towards family life, violence in the family, and intergenerational relationships.

Mirjana Ule, Ph.D., is Professor of Social Psychology at the Faculty of Social Sciences, University of Ljubljana, Slovenia. She is the Head of the Center for Social Psychology and the coordinator of the postgraduate program "Sociology of everyday life." Her main topics of research are identity, life course, everyday life, youth and women studies, family and lifestyles research. Prof. Ule is the author of many books, i.e.: *Youth and Ideology* (1988), *Woman, Private, Political* (1990), *Social Psychology* (1992, 1994, 1997, 2000), *Psychology of Everyday Life* (1993), *The Future/Transition of Youth* (1995), *Time-out for student youth* (ed., 1996), *Youth in Slovenia, New Perspectives from the Nineties* (in English), *Prejudice and Discriminations* (1999), *Social vulnerability of young people* (2000), and *Youth, family and parenthood: Changes of life course in Slovenia* (2003).

Valentina I. Uspenskaya, Ph.D., is Professor of Sociology at the Department of Sociology and Political Science at Tver State University, Tver, Russia. She heads the University Center of Women's History and Gender Studies and edits the annual series *Women, History, Society*, published by the center. She has written many articles on women's question and is currently working on a book devoted to the history of feminist thought.

Tatiana Zhurzhenko, Ph.D., is Associate Professor at V. Karazin Kharkiv National University in Ukraine. From 1994 to 1999 she was member of the Kharkiv Center for Gender Studies. Her research interests focus on transformation processes in post-Soviet Ukraine: feminism(s) and nationalism(s); gender aspects of the transition to market economy; nation-building, language politics, new national borders and regional identities. She currently is a Lise Meitner Fellow at the University of Vienna, Austria, Institute for East European History where she examines the political and social ramifications of the new Ukrainian-Russian border. Recent publications include *Social Reproduction and Gender Politics in Ukraine, Kharkiv 2001* (in Russian); (Anti)national feminisms, Post-Soviet Gender Studies: Women's Voices of Transition and Nation Building in Ukraine, in *Oesterreichische Osthefte, Wien 2001* (in English); Strong Women, Weak State: Family Politics and Nation Building in Post-Soviet Ukraine, in *Post-Soviet Women Encountering Transition*, ed. by K. Kuehnast and C. Nechemias, Johns Hopkins University Press, 2004 (forthcoming); The Old Ideology of the New Family: Demographic Nationalism in Russia and Ukraine, in *Family Ties: Models for Assembling*, ed. by S. Oushakine, Moscow: NLO, (forthcoming 2004, in Russian).